D1528761

THE TENTH MUSE

THE TENTH MUSE

(1650)

AND, FROM THE MANUSCRIPTS,

Meditations Divine and Morall

TOGETHER WITH

Letters and Occasional Pieces

BY

ANNE BRADSTREET

FACSIMILE REPRODUCTIONS
WITH AN INTRODUCTION

BY

JOSEPHINE K. PIERCY

GAINESVILLE, FLORIDA

SCHOLARS' FACSIMILES & REPRINTS

1965

SCHOLARS' FACSIMILES & REPRINTS

1605 N.W. 14TH AVENUE

GAINESVILLE, FLORIDA, 32601, U.S.A.

HARRY R. WARFEL, GENERAL EDITOR

REPRODUCED FROM A COPY IN

AND WITH THE PERMISSION OF

INDIANA UNIVERSITY LIBRARY

L.C. CATALOG CARD NUMBER: 65-10345

MANUFACTURED IN THE U.S.A.

TYPESETTING BY PEPPER PRINTING COMPANY

LITHOGRAPHY BY EDWARDS BROTHERS

BINDING BY UNIVERSAL-DIXIE BINDERY

TABLE OF CONTENTS

(vi)

Manuscripts

INTRODUCTION

The Tenth Muse Lately Sprung Up in America,
published in London in 1650, is something more than
an historical oddity. To be sure, it deserves its place
in the history of American literature as the first
volume of poetry to be published by a British Amer-
ican; but the fact that it has gone through five edi-
tions and two reprints, the latter in 1932 and 1962,
certainly indicates that there is something in Anne
Bradstreet's poetry that outlasts her time. It has,
in fact, proved to be more durable than that of her
English female contemporaries whose poetry, en-
joying greater popularity than hers in their time,
is now neglected or forgotten. It should be noted,
however, that Anne Bradstreet was also read in Eng-
land and that Edward Phillips paid tribute to her
in his *Theatrum Poetarium* (1675).

A volume of poetry out of the English colonies
of the seventeenth century is remarkable. Amid
the adverse circumstances attendant upon building
a new home in a country still battling the wilder-
ness, there would seem to be neither time nor proper
environment to encourage creative effort. Every
Puritan was busy founding a Kingdom of God in a
heathen land. He cut down forests, he built dwell-
ing houses, he grew crops out of almost untillable
soil, and he fought the Indians. And the women,
literally and figuratively, put their hands to the
plough.

Such efforts meant constant, co-operative industry under strong leadership. Anne Bradstreet's father, Thomas Dudley, and her husband, Simon Bradstreet, were able administrators. As the daughter and wife of prominent men and as a Puritan woman, Anne fitted her station in life most admirably. She did so in spite of chronic ill health and the rearing of eight children, a task that must have filled her days from sun-up to candle-light. Yet, in spite of all this, she found time to write poetry, and she did so, also, at a time when writing among women was considered by most Puritans as unbecoming and frivolous. Yet she completely charmed her family and friends with whom she shared the reading of her verse. Presently her brother-in-law, The Rev. John Woodbridge, carried off her manuscript to England, — without her knowledge but obviously at the connivance of friends and family, — and had it published under its immodest title.

The background for Anne Bradstreet's writing was a propitious one: She had spent most of her life until she was eighteen in the household of the Earl of Lincoln, where her father was a trusted steward and friend. The Earl's excellent library was accessible to Anne, and her father encouraged her reading and study. She had done a great deal of intelligent reading before she set sail on the *Arbella* with her parents and her husband of two years. And as every one remembers, after more than six weeks of sailing on unpredictable seas, the Puritans landed at Massachusetts Bay in the summer of 1630. Here Anne Bradstreet "found a new world and new manners at which [her] heart rose."

Writing poetry must have been her outlet for her discontent. We do not know that she wrote poetry while she was in England, but she must have begun soon after she came to Massachusetts if we may judge her industry in writing her volume of over two hundred pages.

The Tenth Muse is highly imitative, the work of an apprentice learning to write by imitating authors whom she admired. She is obviously indebted to Joshua Sylvester's translation of Du Bartas' *La Premiere Semaine* for her pattern of verse, to Sir Walter Raleigh's *History of the World* for stories which she paraphrased, and to the Bible for a rich source book. It would be easy but unsafe to say that these, to all intents and purposes, were her sources. On closer examination, however, one can discover the remarkable breadth of her reading, broad for any educated person of the day, man or woman, except, of course, the giants of that great literary period.

The poetry in her first volume has many faults, the faults of a beginner doing finger exercises, although there is much more to *The Tenth Muse* than just that. It is possible it might have been less amateurish if she had known her work was to be published and she had had the opportunity for revision. At any rate, when she saw her "rambling brat in print," her "blushing was not small." She set about correcting errors, rewriting passages, and adding new and better poems, — all preparatory to a new edition, which, unfortunately, was not published until six years after her death in 1678. In this volume is some of her best poetry like "Contemplations" and "The Flesh and the Spirit." A third edition, actually a reprint of the second, appeared in 1758. In 1867 John Harvard Ellis published his, the fourth and most scholarly, edition of Anne Bradstreet's poetry, to which he added hitherto unpublished work of occasional pieces of poetry and prose and her admirable prose meditations. This is the edition reprinted in 1932 and 1962 by Peter Smith. In 1897, Charles Eliot Norton, a descendant, published his version, in which, with considerable condescension, as if the poetry of Anne Bradstreet needed an apology, he made "corrections" in spelling and grammar.

The only known extant manuscript in Anne Bradstreet's handwriting is that of the meditations, used by Ellis and now in the appropriate possession of the Stevens Memorial Library at North Andover, the home of Anne Bradstreet. Always interested in early Americana and proud of the tradition of Anne Bradstreet in particular, it was with particular satisfaction that the trustees purchased the manuscript shortly before the celebration of the library's fiftieth anniversary. The purchase was made possible through the generous gifts of three distinguished bibliophiles, Mr. Clifton Waller Barrett of New York City, Mr. Lessing J. Rosenwald of Jenkintown, Pennsylvania, and Mr. Buchanan Charles of North Andover, Massachusetts; and also of an anonymous donor; Miss Elizabeth Wade White of Middlebury, Connecticut, and Oxford, England; and Mrs. Buchanan Charles. The transaction was described by the London *Times* under the headline "Historic Manuscript Goes Home." Noting this, *The Bay State Librarian* commented that "The man-

uscript is well known in the rare book world because
of the continuous efforts to sell it after it was ob-
tained by a dealer from a Bradstreet descendant
some twenty years ago. It is called one of the ma-
jor American library treasures, being in the hand-
writing of the author considered the first signifi-
cant woman poet in the English language and the
first American poet of either sex."

It is with particular gratitude and pleasure that
we acknowledge the privilege given us by Mr. Buch-
anan Charles and the other trustees of the Stevens
Memorial Library to reproduce a facsimile copy of
the manuscript. Indiana University Library has
permitted the reproduction, somewhat enlarged, of
The Tenth Muse.

JOSEPHINE K. PIERCY

Indiana University
10 March 1964

THE TENTH MUSE

THE
TENTH MUSE

Lately fprung up in AMERICA.

OR

Severall Poems, compiled

with great variety of VVit
and Learning, full of delight.
Wherein efpecially is contained a com-
pleat difcourfe and defcription of

The Four
{ *Elements,*
Conftitutions,
Ages of Man,
Seafons of the Year. }

Together with an Exact Epitomie of
the Four Monarchies, viz.

The
{ *Affyrian,*
Perfian,
Grecian,
Roman. }

Alfo a Dialogue between Old *England* and
New, concerning the late troubles.
With divers other pleafant and ferious Poems.

By a Gentlewoman in thofe parts.

Printed at London for *Stephen Bowtell* at the figne of the
Bible in Popes Head-Alley. 1650.

Kind Reader:

Had I opportunity but to borrow some of the *Authors* wit, 'tis pos-sible I might so trim this curious Work with such quaint expressions, as that the Preface might bespeake thy further peru-sall; but I feare 'twil be a shame for a man that can speak so little, to be seene in the title page of this *Womans Book*, left by comparing the one with the other, the *Reader* should passe his sentence, that it is the gift of wo-men, not only to speak most, but to speake best; I shall leave therefore to commend that, which with any ingenious *Reader* will too much commend the *Author*, unlesse men turne more peevish then women, to envie the excellency of the inferiour *Sex*. I doubt not but the *Reader* will quickly finde more then I can say, and the worst effect of his rea-ding will be unbeleif, which will make him question whether it be a womans *Work*, and aske, Is it posible? If any doe, take this as an answer from him that dares avow it; It is the VVork of a VVoman, honoured, and e-

A 3.   steemed

steemed where she lives, for her gracious de-
meanour, her eminent parts, her pious con-
versation, her courteous disposition, her exact
diligence in her place, and discreet mannag-
ing of her family occasions; and more then
so, these Poems are the fruit but of some few
houres, curtailed from her sleep, and other re-
freshments. I dare adde little, lest I keepe
thee too long, if thou wilt not beleeve the
worth of these things (in their kind) when
a man sayes it, yet beleeve it from a woman
when thou seest it. This only I shall annex,
I feare the displeasure of no person in the pub-
lishing of these Poems but the Authors, without
whose knowledge, and contrary to her expe-
ctation, I have presumed to bring to publick
view what she resolved should never in such
a manner see the Sun; but I found that di-
vers had gotten some scattered papers, affe-
cted them wel, were likely to have sent forth
broken peices to the Authors prejudice, which
I thought to prevent, as well as to pleasure
those that earnestly desired the view of the
whole.   Mercu-

MErcury shew'd *Apollo*, *Bartas* Book,
Minerva this, and wisht him well to
   look,
And tell uprightly, which, did which excell;
He view'd, and view'd, and vow'd he could
   not tell.
They bid him Hemisphear his mouldy nose,
With's crackt leering-glasses, for it would
   pose
The best brains he had in's old pudding-pan,
Sex weigh'd, which best, the Woman, or the
   Man?
He peer'd, and por'd, and glar'd, and said for
   wore,
I'me even as wise now, as I was before :
They both 'gan laugh, and said, it was no
   mar'l
The Auth'resse was a right *Du Bartas* Girle.
Good sooth quoth the old *Don*, tel ye me so,
I muse whither at length these Girls wil go;
It half revives my chil frost-bitten blood,
To see a woman, once, do ought that's good;
And chode buy *Chaucers* Boots, and *Homers*
   Furrs,
Let men look to't, least women weare the
   Spurs.

                              N. Ward.
              A 4   To

To my deare Sister, the Author of these Poems.

Though most that know me, dare (I think) affirm
I ne're was borne to doe a Poet harm,
   Yet when I read your pleasant witty strains,
It wrought so strongly on my addle braines;
That though my verse be not so finely spun,
And so (like yours) cannot so neatly run:
Yet am I willing, with upright intent,
To shew my love without a complement.
There needs no painting to that comely face,
That in its native beauty hath such grace;
What I (poore silly I) prefix therefore,
Can but doe this, make yours admir'd the more;
And if but only this, I doe attaine
Content, that my disgrace may be your gaine.

   If women, I with women, may compare,
Your Works are solid, others weake as aire;
Some books of Women I have heard of late,
Perused some, so witlesse, intricate,
So void of sence, and truth, as if to cire
Were only wisht (acting above their sphear)

                       And

And all to get, what (filly foules) they lack,
Esteeme to be the wiseft of the pack ;
Though (for your fake) to fome this be permitted,
To print, yet wifh I many better witted ;
Their vanity make this to be inquired,
If women are with wit, and fence infpired.
Yet when your Works fhall come to publick view,
'Twill be affirm'd, 'twill be confirm'd by you :
And I, when ferioufly I had revolved
What you had done, I prefently refolved,
Theirs was the Perfons, not the Sexes failing,
And therefore did be-fpeak a modeft vailing.
You have acutely in *Eliza's* ditty
Acquitted women, elfe I might with pitty,
Have wifht them all to womens Works to look,
And never more to meddle with their book.
What you have done, the Sun fhall witneffe beare,
That for a womans Worke 'tis very rare ;
And if the Nine vouchfafe the Tenth a place,
I think they rightly may yeeld you that grace.
   But leaft I fhould exceed, and too much love,
Should too too much endear'd affection move,
To fuper-adde in praifes I fhall ceafe,
Leaft while I pleafe my felfe I fhould difpleafe
The longing Reader, who may chance complaine,
And fo requite my love with deep difdaine ;
That I your filly Servant, ftand i' th' porch,
Lighting your Sun-light with my blinking torch ;
Hindring his minds content, his fweet repofe,
Which your delightfull *Poems* doe difclofe,
When once the Caskets op'ned ; yet to you
Let this be added, then i'le bid adieu.

If you shall think, it will be to your shame
To be in print, then I must beare the blame :
If't be a fault, 'tis mine, 'tis shame that might
Deny so faire an infant of its right,
To looke abroad ; I know your modest minde,
How you will blush, complaine, 'tis too unkinde,
To force a womans birth, provoke her paine,
Expose her Labours to the world's disdaine :
I know you'l say, you doe defie that mint,
That stampt you thus, to be a foole in print.
'Tis true, it doth not now so neatly stand,
As ift 'twere pollisht with your owne sweet hand ;
'Tis not so richly deckt, so trimly tir'd,
Yet it is such as justly is admir'd.
If it be folly, 'tis of both, or neither,
Both you and I, we'l both be fools together ;
And he that sayes, 't is foolish (if my word
May sway) by my consent shall make the third.
I dare out-face the worlds disdaine for both,
If you alone professe you are not wroth ;
Yet if you are, a womans wrath is little,
When thousands else admire you in each tittle.

I. W.

Upon

Upon the Author, by a knowne Friend.

Now I beleeve Tradition, which doth call
The Muses, Vertues, Graces, Females all;
Only they are not nine, eleaven, nor three,
Our Authresse proves them but one unity.
Mankind take up some blushes on the score,
Menopolize perfection no more:
In your owne Arts, confesse your selves out-done,
The Moone hath totally ecclips'd the Sun,
Not with her sable mantle musling him,
But her bright silver makes his gold looke dim:
Just as his beams force our pale Lamps to winke,
And earthly Fires within their ashes shrinke.

I cannot wonder at Apollo now
That he with Female Lawrell crown'd his brow,
That made him witty: had I leave to chuse,
My Verse should be a Page unto your Muse.

C. B.

Arme

ARme, arme, Soldado's arme, Horfe,
   Horfe, fpeed to your Horfes,
Gentle-women, make head, they vent
   their plots in Verfes;
They write of Monarchies, a moſt ſe-
   ditious word,
It ſignifies Oppreſſion, Tyranny, and
   Sword:
March amain to *London*, they'l riſe, for
   there they flock,
But ſtay a while, they ſeldome riſe till
   ten a clock.

R. 2.

In

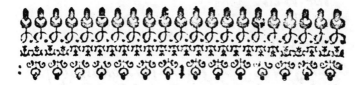

In praise of the Author,

Miſtris *Anne Bradſtreet*, Vertue's true and lively Patterne, Wife of the Worſhipfull *Simon Brad-ſtreet* Eſquire.

At preſent reſiding in the Occi-dentall parts of the World, in *America*, alias

NOV-ANGLIA.

VVHat Golden ſplendent *STAR is this, ſo bright,*
One thouſand miles thrice told, both day and night,

(From

(*From th' Orient firſt ſprung*) *now from the Weſt*
That ſhines; ſwift-winged Phœbus, *and the reſt,*
Of all Joves *fiery flames ſurmounting far,*
As doth each Planet, *every falling Star;*
By whoſe divine, and lucid light moſt cleare,
Natures darke ſecret Myſteries appeare;
Heaven's, Earths, *admired wonders, noble acts*
Of Kings, and Princes *moſt heroyick facts,*
And what e're elſe in darknes ſeem'd to dye,
Revives all things ſo obvious now to th' eye;
That he who theſe, its glittering Rayes viewes o're,
Shall ſee what's done, in all the world before.

N. H.

Upon

Upon the Author.

'TWere extreame folly should I dare attempt,
To praise this Authors worth with complement;
None but her self must dare commend her parts,
Whose sublime brain's the Synopsis of Arts:
Nature and Skil, here both in one agree,
To frame this Master-peice of Poetry:
False Fame, belye their Sex, no more, it can,
Surpasse, or parallel, the best of man.

C. B.

Another to M^ris. *Anne Bradstreete*, Author of this Poem.

I'Ve read your Poem (Lady) and admire,
Your Sex, to such a pitch should e're aspire;
Goe on to write, continue to relate,
New Histories, of Monarchy and State:
And what the *Romans* to their Poets gave,
Be sure such honour, and esteeme you'l have.

H. S.

An

An Anagram.

Anna Bradeſtreate.

Deer Neat *An Bartas.*

So *Bartas* like thy fine ſpun Poems been,
That *Bartas* name will prove an Epicene.

Another.

Anne Bradſtreate.

Artes bred neat *An.*

To

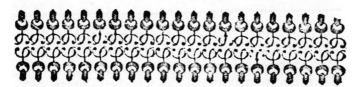

To her most Honoured Father *Thomas Dudley Esq;* *these humbly presented.*

DEare Sir, of late delighted with the sight,   *T D onthe*
Of your *four sisters, deckt in black & white *four parts*
Of fairer Dames, the sun near saw the face , *of the*
(though made a pedestall for *Adams* Race)   *world*
Their worth so shines, in those rich lines you show.
Their paralells to find I scarcely know,
To climbe their Climes, I have nor strength, nor skill,
To mount so high, requires an Eagles quill :
Yet view thereof, did cause my thoughts to soare,
My lowly pen, might wait upon those four,
I bring my four; and four, now meanly clad,
To do their homage unto yours most glad,
Who for their age, their worth, and quality,
Might seem of yours to claime precedency ;
But by my humble hand thus rudely pen'd
They are your bounden handmaids to attend.
These same are they, of whom we being have,
These are of all, the life, the nurse, the grave,
These are, the hot, the cold, the moist, the dry,
That sinke, that swim, that fill, that upwards flye,

                 B   Of

Of these consists, our bodyes, cloathes, and food,
The world, the usefull, hurtfull, and the good:
Sweet harmony they keep, yet jar oft times,
Their discord may appear, by these harsh rimes.
Yours did contest, for Wealth, for Arts, for Age,
My first do shew, their good, and then their rage,
My other four, do intermixed tell
Each others faults, and where themselves excell :
How hot, and dry, contend with moist, and cold,
How Aire, and Earth, no correspondence hold,
And yet in equall tempers, how they gree,
How divers natures, make one unity.
Some thing of all (though mean) I did intend,
But fear'd you'ld judge, one *Bartas* was my friend,
I honour him, but dare not wear his wealth,
My goods are true (though poor) I love no stealth,
But if I did, I durst not send them you;
Who must reward a theife, but with his due.
I shall not need my innocence to clear,
These ragged lines, will do't, when they appear.
On what they are, your mild aspect I crave,
Accept my best, my worst vouchsafe a grave.

From her, that to your selfe more duty owes,
Then waters, in the boundlesse Ocean flowes.

ANNE BRADSTREET.

The

THE
PROLOGUE.

1.

TO sing of Wars, of Captaines, and of Kings,
  Of Cities founded, Common-wealths begun,
For my mean Pen, are too superiour things,
And how they all, or each, their dates have run :
Let Poets, and Historians set these forth,
My obscure Verse, shal not so dim their worth.

2.

But when my wondring eyes, and envious heart,
Great *Bartas* sugar'd lines doe but read o're ;
Foole, I doe grudge, the Muses did not part
'Twixt him and me, that over-fluent store ;
A *Bartas* can, doe what a *Bartas* wil,
But simple I, according to my skill.

3.

From School-boyes tongue, no Rhethorick we expect,
Nor yet a sweet Consort, from broken strings,
Nor perfect beauty, where's a maine defect,
My foolish, broken, blemish'd Muse so sings ;
And this to mend, alas, no Art is able,
'Cause Nature made it so irreparable.

4.

Nor can I, like that fluent sweet tongu'd *Greek*
Who lisp'd at first, speake afterwards more plaine
By Art, he gladly found what he did seeke,
A full requitall of his striving paine :

B 2

Art

Art can doe much, but this maxime's most sure,
A weake or wounded braine admits no cure.

5.

Iam obnoxious to each carping tongue,
Who sayes, my hand a needle better fits,
A Poets Pen, all scorne, I should thus wrong;
For such despight they cast on female wits:
If what I doe prove well, it wo'nt advance,
They'l say its stolne, or else, it was by chance.

6.

But sure the antick *Greeks* were far more milde,
Else of our Sex, why feigned they those nine,
And poesy made, *Calliope's* owne childe,
So 'mongst the rest, they plac'd the Arts divine :
But this weake knot they will full soone untye,
The *Greeks* did nought, but play the foole and lye.

7.

Let *Greeks* be *Greeks*, and Women what they are,
Men have precedency, and still excell,
It is but vaine, unjustly to wage war,
Men can doe best, and Women know it well;
Preheminence in each, and all is yours,
Yet grant some small acknowledgement of ours.

8.

And oh, ye high flown quils, that soare the skies,
And ever with your prey, still catch your praise,
If e're you daigne these lowly lines, your eyes
Give wholsome Parsley wreath, I aske no Bayes :
This meane and unrefined stuffe of mine,
Will make your glistering gold but more to shine.

A. B.
The

The
Foure Elements.

Ire, Aire, Earth, and Water, did all contest
which was the strongest, noblest, & the best,
Who the most good could shew, & who most
    rage
For to declare, themselves they all ingage;
And in due order each her turne should speake,
But enmity, this amity did breake;
All would be cheife, and all scorn'd to be under,
Whence issu'd raines, and winds, lightning and thunder;
The quaking Earth did groan, the skie look't black,
The Fire, the forced Aire, in sunder crack;
The sea did threat the heavens, the heavens the earth,
All looked like a Chaos, or new birth;
Fire broyled Earth, and scorched Earth it choaked,
Both by their darings; Water so provoked,
That roaring in it came, and with its source
Soone made the combatants abate their force,
The rumbling, hissing, puffing was so great,
The worlds confusion it did seeme to threat;
But Aire at length, contention so abated,
That betwixt hot and cold, she arbitrated
The others enmity: being lesse, did cease
All stormes now laid, and they in perfect peace,
That Fire should first begin, the rest consent,
Being the most impatient Element.

Fire.

Fire.

WHat is my worth (both ye) and all things know,
   Where little is, I can but little show,
But what I am, let learned *Grecians* say;
What I can doe, well skill'd Mechanicks may,
The benefit all Beings, by me finde;
Come first ye Artists, and declare your minde.
What toole was ever fram'd, but by my might,
O Martialist ! what weapon for your fight?
To try your valour by, but it must feele
My force ? your sword, your Pike, your flint and steele,
Your Cannon's bootlesse, and your powder too
Without mine ayd, alas, what can they doe?
The adverse wall's not shak'd, the Mine's not blowne,
And in despight the City keeps her owne,
But I with one Granado, or Petard,
Set ope those gates, that 'fore so strong was barr'd.
Ye Husband-men, your coulter's made by me,
Your shares, your mattocks, and what e're you see,
Subdue the earth, and fit it for your graine,
That so in time it might requite your paine;
Though strong limb'd *Vulcan* forg'd it by his skill,
I made it flexible unto his will.
Ye Cooks, your kitchin implements I fram'd,
Your spits, pots, jacks, what else I need not name,
Your dainty food, I wholsome make, I warme
Your shrinking limbs, which winters cold doth harme;
Ye Paracelsians too, in vaine's your skil
In chymestry, unlesse I help you Stil,

                                        And

And you Philofophers, if ere you made
A tranfmutation,it was through mine aide.
Ye Silver-fmiths, your ure I do refine,
What mingled lay with earth, I caufe to fhine.
But let me leave thefe things, my flame afpires
To match on high with the Celeftiall fires.
The Sun,an Orbe of Fire was held of old,
Our Sages new, another tale have told :
But be he what they lift, yet his afpeƈt,
A burning fiery heat we find refleƈt;
And of the felfe fame nature is with mine,
Good fifter Earth, no witneffe needs but thine ;
How doth his warmth refrefh thy frozen backs,
And trim thee gay, in green, after thy blacks ?
Both man and beaft, rejoyce at his approach,
And birds do fing,to fee his glittering Coach.
And though nought but *Sal'manders* live in fire ;
The Flye *Pyraufta* cal'd, all elfe expire.
Yet men and beafts,Aftronomers can tell,
Fixed in heavenly conftellations dwell,
My Planets, of both Sexes, whofe degree,
Poor Heathen judg'd worthy a Diety :
With *Orion* arm'd, attended by his dog,
The *Theban* ftout *Alcides*, with his club:
The Valiant *Perfeus* who *Medufa* flew,
The Horfe that kill'd *Bellerophon*, then flew.
My Crabbe, my Scorpion, fifhes, you may fee,
The maid with ballance, wayn with horfes three ;
The Ram,the Bull,the Lyon, and the Beagle ;
The Bear, the Goate,the Raven,and the Eagle,
The Crown, the Whale,the Archer, Bernice Hare,
The Hidra,Dolphin,Boys,that waters bear.

Nay

Nay more then thefe, Rivers 'mongft ftars are found,
Eridanus, where *Phaeton* was drown'd,
Their magnitude and height fhould *I* recount,
My ftory to a Volume would amount:
Out of a multitude, thefe few *I* touch,
Your wifdom out of little gathers much,
I'le here let paffe, my Choler caufe of warres,
And influence of divers of thofe ftarres,
When in conjunction with the fun, yet more,
Augment his heat, which was too hot before :
The Summer ripening feafon I do claime;
And man from thirty unto fifty frame.
Of old, when Sacrifices were divine,
I of acceptance was the holy figne.
'Mong all my wonders which I might recount ;
There's none more ftrange then *Ætna's* fulphery mount
The choaking flames, that from *Vefuvius* flew
The over-curious fecond *Pliny* flew:
And with the afhes, that it fometimes fhed
Apulia's jacent parts were covered ;
And though I be a fervant to each man;
Yet by my force, mafter my mafter can.
What famous Townes to cinders have I turn'd ?
What lafting Forts my kindled wrath hath burn'd ?
The ftately feats of mighty Kings by me :
In confus'd heaps of afhes may ye fee.
Where's *Ninus* great wal'd Town, and *Troy* of old ?
Carthage, and hundred moe, in ftories told,
Which when they could not be o're come by foes
The Army through my helpe victorious rofe ;
Old facred *Zion*, I demolifh'd thee;
So great *Diana's* Temple was by me.

                                   And

And more then bruitish *Sodome* for her lust,
With neighbouring Townes I did consume to dust,
What shal I say of Lightning, and of Thunder,
Which Kings, and mighty ones; amaz'd with wonder,
Which made a *Cæsar*, (*Romes*) the worlds proud head,
Foolish *Caligula*, creep under's bed
Of Metors, *Ignis Fatuus*, and the rest,
But to leave those to'th' wise, I judge is best,
The rich I oft make poore, the strong I maime,
Not sparing life when I can take the same;
And in a word, the World I shal consume,
And all therein at that great day of doome;
Not before then, shal cease my raging ire,
And then, because no matter more for fire:
Now Sisters, pray proceed, each in her course,
As I; impart your usefulnesse, and force.

Earth.

THe next in place, Earth judg'd to be her due,
   Sister, in worth I come not short of you;
In wealth and use *I* doe surpasse you all,
And Mother Earth, of old, men did me call,
Such was my fruitfulnesse; an Epithite
Which none ere gave, nor you could claime of right,
Among my praises this I count not least,
I am th' originall of man and beast,
To tell what sundry fruits my fat soyle yeelds,
In vine-yards, orchards, gardens, and corne fields,
Their kinds, their taste, their colours, and their smels,
Would so passe time, I could say nothing else;

                                        The

The rich and poore, wife, foole, and every fort,
Of thefe fo common things, can make report:
To tell you of my Countries, and my regions
Soone would they paffe, not hundreds, but legions,
My cities famous, rich, and populous,
Whofe numbers now are growne innumerous ;
I have not time to thinke of every part,
Yet let me name my *Græcia*, 'tis my heart
For Learning, Armes, and Arts, I love it well :
But chiefly, 'caufe the Mufes there did dwell ;
I'le here skip o're my mountaines, reaching skies
Whether Pyrenian, or the Alpes; both lyes
On either fide the country of the *Gaules*,
Strong forts from *Spanifh* and *Italian* braules,
And huge great *Taurus*, longer then the reft.
Dividing great *Armenia* from the leaft,
And *Hemus*, whofe fteep fides, none foote upon,
But farewell all, for deare mount *Helicon*,
And wonderous high *Olimpus*, of fuch fame,
That heaven it felfe was oft call'd by that name ;
Sweet *Parnaffus*, I dote too much on thee,
Unleffe thou prove a better friend to me ;
But ile skip o're thefe Hills, not touch a Dale,
Nor yet expatiate, in Temple vale ;
Ile here let goe, my Lions of *Numedia*,
My Panthers, and my Leopards of *Libia*,
The Behemoth, and rare found Unicorne,
Poyfons fure antidote lyes in his horne.
And my *Hyæna* (imitates mans voyce)
Out of huge numbers, I might pick my choyce,
Thoufands in woods, and planes, both wild, and tame,
But here, or there, I lift now none to name ;

                                    No,

No, though the fawning dog did urge me fore
In his behalfe to fpeak a word the more ;
Whofe truft, and valour I might here commend :
But time's too fhort, and precious fo to fpend.
But hark, ye worthy Merchants who for prize
Send forth your well man'd fhips, where fun doth rife.
After three years, when men and meat is fpent,
My rich commodities payes double rent.
Ye *Galenifts*, my Drugs that come from thence
Doe cure your patients, fill your purfe with pence;
Befides the ufe you have, of Hearbs and Plants,
That with leffe coft, neare home, fupplyes your wants.
But Marriners, where got you fhips and failes ?
And Oares to row, when both my fifters failes ?
Your Tackling, Anchor, Compaffe too, is mine ;
Which guides, when Sun, nor Moon, nor *Stars* do fhine.
Ye mighty Kings, who for your lafting fames
Built Cities, Monuments call'd by your names ;
Was thofe compiled heapes of maffy ftones ?
That your ambition laid, ought but my bones ?
Ye greedy mifers who do dig for gold ;
For gemmes, for filver, treafures which I hold :
Will not my goodly face, your rage fuffice ?
But you will fee what in my bowels lyes ?
And ye Artificers, all trades and forts;
My bounty calls you forth to make reports,
If ought you have to ufe, to wear, to eate ?
But what I freely yeeld upon your fweat ?
And cholerick fifter, thou (for all thine ire)
Well knoweft, my fuell muft maintain thy fire.
As I ingenuoufly (with thanks) confeffe
My cold, thy (fruitfull) heat, doth crave no leffe:

                               But

But how my cold, dry temper, works upon
The melancholy conftitution.
How the Autumnal feafon I do fway;
And how I force the grey head to obey.
I fhould here make a fhort, yet true narration,
But that thy method is my imitation.
Now might I fhew my adverfe quality,
And how I oft work mans mortality.
He fometimes findes, maugre his toyling paine,
Thiftles and thornes, where he expected graine;
My fap, to plants and trees, I muft not grant,
The Vine, the Olive, and the Figtree want:
The Corne, and Hay, both fall before they'r mowne;
And buds from fruitfull trees, before they'r blowne:
Then dearth prevailes, that Nature to fuffice,
The tender mother on her Infant flyes:
The Husband knowes no Wife, nor father fons;
But to all outrages their hunger runnes.
Dreadfull examples, foon I might produce,
But to fuch auditours 'twere of no ufe.
Again, when Delvers dare in hope of gold,
To ope thofe veines of Mine, audacious bold:
While they thus in my intralls feem to dive;
Before they know, they are inter'd alive.
Ye affrighted wights, appall'd how do you fhake
If once you feele me, your foundation, quake,
Becaufe in the abyffe of my darke wombe:
Your Cities and your felves I oft intombe.
O dreadfull Sepulcher! that this is true,
Korah and all his Company well knew.
And fince, faire *Italy* full fadly knowes
What fhe hath loft by thefe my dreadfull woes.

                                                    And

And *Rome*, her *Curtius*, can't forget I think;
Who bravely rode into my yawning chinke.
Again, what veines of poyson in me lye ;
As *Stibium* and unfixt *Mercury* :
With divers moe, nay, into plants it creeps ;
In hot, and cold, and some benums with fleeps,
Thus I occasion death to man and beaft,
When they feek food, and harme miftruft the leaft.
Much might I fay, of the *Arabian* fands ;
Which rife like mighty billowes on the lands :
Wherein whole Armies I have overthrown ;
But windy fifter, 'twas when you have blown.
Ile fay no more, yet this thing adde I muft,
Remember fonnes, your mould is of my duft,
And after death, whether inter'd, or burn'd ;
As earth at firft, fo into earth return'd.

Water.

SCarce Earth had done, but th' angry waters mov'd;
  Sifter (quoth fhe) it had full well behov'd
Among your boaftings to have praifed me;
Caufe of your fruitfulneffe, as you fhall fee :
This your neglect, fhewes your ingratitude ;
And how your fubtilty would men delude.
Not one of us, all knowes, that's like to thee,
Ever in craving, from the other three :
But thou art bound to me, above the reft ;
Which am thy drink, thy blood, thy fap, and beft.
If I withhold, what art thou, dead, dry lump
Thou bear'ft no graffe, nor plant, nor tree, nor ftump.
                                              Thy

Thy extream thirst is moistened by my love,
With springs below,and showers from above;
Or else thy sun-burnt face, and gaping chapps;
Complaines to th'heaven, when I withhold my drops:
Thy Bear, thy Tyger, and thy Lyon stout,
When I am gone, their fiercenesse none need doubt;
The Camell hath no strength, thy Bull no force;
Nor mettl's found in the couragious Horse:
Hindes leave their Calves, the Elephant the Fens;
The Woolves and savage Beasts, forsake their Dens.
The lofty Eagle and the Storke flye low,
The Peacock, and the Ostrich, share in woe:
The Pine,the Cedars, yea and *Daph'nes* tree;
Do cease to flourish in this misery.
Man wants his bread,and wine,and pleasant fruits;
He knowes such sweets,lyes not in earths dry roots,
Then seeks me out, in River and in Well;
His deadly mallady, I might expell.
If I supply, his heart and veines rejoyce;
If not,soon ends his life,as did his voyce.
That this is true, earth thou canst not deny;
I call thine *Egypt*,this to verifie;
Which by my fatting Nile, doth yeeld such store,
That she can spare,when Nations round are poore.
When I run low,and not o'reflow her brinks;
To meet with want, each woefull man bethinks.
But such I am, in Rivers,showers and springs;
But what's the wealth that my rich Ocean brings?
Fishes so numberlesse I there do hold;
Shouldst thou but buy, it wou'd exhaust thy gold.
There lives the oyly Whale,whom all men know,
Such wealth, but not such like, Earth thou mayst shew.
                                                    The

The Dolphin (loving muſique) *Arions* friend.
The crafty Barbell, whoſe wit doth her commend;
With thouſands moe, which now I liſt not name,
Thy ſilence of thy beaſts, doth cauſe the ſame.
My pearles that dangle at thy darlings ears ;
Not thou, but ſhell-fiſh yeelds, as *Pliny* clears.
Was ever gem ſo rich found in thy trunke ?
As *Ægypts* wanton *Cleopatra* drunke.
Or haſt thou any colour can come nigh ;
The *Roman* Purple, double *Tirian* dye.
Which *Cæſars, Conſuls, Tribunes* all adorne ;
For it, to ſearch my waves, they thought no ſcorne.
Thy gallant rich perfuming Amber-greece:
I lightly caſt a ſhoare as frothy fleece.
With rowling graines of pureſt maſſy gold :
Which *Spaines Americans,* do gladly hold.
Earth, thou haſt not more Countrys, Vales and Mounds,
Then I have Fountaines, Rivers, Lakes and Ponds:
My ſundry Seas, Black, VVhite, and Adriatique
Ionian, Balticke, and the vaſt *Atlantique* ;
The *Pontieke, Caſpian,* Golden Rivers fine.
Aſphaltis Lake, where nought remains alive.
But I ſhould go beyond thee in thy boaſts,
If I ſhould ſhew, more Seas, then thou haſt Coaſts.
But note this maxime in Philoſophy :
Then Seas are deep, Mountains are never high.
To ſpeake of kinds of VVaters I'le negleƈt,
My divers Fountaines and their ſtrange effeƈt ;
My wholeſome Bathes, together with their cures.
My water *Syrens,* with their guilefull lures:
Th' uncertain cauſe, of certain ebbs and flowes ;
VVhich wondring *Ariſtotles* wit, ne'r knowes.

Nor

Nor will I speake of waters made by Art,
Which can to life, restore a fainting heart:
Nor fruitfull dewes, nor drops from weeping eyes;
VVhich pitty moves, and oft deceives the wise.
Nor yet of Salt, and Sugar, sweet and smart,
Both when we list, to water we convert.
Alas; thy ships and oares could do no good
Did they but want my Ocean, and my Flood.
The wary Merchant, on his weary beast
Transfers his goods, from North and South and East;
Unlesse I ease his toyle, and doe transport,
The wealthy fraught, unto his wished Port.
These be my benefits which may suffice:
I now must shew what force there in me lyes.
The fleg my constitution I uphold;
All humours, Tumours, that are bred of cold.
O're childehood, and Winter, I bear the sway;
Yet *Luna* for my Regent I obey.
As I with showers oft time refresh the earth;
So oft in my excesse, I cause a dearth:
And with aboundant wet, so coole the ground,
By adding cold to cold, no fruit proves found;
The Farmer, and the Plowman both complain
Of rotten sheep, lean kine, and mildew'd grain.
And with my wasting floods, and roaring torrent;
Their Cattle, Hay, and Corne, I sweep down current,
Nay many times, my Ocean breaks his bounds:
And with astonishment, the world confounds.
And swallowes Countryes up, ne're seen againe:
And that an Island makes, which once was maine.
Thus *Albion* (tis thought) was cut from *France*,
Cicily from *Italy*, by th'like chance.

And

And but one land was *Affriea* and *Spayne*,
Untill ſtraight *Gibralter*, did make them twaine.
Some ſay I ſwallowed up(ſure 'tis a notion)
A mighty Country ith' *Atlanticke* Ocean.
I need not ſay much of my Haile and Snow,
My Ice and extream cold, which all men know.
VVhereof the firſt, ſo ominous I rain'd,
That *Iſraels* enemies, therewith was brain'd.
And of my chilling colds,ſuch plenty be;
That *Caucaſus* high mounts, are ſeldom free.
Mine Ice doth glaze *Europs* big'ſt Rivers o're,
Till Sun releaſe, their ſhips can ſaile no more.
All know, what innundations I have made;
VVherein not men, but mountaines ſeem'd to wade
As when *Achaia*,all under water ſtood,
That in two hundred year, it ne'r prov'd good.
Ducalions great deluge, with many moe ;
But theſe are trifles to the Flood of *Noe*.
Then wholly periſh'd, earths ignoble race;
And to this day, impaires her beautious face.
That after times, ſhall never feel like woe :
Her confirm'd ſonnes, behold my colour'd bow.
Much might I ſay of wracks, but that Ile ſpare,
And now give place unto our ſiſter *Aire*.

Aire.

COntent (quoth Aire) to ſpeake the laſt of you,
   Though not through ignorance, firſt was my due,
I doe ſuppoſe, you'l yeeld without controle;
I am the breath of every living ſoul.

C

Mor-

Mortalls, what one of you, that loves not me,
Aboundantly more then my fifters three?
And though you love Fire, Earth, and VVater wel;
Yet Aire, beyond all thefe ye know t'excell.
I aske the man condemn'd, that's near his death :
How gladly fhould his gold purchafe his breath,
And all the wealth, that ever earth did give,
How freely fhould it go, fo he might live.
No world, thy witching trafh, were all but vain.
If my pure Aire, thy fonnes did not fuftain.
The famifht, thirfty man, that craves fupply :
His moveing reafon is, give leaft I dye.
So loath he is to go, though nature's fpent,
To bid adue, to his dear Element.
Nay, what are words, which doe reveale the mind ?
Speak, who, or what they will, they are but wind.
Your Drums, your Trumpets, and your Organs found,
VVhat is't? but forced Aire which muft rebound,
And fuch are Ecchoes, and report o'th gun
VVhich tells afar, th' exployt which he hath done.
Your fongs and pleafant tunes, they are the fame,
And fo's the notes which Nightingales do frame.
Ye forging Smiths, if Bellowes once were gone;
Your red hot work, more coldly would go on.
Ye Mariners, tis I that fill your Sailes,
And fpeed you to your Port, with wifhed gales.
VVhen burning heat, doth caufe you faint, I coole,
And when I fmile, your Ocean's like a Poole.
I ripe the corne, I turne the grinding mill;
And with my felfe, I every vacuum fill.
The ruddy fweet fanguine, is like to Aire,
And youth, and fpring, fages to me compare.

My

My moiſt hot nature, is ſo purely thinne,
No place ſo ſubtilly made, but I get in.
I grow more pure and pure, as I mount higher,
And when I'm throughly rarifi'd, turn fire.
So when I am condens'd, I turne to water;
VVhich may be done, by holding down my vapour.
Thus I another body can aſſume,
And in a trice, my own nature reſume.
Some for this cauſe (of late) have been ſo bold,
Me for no Element, longer to hold.
Let ſuch ſuſpend their thoughts, and ſilent be;
For all Philoſophers make one of me.
And what thoſe Sages, did, or ſpake, or writ,
Is more authentick then their moderne wit.
Next, of my Fowles ſuch multitudes there are;
Earths Beaſts, and VVaters Fiſh, ſcarce can compare.
The Oſtrich with her plumes, th'Eagle with her eynes;
The Phœnix too (if any be) are mine;
The Stork, the Crane, the Partrich, and the Pheſant;
The Pye, the Jay, the Larke, a prey to th' Peaſant.
VVith thouſands moe, which now I may omit;
VVithout impeachment, to my tale or wit.
As my freſh Aire preſerves, all things in life;
So when'ts corrupt, mortality is rife.
Then Feavours, Purples, Pox, and Peſtilence;
VVith divers moe, worke deadly conſequence.
VVhereof ſuch multitudes have dy'd and fled,
The living, ſcarce had power, to bury dead.
Yea ſo contagious, Countries have me known;
That birds have not ſcap'd death, as they have flows,
Of murrain, Cattle numberleſſe did fail.
Men fear'd deſtruction epidemicall.

Then

Then of my tempests, felt at Sea and Land,
Which neither ships nor houses could withstand.
What woeful wracks I've made, may wel appear,
If nought was known, but that before *Algire*.
Where famous *Charles* the fift, more losse sustain'd,
Then in his long hot wars, which *Millain* gain'd.
How many rich fraught vessells, have I split?
Some upon sands, some upon rocks have hit.
Some have I forc'd, to gaine an unknown shoare;
Some overwelm'd with waves, and seen no more.
Again, what tempests, and what hericanoes
Knowes VVestern Isles, *Christophers*, *Barbadoes*;
VVhere neither houses, trees, nor plants, I spare;
But some fall down, and some flye up with aire.
Earth-quaks so hurtful and so fear'd of all,
Imprisoned I, am the original.
Then what prodigious sights, sometimes I show:
As battells pitcht ith' Aire (as Countries know;)
Their joyning, fighting, forcing, and retreat;
That earth appeares in heaven, oh wonder great!
Sometimes strange flaming swords, and blazing stars,
Portentious signes, of Famines, Plagues and VVars.
VVhich makes the mighty Monarchs fear their Fates,
By death, or great mutations of their States.
I have said lesse, then did my sisters three;
But what's their worth, or force, but more's in me.
To adde to all I've said, was my intent,
But dare not go, beyond my Element.

Of

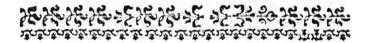

Of the foure Humours in Mans constitution.

He former foure, now ending their Dis-
    course,
Ceasing to vaunt, their good, or threat their
    force.
Loe! other foure step up, crave leave to shew
The native qualities, that from each flow,
But first they wisely shew'd their high descent,
Each eldest Daughter to each Element ;
Choler was own'd by Fire, and Blood by Aire,
Earth knew her black swarth childe, Water her faire ;
All having made obeysance to each Mother,
Had leave to speake, succeeding one the other ;
But 'mongst themselves they were at variance,
Which of the foure should have predominance ;
Choler hotly claim'd, right by her mother,
Who had precedency of all the other.
But Sanguine did disdaine, what she requir'd,
Pleading her selfe, was most of all desir'd ;
Proud Melancholy, more envious then the rest,
The second, third, or last could not digest ;
She was the silencest of all the foure,
Her wisedome spake not much, but thought the more.

C 3

Cold

Cold flegme, did not conteſt for higheſt place,
Only ſhe crav'd, to have a vacant ſpace.
Wel, thus they parle, and chide, but to be briefe,
Or wil they nil they, Choler wil be cheife;
They ſeeing her imperioſity,
At preſent yeelded, to neceſſity.

Choler.

TO ſhew my great deſcent, and pedigree,
Your ſelves would judge, but vain prolixity.
   It is acknowledged, from whence I came,
It ſhal ſuffice, to tel you what I am :
My ſelf, and Mother, one as you ſhal ſee,
But ſhe in greater, I in leſſe degree ;
We both once Maſculines, the world doth know,
Now Feminines (a while) for love we owe
Unto your Siſter-hood, which makes us tender
Our noble ſelves, in a leſſe noble Gender.
Though under fire, we comprehend all heat,
Yet man for Choler, is the proper ſeat.
I in his heart erect my regal throne,
Where Monarch-like I play, and ſway alone.
Yet many times, unto my great diſgrace,
One of your ſelves are my compeers, in place:
Where if your rule once grow predominant,
The man proves boyiſh, ſottiſh, ignorant,
But if ye yeeld ſub-ſervient unto me,
I make a man, a man i'th higheſt degree,
Be he a Souldier, I more fence his heart
Then Iron Corſlet, 'gainſt a ſword or dart ;

Wh

What makes him face his foe, without appal?
To ftorme a Breach, or fcale a City wal?
In dangers to account himfelf more fure,
Then timerous Hares, whom Caftles doe immure?
Have ye not heard of Worthies, Demi-gods?
'Twixt them and others, what ift makes the odds
But valour,whence comes that? from none of you;
Nay milk-fops,at fuch brunts you look but blew,
Here's Sifter Ruddy, worth the other two,
That much wil talk, but little dares fhe do,
Unleffe to court, and claw, and dice, and drink,
And there fhe wil out-bid us all, I think;
She loves a Fiddle, better then a Drum,
A Chamber wel, in field fhe dares not come;
She'l ride a Horfe as bravely, as the beft,
And break a ftaffe, provided't be in jeft,
But fhuns to look on wounds, and bloud that's fpilt,
She loves her fword, only becaufe its gilt;
Then here's our fad black Sifter, worfe then you,
She'l neither fay, fhe wil, nor wil fhe doe:
But peevifh, Male-content, mufing fhe fits,
And by mifprifions,like to loofe her wits;
If great perfwafions, caufe her meet her foe;
In her dul refolution, fhe's flow.
To march her pace,to fome is greater pain,
Then by a quick encounter, to be flaine;
But be fhe beaten, fhe'l not run away,
She'l firft advife, if't be not beft to ftay.
But let's give, cold,white;Sifter Flegme her right.
So loving unto all, fhe fcornes to fight.
If any threaten her, fhe'l in a trice,
Convert from water, to conjealed Ice;

Her

Her teeth wil chatter, dead and wan's her face,
And 'fore she be assaulted, quits the place,
She dare, not challenge if I speake amisse;
Nor hath she wit, or heat, to blush at this.
Here's three of you, all sees now what you are,
Then yeeld to me, preheminence in War.
Again, who fits, for learning, science, Arts?
Who rarifies the intellectuall parts?
Whence flow fine spirits, and witty notions?
Not from our dul slow Sisters motions:
Nor sister Sanguine, from thy moderate heat,
Poor spirits the Liver breeds, which is thy seat,
What comes from thence, my heat refines the same,
And through the arteries sends o're the frame,
The vitall spirits they're call'd, and wel they may,
For when they faile, man turnes unto his clay:
The Animal I claime, as wel as these,
The nerves should I not warm, soon would they freeze.
But Flegme her self, is now provok'd at this,
She thinks I never shot so farre amisse;
The Brain she challenges, the Head's her seat,
But know'ts a foolish brain, that wanteth heat;
My absence proves, it plain, her wit then flyes
Out at her nose, or melteth at her eyes;
Oh, who would misse this influence of thine,
To be distill'd a drop on every line!
No, no, thou hast no spirits, thy company
Wil feed a Dropsie, or a Timpany,
The Palsie, Gout, or Cramp, or some such dolor,
Thou wast not made for Souldier, or for Schollar;
Of greasie paunch, and palled checks, go vaunt,
But a good head from these are disonant;

But

But Melancholy, wouldſt have this glory thine ?
Thou ſayſt, thy wits are ſtai'd, ſubtle and fine:
Tis true, when I am midwife to thy birth;
Thy ſelf's as dul, as is thy mother Earth.
Thou canſt not claime, the Liver, Head nor Heart;
Yet haſt thy ſeat aſſign'd, a goodly part,
The ſinke of all us three, the hatefull ſpleen;
Of that black region, Nature made thee Queen;
Where paine and ſore obſtructions, thou doſt work ;
Where envy, malice, thy companions lurke.
If once thou'rt great, what followes thereupon ?
But bodies waſting, and deſtruction.
So baſe thou art, that baſer cannot be ;
The excrement, aduſtion of me.
But I am weary to dilate thy ſhame ;
Nor is't my pleaſure, thus to blur thy name:
Onely to raiſe my honours to the Skyes,
As objects beſt appear, by contraries.
Thus arms, and arts I claim, and higher things;
The Princely quality, befitting Kings.
Whoſe Serene heads, I line with policies,
They're held for Oracles, they are ſo wiſe.
Their wrathfull looks are death, their words are laws;
Their courage, friend, and foe, and ſubject awes.
But one of you would make a worthy King :
Like our ſixt *Henry*, that ſame worthy thing.
That when a Varlet, ſtruck him o're the ſide,
Forſooth you are to blame, he grave reply'd.
Take choler from a Prince, what is he more,
Then a dead Lyon? by beaſts triumpht ore.
Again, ye know, how I act every part:
By th' influence I ſend ſtill from the heart.

Its

Its not your mufcles, nerves, nor this nor that:
Without my lively heat, do's ought thats flat.
The fpongy Lungs, I feed with frothy blood.
They coole my heat, and fo repay my good.
Nay, th' ftomach, magazeen to all the reft,
Without my boiling heat cannot digeft.
And yet to make, my greatneffe far more great:
What differences the Sex, but only heat?
And one thing more to clofe with my narration.
Of all that lives, I caufe the propagation.
I have been fparing, what I might have faid,
I love no boafting, that's but childrens trade:
To what you now fhal fay, I wil attend,
And to your weakneffe, gently condefcend.

Blood.

GOod fifters give me leave (as is my place)
   To vent my griefe, and wipe off my difgrace.
Your felves may plead, your wrongs are no whit leffe,
Your patience more then mine, I muft confeffe.
Did ever fober tongue, fuch language fpeak?
Or honeftie fuch ties, unfriendly break?
Do'ft know thy felfe fo well, us fo amiffe?
Is't ignorance, or folly caufeth this?
Ile only fhew the wrongs, thou'ft done to me:
Then let my fifters, right their injury.
To pay with railings, is not mine intent,
But to evince the truth, by argument.
I will annalife, thy fo proud relation;
So ful of boafting, and prevarication.

                                        Thy

Thy childiſh incongruities, Ile ſhow ;
So walke thee til thou'rt cold, then let thee go.
There is no Souldier, but thy ſelfe thou ſay'ſt,
No valour upon earth, but what thou haſt.
Thy fooliſh provocations, I deſpiſe.
And leave't to all, to judge where valour lyes.
No pattern, nor no Patron will I bring,
But *David*, *Judah*'s moſt heroyick King:
Whoſe glorious deeds in armes, the world can tel,
A roſie cheek'd muſitian, thou know'ſt wel.
He knew how, for to handle, Sword and Harpe,
And how to ſtrike ful ſweet, as wel as ſharpe.
Thou laugh'ſt at me, for loving merriment:
And ſcorn'ſt all Knightly ſports, at turnament.
Thou ſayſt I love my ſword, becauſe tis guilt:
But know, I love the blade, more then the hilt.
Yet do abhorre, ſuch timerarious deeds,
As thy unbridled, barb'rous Choler yeelds.
Thy rudeneſſe counts, good manners vanity,
And real complements, baſe flattery.
For drink, which of us twain, like it the beſt,
Ile go no further then thy noſe for teſt.
Thy other ſcoffes not worthy of reply:
Shal vaniſh as of no validity.
Of thy black calumnies, this is but part:
But now Ile ſhew, what Souldier thou art.
And though thou'ſt uſ'd me, with opprobrious ſpight,
My ingenuity muſt give thee right.
Thy Choler is but rage, when tis moſt pure.
But uſeful, when a mixture can indure.
As with thy mother Fire, ſo 'tis with thee,
The beſt of al the four, when they agree.

But

But let her leave the rest, and I presume,
Both them and all things elſe, ſhe will conſume.
Whil'ſt us, for thine aſſociates thou takeſt,
A Souldier moſt compleat in al points makeſt.
But when thou ſcorn'ſt to take the helpe we lend,
Thou art a fury, or infernal Fiend.
Witneſſe the execrable deeds thou'ſt done:
Nor ſparing Sex, nor age, nor ſire, nor ſon.
To ſatisfie thy pride, and cruelty
Thou oft haſt broke bounds of humanity.
Nay ſhould I tel, thou wouldſt count me no blab,
How often for the lye, thou'ſt giv'n the ſtab.
To take the wal's a ſin, of ſuch high rate,
That naught but blood, the ſame may expiate.
To croſſe thy wil, a challenge doth deſerve.
So ſpils that life, thou'rt bounden to preſerve,
Wilt thou this valour, manhood, courage cal:
Nay, know 'tis pride, moſt diabolical.
If murthers be thy glory, tis no leſſe.
Ile not envy thy feats, nor happineſſe.
But if in fitting time, and place, on foes;
For Countries good, thy life thou darſt expoſe.
Be dangers neer ſo high, and courage great,
Ile praiſe that fury, valour, choler, heat.
But ſuch thou never art, when al alone;
Yet ſuch, when we al four are joyn'd in one.
And when ſuch thou art, even ſuch are we.
The friendly coadjutors, ſtil to thee.
Nextly, the ſpirits thou do'ſt wholly claime,
Which natural, vital, animal we name.
To play Philoſopher, I have no liſt;
Nor yet Phiſician, nor Anatomiſt.

For

For acting theſe, I have nor wil, nor art,
Yet ſhal with equity give thee thy part,
For th' natural, thou doſt not much conteſt,
For there are none, thou ſay'ſt, if ſome, not beſt.
That there are ſome, and beſt, I dare averre;
More uſeful then the reſt, don't reaſon erre ;
What is there living, which cannot derive
His life now animal, from vegative ?
If thou giv'ſt life, I give thee nouriſhment,
Thine without mine, is not, 'tis evident:
But I, without thy help can give a growth,
As plants, trees, and ſmall Embryon know'th,
And if vital ſpirits do flow from thee,
I am as ſure, the natural from me;
But thine the nobler, which I grant, yet mine
Shal juſtly claime priority of thine ;
I am the Fountaine which thy Ciſterns fils,
Through th' warme, blew conduits of my veinal rils ;
What hath the heart, but what's ſent from the liver ?
If thou'rt the taker, I muſt be the giver :
Then never boaſt of what thou do'ſt receive,
For of ſuch glory I ſhal thee bereave ;
But why the heart, ſhould be uſurpt by thee,
I muſt confeſſe, is ſomewhat ſtrange to me,
The ſpirits through thy heat, are made perfect there,
But the materials none of thine, that's cleare,
Their wondrous mixture, is of blood, and ayre,
The firſt my ſelf, ſecond my ſiſter faire,
But i'le not force retorts, nor do thee wrong,
Thy fiery yellow froth, is mixt among.
Challenge not all, 'cauſe part we do allow,
Thou know'ſt I've there to do, as wel as thou ;

But

But thou wilt fay, I deale unequally,
There lives the irafcible faculty:
Which without all difpute, is Cholers owne ;
Befides the vehement heat, only there known,
Can be imputed unto none, but Fire ;
Which is thy felf, thy *Mother*, and thy Sire ;
That this is true, I eafily can affent,
If ftil thou take along my Aliment,
And let me be thy Partner, which is due,
So wil I give the dignity to you.
Again, ftomachs concoction thou doft claime,
But by what right, nor do'ft, nor canft thou name ;
It is her own heat, not thy faculty,
Thou do'ft unjuftly claime, her property,
The help fhe needs, the loving Liver lends,
Who th'benefit o'th' whole ever intends :
To meddle further, I fhal be but fhent,
Th'reft to our Sifters, is more pertinent.
Your flanders thus refuted, takes no place,
Though caft upon my guiltleffe blufhing face ;
Now through your leaves, fome little time i'le fpend ;
My worth in humble manner, to commend.
This hot, moift, nurtritive humour of mine,
When 'tis untaint, pure, and moft genuine
Shal firftly take her place, as is her due,
Without the leaft indignity to you ;
Of all your qualities I do partake,
And what you fingly are, the whole I make.
Your hot, dry, moyft, cold, natures are foure,
I moderately am all, what need I more :
As thus, if hot, then dry ; if moift, then cold ;
If this can't be difprov'd, then all I hold :

My

My vertues hid, i've let you dimly ſee ;
My ſweet complexion, proves the verity,
This ſcarlet die's a badge of what's within,
One touch thereof ſo beautifies the skin ;
Nay, could I be from all your tangs but pure,
Mans life to boundleſſe time might ſtil endure ;
But here's one thruſts her heat, where'ts not requir'd
So ſuddenly, the body all is fir'd:
And of the ſweet, calme temper, quite bereft,
Which makes the manſion, by the ſoul ſoon left ;
So Melancholly ceaſes on a man ;
With her uncheerful viſage, ſwarth and wan;
The body dryes, the minde ſublime doth ſmother,
And turns him to the wombe of 's earthy mother,
And Flegme likewiſe can ſhew, her cruel art,
With cold diſtempers, to pain every part ;
The Lungs, ſhe rots, the body weares away,
As if ſhe'd leave no fleſh to turn to clay,
Her languiſhing diſeaſes, though not quick,
At length demoliſhes the faberick,
All to prevent, this curious care I take;
Ith' laſt concoction, ſegregation make.
Of all the perverſe humours from mine owne,
The bitter choler, moſt malignant knowne
I turn into his cel, cloſe by my ſide,
The Melancholly to the Spleen to 'bide ;
Likewiſe the Whey, ſome uſe I in the reines,
The over plus I ſend unto the reines ;
But yet for all my toyl, my care, my skil,
It's doom'd by an irrevocable wil :
That my intents ſhould meet with interruption,
That mortal man, might turn to his corruption.

I

I might here shew, the noblenesse of minde,
Of such as to the Sanguine are inclin'd,
They're liberal, pleasant, kinde, and courteous,
And like the Liver, all benignious;
For Arts, and Sciences, they are the fittest,
And maugre (Choler) stil they are the wittest,
An ingenious working phantasie,
A most volumnious large memory,
And nothing wanting but solidity.
But why, alas, thus tedious should I be?
Thousand examples, you may daily see
If time I have transgrest, and been too long,
Yet could not be more breif, without much wrong.
I've scarce wip'd off the spots, proud Choler cast,
Such venome lyes in words, though but a blast,
No braggs i've us'd, t'your selves I dare appeale,
If modesty my worth do not conceale.
I've us'd no bitternesse, nor taxt your name,
As I to you, to me, do ye the same.

Melancholy.

HE that with two assaylents hath to do,
Had need be armed wel, and active too,
Especially when freindship is pretended:
That blow's most deadly, where it is intended;
Though Choler rage, and raile, i'le not do so,
The tongue's no weapon to assault a foe,
But sith we fight with words, we might be kind,
To spare our selves, and beat the whistling winde.

Faire

Faire roſie Siſter, ſo might'ſt thou ſcape free,
I .e flatter for a time, as thou did'ſt me,
But when the firſt offenders I have laid,
Thy ſoothing girds ſhal fully be repaid ;
But Choler, be thou cool'd, or chaf'd, i'le venter,
And in contentions liſts, now juſtly enter.
Thy boaſted valour ſtoutly's been repell'd,
If not as yet, by me, thou ſhalt be quell'd :
What mov'd thee thus to villifie my name?
Not paſt all reaſon, but in truth all ſhame:
Thy fiery ſpirit ſhal bear away this prize,
To play ſuch furious pranks I am too wiſe ;
If in a Souldier raſhneſſe be ſo precious,
Know, in a General its moſt pernicious.
Nature doth teach, to ſheild the head from harm,
The blow that's aim'd thereat is latch'd by th'arm,
When in Battalia my foes I face,
I then command, proud Choler ſtand thy place,
To uſe thy ſword, thy courage, and thy Art,
For to defend my ſelf, thy better part ;
This warineſſe count not for cowardiſe,
He is not truly valiant that's not wiſe ;
It's no leſſe glory to defend a town,
Then by aſſault to gain one, not our own.
And if *Marccius* bold, be call'd *Romes* ſword,
Wiſe *Fabius* is her buckler : all accord.
And if thy haſte, my ſlowneſſe ſhould not temper,
'Twere but a mad, irregular diſtemper.
Enough of that, by our Siſter heretofore,
I'le come to that which wounds me ſomewhat more :
Of Learning, and of Policie, thou would'ſt bereave me,
But's not thy ignorance ſhal thus deceive me.

D

What

What greater Clerke, or polititian lives?
Then he whose brain a touch my humour gives.
What is too hot, my coldnesse doth abate;
What's diffluent, I do consolidate.
If I be partial judg'd, or thought to erre,
The melancholy Snake shal it aver.
Those cold dry heads, more subtilly doth yeild,
Then all the huge beasts of the fertile field.
Thirdly, thou dost confine me to the spleen,
As of that only part I was the Queen:
Let me as wel make thy precincts, the gal;
To prison thee within that bladder smal.
Reduce the man to's principles, then see
If I have not more part, then al ye three:
What is without, within, of theirs, or thine.
Yet time and age, shal soon declare it mine.
When death doth seize the man, your stock is lost,
When you poor bankrupts prove, then have I most.
You'l say, here none shal ere disturbe my right;
You high born (from that lump) then take your flight
Then who' mans friend, when life and all forsakes?
His mother (mine) him to her wombe retakes,
Thus he is ours, his portion is the grave.
But whilst he lives, Ile shew what part I have.
And first, the firme dry bones, I justly claim:
The strong foundation of the stately frame.
Likewise the useful spleen, though not the best,
Yet is a bowel cal'd wel as the rest.
The Liver, Stomach, owes it thanks of right:
The first it draines, o'th' last quicks appetite,
Laughter (though thou sayst malice) flowes from hence,
These two in one cannot have residence.

                                                          Eu:

But thou moſt groſly do'ſt miſtake, to thinke
The Spleen for al you three, was made a ſinke,
Of al the reſt, thou'ſt nothing there to do;
But if thou haſt, that malice comes from you.
Again, you often touch my ſwarthy hew,
That black is black, and I am black, tis true;
But yet more comely far, I dare avow,
Then is thy torrid noſe, or braſen brow.
But that which ſhewes how high thy ſpight is bent,
In charging me, to be thy excrement.
Thy loathſome imputation I defie;
So plain a ſlander needeth no reply.
When by thy heat, thou'ſt bak'd thy ſelfe to cruſt,
Thou do'ſt aſſume my name, wel be it juſt;
This tranſmutation is, but not excretion,
Thou wants Philoſophy, and yet diſcretion.
Now by your leave, Ile let your greatneſſe ſee;
What officer thou art to al us three.
The Kitchin Drudge, the cleanſer of the ſinks,
That caſts out ail that man or eates, or drinks.
Thy bittering quality, ſtil irretates,
Til filth and thee, nature exhonorates.
If any doubt this truth, whence this ſhould come;
Show them thy paſſige to th' *Duodenum.*
If there thou'rt ſtopt, to th' Liver thou turn'ſt in,
And ſo with jaundiſe, Safferns al the skin.
No further time ile ſpend, in conſutations,
I truſt I've clear'd your ſlandrous imputations.
I now ſpeake unto al, no more to one;
Pray hear, admire, and learn inſtruction.
My vertues yours ſurpaſſe, without compare;
The firſt, my conſtancy, that jewel rare.

D 2   Choler's

Choler's too rash, this golden gift to hold.
And Sanguine is more fickle many fold.
Here, there, her reſtleſſe thoughts do ever flye;
Conſtant in nothing, but inconſtancy,
And what Flegme is, we know, likewiſe her mother,
Unſtable is the one, ſo is the other.
With me is noble patience alſo found,
Impatient Choler loveth not the ſound.
VVhat Sanguine is, ſhe doth not heed, nor care.
Now up, now down, transported like the Aire.
Flegm's patient, becauſe her nature's tame.
But I by vertue, do acquire the ſame.
My temperance, chaſtity, is eminent,
But theſe with you, are ſeldome reſident.
Now could I ſtain my ruddy ſiſters face,
With purple dye, to ſhew but her diſgrace.
But I rather with ſilence, vaile her ſhame;
Then cauſe her bluſh, while I dilate the ſame.
Nor are ye free, from this inormity,
Although ſhe beare the greateſt obloquie.
My prudence, judgement, now I might reveale,
But wiſdome 'tis, my wiſdom to conceale.
Unto diſeaſes not inclin'd as ye:
Nor cold, nor hot, Ague, nor Pluriſie;
Nor Cough, nor Quinſie, nor the burning Feavor.
I rarely feel to act his fierce indeavour.
My ſickneſſe cheifly in conceit doth lye,
What I imagine, that's my malady.
Strange Chymera's are in my phantaſie,
And things that never were, nor ſhal I ſee.
Talke I love not, reaſon lyes not in length,
Nor multitude of words, argues our ſtrength;

I'e

I've done, pray Siſter Flegme proceed in courſe,
We ſhal expeſt much ſound, but little force.

Flegme.

PAtient I am, patient i'd need to be,
  To bear the injurious taunts of three ;
   Though wit I want, and anger I have leſſe,
Enough of both, my wrongs for to expreſſe ;
I've not forgot how bitter Choler ſpake,
Nor how her Gaul on me ſhe cauſleſſe brake ;
Nor wonder 'twas, for hatred there's not ſmal,
Where oppoſition is diametrical :
To what is truth, I freely wil aſſent,
(Although my name do ſuffer detriment)
What's ſlanderous, repel; doubtful, diſpute ;
And when i've nothing left to ſay, be mute ;
Valour I want, no Souldier am, 'tis true,
I'le leave that manly property to you ;
I love no thundering Drums, nor bloody Wars,
My poliſh'd skin was not ordain'd for skars,
And though the pitched field i've ever fled,
At home, the Conquerours, have conquered :
Nay, I could tel you (what's more true then meet)
That Kings have laid their Scepters at my feet,
When ſiſter Sanguine paints my Ivory face,
The Monarchs bend, and ſue, but for my grace ;
My Lilly white, when joyned with her red,
Princes hath ſlav'd, and Captains captived :
Country with Country, *Greece* with *Aſia* fights,
Sixty nine Princes, all ſtout *Hero* Knights.

Under *Troy's* wals, ten years wil wast away,
Rather then loose, one beauteous *Hellena* ;
But 'twere as vain, to prove the truth of mine,
As at noon day to tel, the Sun doth shine.
Next difference betwixt us twain doth lye,
Who doth possesse the Brain, or thou, or I ;
Shame forc'd thee say, the matter that was mine,
But the spirits, by which it acts are thine ;
Thou speakest truth, and I can speak no lesse,
Thy heat doth much, I candidly confesse,
But yet thou art as much, I truly say,
Beholding unto me another way.
And though *I* grant, thou art my helper here,
No debtor I, because 'tis paid else where ;
With all your flourishes, now Sisters three,
Who is't or dare, or can compare with me ;
My excellencies are so great, so many,
I am confounded, 'fore I speak of any:
The Brain's the noblest member all allow,
The scituation, and form wil it avow,
Its ventricles, membranees, and wond'rous net,
Galen, Hipocrates, drives to a set.
That divine Essence, the immortal Soul,
Though it in all, and every part be whole :
Within this stately place of eminence,
Doth doubtlesse keep its mighty residence ;
And surely the Souls sensative here lives,
Which life and motion to each Creature gives,
The conjugations of the parts toth' brain
Doth shew, hence flowes the power which they retain ;
Within this high built Cittadel doth lye,
The Reason, Fancy, and the Memory ;

The

The faculty of ſpeech doth here abide,
The ſpirits animal,from whence doth ſlide,
The five moſt noble Sences, here do dwel,
Of three, its hard to ſay, which doth excel ;
This point for to diſcuſſe longs not to me,
I'le touch the Sight, greateſt wonder of the three ;
The optick nerve, coats, humours, all are mine,
Both watry, glaſſie, and the chriſtaline.
O ! mixture ſtrange, oh colour, colourleſſe,
Thy perfect temperament, who can expreſſe ?
He was no foole, who thought the Soul lay here,
Whence her affections, paſſions, ſpeak ſo clear ;
O ! good, O bad, O true, O traiterous eyes !
What wonderments, within your bals there lyes?
Of all the Sences, Sight ſhal be the Queen ;
Yet ſome may wiſh, oh, had mine eyes ne're ſeene.
Mine likewiſe is the marrow of the back,
Which runs through all the ſpondles of the rack,
It is the ſubſtitute o'th royal Brain,
All nerves (except ſeven paire) to it retains
And the ſtrong ligaments, from hence ariſe,
With joynt to joynt, the entire body tyes ;
Some other parts there iſſue from the Brain,
Whoſe uſe and worth to tel, I muſt refrain ;
Some worthy learned *Crooke* may theſe reveal,
But modeſty hath charg'd me to conceal ;
Here's my epitome of excellence,
For what's the Brains, is mine, by conſequence ;
A fooliſh Brain (ſaith Choler) wanting heat,
But a mad one, ſay I, where 'tis too great,
Phrenſie's worſe,then folly,one would more glad,
With a tame foole converſe, then with a mad.

D 4

Then

Then, my head for learning is not the fittest,
Ne're did I heare that Choler was the witt'est;
Thy judgement is unsafe, thy fancy little,
For memory, the fand is not more brittle.
Again, none's fit for Kingly place but thou,
If Tyrants be the best, i'le it allow;
But if love be, as requisite as feare,
Then I, and thou, must make a mixture here:
Wel, to be breif, Choler I hope now's laid,
And I passe by what sister Sanguine said;
To Melancholly i'le make no reply,
The worst she said, was, instability,
And too much talk; both which, I do confesse,
A warning good, hereafter i'le say lesse.
Let's now be freinds, 'tis time our spight was spent,
Lest we too late, this rashnesse do repent,
Such premises wil force a sad conclusion,
Unlesse we 'gree, all fals into confusion.
Let Sanguine, Choler, with her hot hand hold,
To take her moyst, my moistnesse wil be bold;
My cold, cold Melanchollies hand shal clasp,
Her dry, dry Cholers other hand shal grasp;
Two hot, two moist, two cold, two dry here be,
A golden Ring, the Posey, *Unity*:
Nor jars, nor scoffs, let none hereafter see,
But all admire our perfect amity;
Nor be discern'd, here's water, earth, aire, fire,
But here's a compact body, whole, entire:
This loving counsel pleas'd them all so wel,
That Flegme was judg'd, for kindnesse to excel.

The

The Four Ages of Man.

Loe now! four other acts upon the stage,
Childhood, and Youth, the Manly, and
Old-age.
The first : son unto Flegme, grand-child to
water,
Unstable, supple, moist, and cold's his Naure.
The second, frolick, claimes his pedigree,
From blood and aire, for hot, and moist is he.
The third, of fire, and choler is compos'd,
Vindicative, and quarelsome dispos'd.
The last, of earth, and heavy melancholly,
Solid, hating all lightnesse, and al folly.
Childhood was cloath'd in white, and given to show,
His spring was intermixed with some snow.
Upon his head a Garland Nature set :
Of Dazy, Primrose, and the Violet.
Such cold mean flowers (as these) blossome betime,
Before the Sun hath throughly warm'd the clime.
His hobby striding, did not ride, but run,
And in his hand an hour-glasse new begun,
In dangers every moment of a fall,
And when tis broke, then ends his life and all.
But if he held, til it have run its last,
Then may he live, til threescore years or past.

Next

Next, youth came up, in gorgeous attire ;
(As that fond age, doth most of al desire.)
His Suit of Crimson, and his Scarfe of Green :
In's countenance, his pride quickly was seen.
Garland of Roses, Pinks, and Gilliflowers,
Seemed to grow on's head (bedew'd with showers:)
His face as fresh, as is *Aurora* faire,
When blushing first, she 'gins to red the Aire.
No wooden horse, but one of mettal try'd:
He seems to flye, or swim, and not to ride.
Then prauncing on the Stage, about he wheels;
But as he went, death waited at his heeles.
The next came up, in a more graver sort,
As one that cared, for a good report.
His Sword by's side, and choler in his eyes;
But neither us'd (as yet) for he was wise.
Of Autumne fruits a basket on his arme.
His golden god in's purse, which was his charm?
And last of al, to act upon this Stage ;
Leaning upon his staffe, comes up old age.
Under his arme a Sheafe of wheat he bore,
A Harvest of the best, what needs he more.
In's other hand a glasse, ev'n almost run,
This writ about : *This out, then I am done.*
His hoary haires, and grave aspect made way;
And al gave eare, to what he had to say.
These being met, each in his equipage,
Intend to speak, according to their age:
But wise Old-age, did with all gravity,
To childish childhood, give precedency.
And to the rest, his reason mildly told;
That he was young, before he grew so old.

To

To do as he, the reſt ful ſoon aſſents,
Their method was, that of the Elements,
That each ſhould tel, what of himſelfe he knew;
Both good and bad, but yet no more then's true:
With heed now ſtood, three ages of fraile man,
  To hear the child, who crying, thus began.

Childhood.

AH me! conceiv'd in ſin, and born in ſorrow,
  A nothing, here to day, but gone to morrow.
Whoſe mean beginning, bluſhing cann't reveale,
But night and darkeneſſe, muſt with ſhame conceal.
My mothers breeding ſicknes, I will ſpare;
Her nine months weary burden not declare.
To ſhew her bearing pangs, I ſhould do wrong,
To tel that paine, which cann't be told by tongue;
With tears into this world I did arrive;
My mother ſtil did waſte, as I did thrive:
Who yet with love, and all alacrity,
Spending was willing, to be ſpent for me;
With wayward cryes, I did diſturbe her reſt,
Who ſought ſtil to appeaſe me, with her breſt,
With weary armes, ſhe danc'd, and *By, By,* ſung,
When wretched I (ungrate)had done the wrong.
When Infancy was paſt, my Childiſhneſſe,
Did act al folly, that it could expreſſe.
My ſillineſſe did only take delight,
In that which riper age did ſcorn, and ſlight:
In Rattles, Bables, and ſuch toyiſh ſtuffe.
My then ambitious thoughts, were low enough.

                                            My

My high-borne soule, so straitly was confin'd :
That its own worth, it did not know, nor mind.
This little house of flesh, did spacious count:
Through ignorance, all troubles did surmount.
Yet this advantage, had mine ignorance,
Freedome from Envy, and from Arrogance.
How to be rich, or great, I did not carke;
A Baron or a Duke, ne'r made my mark.
Nor studious was, Kings favours how to buy,
With costly presents, or base flattery.
No office coveted, wherein I might
Make strong my selfe, and turne aside weak right.
No malice bare, to this, or that great Peer,
Nor unto buzzing whisperors, gave ear.
I gave no hand, nor vote, for death, or life :
I'd nought to do, 'twixt Prince, and peoples strife.
No Statist I : nor Marti'list i' th' field ;
Where e're I went, mine innocence was shield.
My quarrells, not for Diadems did rise;
But for an Apple, Plumbe, or some such prize,
My stroks did cause no death, nor wounds, nor skars.
My little wrath did cease soon as my wars.
My duel was no challenge, nor did seek.
My foe should weltering, with his bowels reek.
I had no Suits at law, neighbours to vex.
Nor evidence for land, did me perplex.
I fear'd no stormes, nor al the windes that blows,
I had no ships at Sea, no fraughts to loose.
I fear'd no drought; nor wet, I had no crop,
Nor yet on future things did place my hope.
This was mine innocence, but oh the seeds,
Lay raked up ; of all the cursed weeds,

Which

Which fprouted forth, in my infuing age,
As he can tell, that next comes on the ftage.
But yet let me relate, before I go,
The fins, and dangers I am fubject to.
From birth ftayned, with *Adams* finfull fact ;
From thence I 'gan to fin, as foon as act.
A perverfe will, a love to what's forbid:
A ferpents fting in pleafing face lay hid.
A lying tongue as foon as it could fpeak,
And fift Commandement do daily break.
Oft ftubborn, peevifh, fullen, pout, and cry:
Then nought can pleafe, and yet I know not why.
As many was my fins, fo dangers too:
For fin brings forrow, ficknefle, death, and woe.
And though I miffe, the toffings of the mind:
Yet griefs, in my fraile flefh, I ftill do find.
What gripes of wind, mine infancy did pain?
What tortures I, in breeding teeth fuftain?
What crudities my cold ftomach hath bred?
Whence vomits, wormes, and flux have iffued?
What breaches, knocks, and falls I daily have?
And fome perhaps, I carry to my grave.
Some times in fire, fometimes in waters fall:
Strangely preferv'd, yet mind it not at all.
At home, abroad, my danger's manifold.
That wonder tis, my glaffe till now doth hold.
I've done, unto my elders I give way.
For 'tis but little, that a childe can fay.

Youth.

Youth.

MY goodly cloathing, and my beauteous skin,
Declare some greater riches are within ;
But what is best i'le first present to view,
And then the worst, in a more ugly hue ;
For thus to do, we on this Stage assemble,
Then let not him, which hath most craft dissemble ;
Mine education, and my learning's such,
As might my self, and others, profit much :
With nurture trained up in vertues Schools,
Of Science, Arts, and Tongues, I know the rules,
The manners of the Court, I likewise know,
Nor ignorant what they in Country do ;
The brave attempts of valiant Knights I prize,
That dare climbe Battlements, rear'd to the skies ;
The snorting Horse, the Trumpet, Drum I like,
The glistring Sword, and wel advanced Pike ;
I cannot lye in trench, before a Town,
Nor wait til good advice our hopes do crown ;
I scorn the heavy Corslet, Musket-proof,
I fly to catch the Bullet that's aloof ;
Though thus in field, at home, to all most kind ;
So affable that I do suit each mind ;
I can insinuate into the brest,
And by my mirth can raise the heart deprest ;
Sweet Musick rapteth my harmonious Soul,
And elevates my thoughts above the Pole.
My wit, my bounty, and my courtesie,
Makes all to place their future hopes on me.

This

This is my beſt, but youth (is known) alas,
To be as wilde as is the ſnuffing Aſſe,
As vain as froth, as vanity can be,
That who would ſee vain man, may look on me :
My gifts abus'd, my education loſt,
My woful Parents longing hopes all croſt,
My wit, evaporates in meriment :
My valour, in ſome beaſtly quarrel's ſpent ;
Martial deeds I love not, 'cauſe they're vertuous;
But'doing ſo, might ſeem magnanimous.
My Luſt doth hurry me, to all that's ill,
I know no Law, nor reaſon, but my wil ;
Sometimes lay wait to take a wealthy purſe,
Or ſtab the man, in's own defence, that's worſe,
Sometimes I cheat (unkind) a female Heir,
Of all at once, who nor ſo wiſe, as fair,
Truſteth my loving looks, and glozing tongue,
Until her freinds, treaſure, and honour's gone.
Sometimes I ſit carouſing others health,
Until mine own be gone, my wit, and wealth;
From pipe to pot, from pot to words, and blows,
For he that loveth Wine, wanteth no woes ;
Dayes, nights, with Ruffins, Roarers, Fidlers ſpend,
To all obſcenity, my eares I bend.
All counſel hate, which tends to make me wiſe,
And deareſt freinds count for mine enemies ;
If any care I take, 'tis to be fine,
For ſure my ſuit more then my vertues ſhine ;
If any time from company I ſpare,
'Tis ſpent in curling, friſling up my hair ;
Some young *Adonis* I do ſtrive to be,
Sardana Pallas, now ſurvives in me :

Cards,

Cards, Dice, and Oaths, concomitant, I love;
To Masques, to Playes, to Taverns stil I move;
And in a word, if what I am you'd heare,
Seek out a Brittish, bruitish Cavaleer;
Such wretch, such monster am I; but yet more,
I want a heart all this for to deplore.
Thus, thus alas! I have mispent my time,
My youth, my best, my strength, my bud, and prime:
Remembring not the dreadful day of Doom,
Nor yet that heavy reckoning for to come;
Though dangers do attend me every houre,
And gastly death oft threats me with her power.
Sometimes by wounds in idle combates taken,
Sometimes by Agues all my body shaken;
Sometimes by Feavers, all my moisture drinking,
My heart lyes frying, and my eyes are sinking;
Sometimes the Cough, Stitch, painful Plurisie,
With sad affrights of death, doth menace me;
Sometimes the loathsome Pox, my face be-mars,
With ugly marks of his eternal scars;
Sometimes the Phrensie, strangely madds my Brain,
That oft for it, in *Bedlam* I remain.
Too many's my Diseases to recite,
That wonder 'tis I yet behold the light,
That yet my bed in darknesse is not made,
And I in black oblivions den long laid;
Of Marrow ful my bones, of Milk my breasts,
Ceas'd by the gripes of Serjeant Death's Arrests:
Thus I have said, and what i've said you see,
Child-hood and youth is vaine, yea vanity.

Middle

Middle Age.

CHildehood and youth, forgot, sometimes I've seen,
And now am grown more staid, that have been green,
What they have done, the same was done by me,
As was their praise, or shame, so mine must be.
Now age is more, more good ye do expect;
But more my age, the more is my defect.
But what's of worth, your eyes shal first behold,
And then a world of droße among my gold.
When my Wilde Oates, were sown, and ripe, & mown,
I then receiv'd a harvest of mine owne.
My reason, then bad judge, how little hope,
Such empty seed should yeeld a better crop.
I then with both hands, graspt the world together,
Thus out of one extreame, into another.
But yet laid hold, on vertue seemingly,
Who climbes without hold, climbes dangerously.
Be my condition mean, I then take paines;
My family to keep, but not for gaines.
If rich, I'm urged then to gather more.
To bear me out i'th' world, and feed the poor,
If a father, then for children must provide:
But if none, then for kindred near ally'd.
If Noble, then mine honour to maintaine.
If not, yet wealth, Nobility can gain.
Fer time, for place, likewise for each relation,
I wanted not my ready allegation.
Yet all my powers, for self-ends are not spent,
For hundreds bleße me, for my bounty sent.

E   Whose

Whofe loynes I've cloth'd, and bellies I have fed;
With mine owne fleece, and with my houfhold bread.
Yea juftice I have done, was I in place;
To chear the good,and wicked to deface.
The proud I crufh'd, th' oppreffed I fet free,
The lyars curb'd but nourifht verity.
Was I a paftor, I my flock did feed:
And gently lead the lambes, as they had need,
A Captain I, with skil I train'd my band;
And fhew'd them how, in face of foes to ftand.
If a Souldier, with fpeed I did obey,
As readily as could my Leader fay:
Was I a laborer, I wrought all day,
As chearfully as ere I took my pay.
Thus hath mine age(in all) fometimes done wel.
Sometimes mine age (in all) been worfe then hell.
In meannefle, greatnefle, riches, poverty;
Did toile, did broile ; oppreff'd, did fteal and lye.
Was I as poor,as poverty could be,
Then bafenefle was companion unto me.
Such fcum, as Hedges, and High-wayes do yeeld,
As neither fow, nor reape, nor plant, nor build.
If to Agricolture, I was ordain'd;
Great labours, forrows, croffes I fuftain'd.
The early Cock, did fummon but in vaine,
My wakefull thoughts, up to my painefull gaine.
For reftleffe day and night,I'm rob'd of fleep,
By cankered care, who centinel doth keep.
My weary beaft,reft from his toile can find;
But if I reft, the more diftreft my mind.
If happineffe my fordidneffe hath found,
'Twas in the crop of my manured ground :

My

My fatted Oxe, and my exuberous Cow,
My fleeced Ewe, and ever farrowing Sow.
To greater things, I never did aspire,
My dunghil thoughts, or hopes, could reach no higher.
If to be rich, or great, it was my fate;
How was I broyl'd with envy, and with hate?
Greater, then was the great'st, was my desire,
And greater stil, did set my heart on fire.
If honour was the point, to which I steer'd;
To run my hull upon disgrace I fear'd,
But by ambitious sailes, I was so carryed;
That over flats, and sands, and rocks I hurried,
Opprest, and sunke, and sad, all in my way;
That did oppose me, to my longed bay:
My thirst was higher, then Nobility.
And oft long'd fore, to taste on Royalty.
Whence poyson, Pistols, and dread instruments,
Have been curst furtherers of mine intents.
Nor Brothers, Nephewes, Sons, nor Sires I've spar'd.
When to a Monarchy, my way they barr'd.
There set, I rid my selfe straight out of hand,
Of such as might my son, or his withstand.
Then heapt up gold, and riches as the clay;
Which others scatter, like the dew in *May*.
Sometimes vaine-glory is the only bait,
Whereby my empty soule, is lur'd and caught.
Be I of worth, of learning, or of parts;
I judge, I should have room, in all mens hearts.
And envy gnawes, if any do surmount.
I hate for to be had, in small account.
If *Bias* like, I'm stript unto my skin,
I glory in my wealth, I have within.

E 2   Thus

Thus good, and bad, and what I am, you see,
Now in a word, what my diseases be.
The vexing Stone, in bladder and in reines,
Torments me with intollerable paines ;
The windy Cholick oft my bowels rend,
To break the darksome prison, where it's pend ;
The knotty Gout doth sadly torture me,
And the restraining lame Sciatica ;
The Quinsie, and the Feavours, oft distaste me,
And the Consumption, to the bones doth wast me ;
Subject to all Diseases, that's the truth,
Though some more incident to age, or youth :
And to conclude, I may not tedious be,
Man at his best estate is vanity.

Old Age.

WHat you have been, ev'n such have I before,
And all you say, say I, and something more ;
Babes innocence, Youths wildnes I have seen,
And in perplexed Middle-age have bin,
Sicknesse, dangers, and anxieties have past,
And on this Stage am come to act my last :
I have bin young, and strong, and wise as you,
But now, *Bis pueri senes*, is too true ;
In every Age i've found much vanitie,
An end of all perfection now I see.
It's not my valour, honour, nor my gold,
My ruin'd house, now falling can uphold ;
It's not my Learning, Rhetorick, wit so large,
Now hath the power, Deaths Warfare, to discharge ;

It's

It's not my goodly houfe, nor bed of down,
That can refrefh, or eafe, if Confcience frown;
Nor from alliance now can I have hope,
But what I have done wel, that is my prop;
He that in youth is godly, wife, and fage,
Provides a ftaffe for to fupport his age.
Great mutations, fome joyful, and fome fad,
In this fhort Pilgrimage I oft have had;
Sometimes the Heavens with plenty fmil'd on me,
Sometimes again, rain'd all adverfity;
Sometimes in honour, fometimes in difgrace,
Sometime an abject, then again in place,
Such private changes oft mine eyes have feen,
In various times of ftate i've alfo been.
I've feen a Kingdom flourifh like a tree,
When it was rul'd by that Celeftial fhe;
And like a Cedar, others fo furmount,
That but for fhrubs they did themfelves account;
Then faw I *France*, and *Holland* fav'd, *Cales* won,
And *Philip*, and *Albertus*, half undone;
I faw all peace at home, terror to foes,
But ah, I faw at laft thofe eyes to clofe:
And then, me thought, the world at noon grew dark,
When it had loft that radiant Sun-like fpark,
In midft of greifs, I faw fome hopes revive,
(For 'twas our hopes then kept our hearts alive)
I faw hopes dafht, our forwardneffe was fhent,
And filenc'd we, by Act of Parliament.
I've feen from *Rome*, an execrable thing,
A plot to blow up Nobles, and their King;
I've feen defignes at *Ree*, and *Cades* croft,
And poor *Palatinate* for ever loft;

E 3   I've

I've feen a Prince, to live on others lands,
A Royall one, by almes from Subjects hands,
I've feen bafe men, advanc'd to great degree,
And worthy ones, put to extremity:
But not their Princes love, nor ftate fo high;
could once reverfe, their fhamefull deftiny.
I've feen one ftab'd, another loofe his head;
And others fly their Country, through their dread.
I've feen, and fo have ye, for 'tis but late,
The defolation, of a goodly State.
Plotted and acted, fo that none can tell,
Who gave the counfel, but the Prince of hell.
I've feen a land unmoulded with great paine.
But yet may live, to fee't made up again:
I've feen it fhaken, rent, and foak'd in blood,
But out of troubles, ye may fee much good,
Thefe are no old wives tales, but this is truth;
We old men love to tell, what's done in youth.
But I returne, from whence I ftept awry,
My memory is fhort, and braine is dry.
My Almond-tree (gray haires) doth flourifh now,
And back, once ftraight, begins apace to bow.
My grinders now are few, my fight doth faile
My fkin is wrinkled, and my cheeks are pale.
No more rejoyce, at muficke pleafant noyfe,
But do awake, at the cocks clanging voyce.
I cannot fcent, favours of pleafant meat,
Nor fapors find, in what I drink or eat.
My hands and armes, once ftrong, have loft their might,
I cannot labour, nor I cannot fight:
My comely legs, as nimble as the Roe,
Now ftiffe and numb, can hardly creep or go.

My

My heart fometimes as fierce, as Lion bold,
Now trembling, and fearful, fad, and cold ;
My golden Bowl, and filver Cord, e're long,
Shal both be broke, by wracking death fo ftrong ;
I then fhal go, whence I fhal come no more,
Sons, Nephews, leave, my death for to deplore ;
In pleafures, and in labours, I have found.
That earth can give no confolation found.
To great, to rich, to poore, to young, or old,
To mean, to noble, fearful, or to bold:
From King to begger, all degrees fhal finde
But vanity, vexation of the minde ;
Yea knowing much, the pleafant'ft life of all,
Hath yet amongft that fweet, fome bitter gall.
Though reading others Works, doth much refrefh,
Yet ftudying much, brings wearineffe to th' flefh ;
My ftudies, labours, readings, all are done,
And my laft period now e'n almoft run ;
Corruption, my Father, I do call,
Mother, and fifters both ; the worms, that crawl,
In my dark houfe, fuch kindred I have ftore,
There, I fhal reft, til heavens fhal be no more ;
And when this flefh fhal rot, and be confum'd,
This body, by this foul, fhal be affum'd ;
And I fhal fee, with thefe fame very eyes,
My ftrong Redeemer, comming in the skies ;
Triumph I fhal, o're Sin, o're Death, o're Hel,
And in that hope, I bid you all farewel.

The

The four Seasons of the Yeare.

Spring.

ANother Four i've yet for to bring on,
Of four times four, the laſt quaternian ;
The Winter, Summer, Autumne, and the
    Spring,
In ſeaſon all theſe Seaſons I ſhal bring ;
Sweet Spring, like man in his minority,
At preſent claim'd, and had priority,
With ſmiling Sun-ſhine face, and garments green,
She gently thus began, like ſome fair Queen ;
Three months there are allotted to my ſhare,
March, *April*, *May*, of all the reſt moſt faire;
The tenth o' th' firſt *Sol* into *Aries* enters,
And bids defiance to all tedious Winters:
And now makes glad thoſe blinded Northern wights,
Who for ſome months have ſeen but ſtarry lights ;
Croſſes the Line, and equals night and day,
Stil adds to th' laſt, til after pleaſant *May* ;
Now goes the Plow-man to his merry toyl,
For to unlooſe his Winter-locked ſoyl ;
The Seedſ-man now doth laviſh out his Grain,
In hope, the more he caſts, the more to gain ;
The Gardner, now ſuperfluous branches lops,
And Poles erects, for his green clambering Hops ;
Now digs, then ſows, his hearbs, his flowers, and roots,
And carefully manures his trees of fruits.

                            The

The Pleiades, their influence now give,
And all that seem'd as dead, afresh do live.
The croaking Frogs, whom nipping Winter kild,
Like Birds, now chirp, and hop about the field,
The Nitingale, the Black-bird, and the Thrush,
Now tune their layes, on sprays of every bush;
The wanton frisking Kids, and soft fleec'd Lambs,
Now jump, and play, before their feeding Dams,
The tender tops of budding Grasse they crop,
They joy in what they have, but more in hope,
For though the Frost hath lost his binding power,
Yet many a fleece of Snow, and stormy showre,
Doth darken *Sols* bright face, makes us remember
The pinching Nor-west cold, of fierce *December*.
My second month is *April*, green, and fair,
Of longer dayes, and a more temperate air;
The Sun now keeps his posting residence
In *Taurus* Signe, yet hasteth straight from thence;
For though in's running progresse he doth take
Twelve houses of the oblique Zodiack,
Yet never minute stil was known to stand,
But only once at *Joshua's* strange command;
This is the month whose fruitfull showers produces
All Plants, and Flowers, for all delights, and uses;
The Pear, the Plumbe, and Apple-tree now flourish,
And Grasse growes long, the tender Lambs to nourish;
The Primrose pale, and azure Violet,
Among the verduous Grasse hath Nature set,
That when the Sun (on's love) the earth doth shine,
These might as Lace, set out her Garments fine;
The fearful Bird, his little house now builds,
In trees, and wals, in cities, and in fields,

                                        The

The outside strong, the inside warme and neat.
A natural Artificer compleate.
The clocking hen, her chipping brood now leads,
With wings, and beak, defends them from the gleads.
My next, and last, is pleasant fruitfull *May*,
Wherein the earth, is clad in rich aray:
The sun now enters, loving *Gemini*,
And heats us with, the glances of his eye,
Our Winter rayment, makes us lay aside,
Least by his fervor, we be terrifi'd,
All flowers before the sun-beames now discloses,
Except the double Pinks, and matchlesse Roses.
Now swarmes the busie buzzing hony Bee.
Whose praise deserves a page, from more then me.
The cleanly huswives Dary, now's ith' prime,
Her shelves, and Firkins fill'd for winter time.
The Meads with Cowslip, Hony-suckl's dight,
One hangs his head, the other stands upright :
But both rejoyce, at th' heavens clear smiling face,
More at her showers, which water them a space.
For fruits, my season yeelds, the early Cherry,
The hasty Pease, and wholesome red Strawberry,
More solid fruits, require a longer time.
Each season, hath his fruit, so hath each clime.
Each man his owne peculiar excellence,
But none in all that hath preheminence.
Some subject, shallow braines, much matter yeelds,
Sometime a theame that's large, proves barren fields.
Melodious Spring, with thy short pittance flye,
In this harsh strain, I find no melody,
Yet above all, this priviledge is thine,
Thy dayes stil lengthen, without least decline.

Summer

Summer.

WHen Spring had done, then Summer muſt begin,
  With melted tauny face, and garments thinne.
Reſembling choler, fire and middle-age;
As Spring did aire, blood, youth in's equipage.
Wiping her ſweat from off her brow, that ran,
VVith haire all wet, ſhe puffing thus began.
Bright *June, July,* and *Auguſt,* hot are mine,
Ith' firſt, *Sol* doth in crabed *Cancer* ſhine.
His progreſſe to the North; now's fully done,
And retrograde, now is my burningSun.
VVho to his Southward tropick ſtill is bent,
Yet doth his parching heat the more augment,
The reaſon why, becauſe his flames ſo faire,
Hath formerly much heat, the earth and aire.
Like as an oven, that long time hath been hear.
Whoſe vehemency, at length doth grow ſo great,
That if you do, remove her burning ſtore,
She's for a time as fervent as before.
Now go thoſe frolick ſwaines, the ſhepheard lad,
To waſh their thick cloath'd flocks, with pipes ful glad.
In the coole ſtreames they labour with delight,
Rubbing their dirty coates, till they look white.
Whoſe fleece when purely ſpun, and deeply dy'd,
With robes thereof, Kings have been dignifi'd.
'Mongſt all ye ſhepheards, never but one man,
Was like that noble, brave *Archadian.*
Yet hath your life, made Kings the ſame envy,
Though you repoſe on graſſe under the skye.

  Careleſſe

Carelesse of worldly wealth, you sit and pipe,
Whilst they're imbroyl'd in Wars, and troubles ripe;
Which made great *Bajazet* cry out in's woes,
Oh! happy Shepheard, which had not to lose.
Orthobulus, nor yet *Sebastia* great,
But whist'leth to thy Flock in cold, and heat,
Viewing the Sun by day, the Moon by night,
Endimions, Diana's dear delight;
This Month the Roses are distill'd in Glasses,
Whose fragrant scent, all made-perfume surpasses;
The Cherry, Goos-berry, is now i'th prime,
And for all sorts of Pease this is the time.
July my next, the hot'st in all the year,
The Sun in *Leo* now hath his carrear,
Whose flaming breath doth melt us from afar,
Increased by the Star *Canicular*;
This month from *Julius Cæsar* took the name,
By *Romans* celebrated to his fame.
Now go the Mowers to their slashing toyl,
The Medows of their burden to dispoyl;
With weary stroaks, they take all in their way,
Bearing the burning heat of the long day;
The Forks, and Rakes do follow them amain,
Which makes the aged fields look young again,
The groaning Carts to bear away this prise,
To Barns, and Stacks, where it for Fodder lyes.
My next, and last, is *August*, fiery hot,
For yet the South-ward Sun abateth not;
This month he keeps with *Virgo* for a space,
The dryed earth is parched by his face.
August, of great *Augustus* took its name,
Romes second Emperour of peaceful fame;

Wirh

With Sickles now, the painful Reapers go,
The ruffling treſſe of *terra* for to moe,
And bundles up in ſheaves the weighty Wheat,
Which after Manchet's made, for Kings to eat;
The Barley, and the Rye, ſhould firſt had place,
Although their Bread have not ſo white a face.
The Carter leads all home, with whiſtling voyce,
He plow'd with pain, but reaping doth rejoyce;
His ſweat, his toyl, his careful, wakeful nights,
His fruitful crop, abundantly requites.
Now's ripe the Pear, Pear-plumbe, and Apricock,
The Prince of Plumbs, whoſe ſtone is hard as Rock.
The Summer's ſhort, the beauteous Autumne haſtes,
To ſhake his fruit, of moſt delicious taſtes;
Like good Old Age, whoſe younger juycie roots,
Hath ſtil aſcended up in goodly Fruits,
Until his head be gray, and ſtrength be gone,
Yet then appears the worthy deeds be 'ath done:
To feed his boughes, exhauſted hath his ſap,
Then drops his Fruits into the Eaters lap.

Autumne.

OF Autumne months, *September* is the prime,
Now day and night are equal in each clime;
The tenth of this, *Sol* riſeth in the Line,
And doth in poyzing *Libra* this month ſhine.
The Vintage now is ripe, the Grapes are preſt,
Whoſe lively liquor oft is curſt, and bleſt;
For nought's ſo good, but it may be abuſed,
But its a precious juyce, when wel it's uſed.

The

The Raisins now in clusters dryed be,
The Orange, Lemon, Dangle on the tree ;
The Figge is ripe, the Pomgranet also,
And Apples now their yellow sides do show ;
Of Medlar, Quince, of Warden, and of Peach,
The season's now at hand, of all, and each ;
Sure at this time, Time first of all began,
And in this month was made apostate man ;
For then in *Eden* was not only seen
Boughs full of leaves, or fruits, but raw, and green,
Or withered stocks, all dry, and dead,
But trees with goodly fruits replenished ;
Which shewes, nor Summer, Winter, nor the Spring,
Great *Adam* was of Paradice made King.
October is my next, we heare in this,
The Northern Winter blasts begin to hisse ;
In *Scorpio* resideth now the Sun,
And his declining heat is almost done.
The fruitful trees, all withered now do stand,
Whose yellow sapleſſe leaves by winds are fann'd:
Which notes, when youth, and strength, have past their
Decrepit age must also have its time ;   (prime,
The sap doth slily creep towards the earth,
There rests, untill the Sun give it a birth:
So doth Old Age stil tend unto his Grave,
Where also he, his Winter time must have ;
But when the Son of Righteouſneſſe drawes nigh,
His dead old stock, again shall mount on high.
November is my last, for time doth haste,
We now of Winters sharpneſſe 'gin to taste;
This month's the Sun in *Sagitarius*,
So farre remote, his glances warm not us ;

                                        Almost

Almoſt at ſhorteſt is the ſhortned day,
The Northern Pole beholdeth not one ray.
Now *Green-land, Green-land, Lap-land, Fin-land,* ſee
No Sun, to lighten their obſcurity ;
Poor wretches, that in total darkneſſe lye,
With minds more dark, then is the darkned sky ;
This month is timber for all uſes fell'd,
When cold, the ſap to th' roots hath low'ſt repell'd .
Beef, Brawn, and Pork, are now in great'ſt requeſt,
And ſolid'ſt meats, our ſtomachs can digeſt ;
This time warm cloaths, ſul diet, and good fires,
Our pinched fleſh, and empty panch requires :
Old cold, dry age, and earth, Autumne reſembles,
And melancholy, which moſt of all diſſembles.
I muſt be ſhort, and ſhort's, the ſhortned day,
What Winter hath to tel, now let him ſay.

Winter.

COld, moiſt, young, flegmy Winter now doth lye
In Swadling clouts, like new-born infancy,
Bound up with Froſts, and furr'd with Hails, and
And like an Infant, ſtil he taller growes.   (Snows,
December is the firſt, and now the Sun
To th' Southward tropick his ſwift race hath run ;
This month he's hous'd in horned *Capricorn,*
From thence he 'gins to length the ſhortned morn,
Through Chriſtendome, with great feſtivity
Now's held, a Gueſt, (but bleſt)Nativity.
Cold frozen *January* next comes in,
Chilling the blood, and ſhrinking up the skin.

In

In *Aquarius*, now keeps the loved Sun,
And North-ward his unwearied race doth run;
The day much longer then it was before,
The cold not lessened, but augmented more.
Now toes, and eares, and fingers often freeze,
And *Travellers* sometimes their noses leese.
Moyst snowie *February* is my last,
I care not how the Winter time doth haste;
In *Pisces* now the golden Sun doth shine,
And North-ward stil approaches to the Line;
The Rivers now do ope, and Snows do melt,
And some warm glances from the Sun are felt,
Which is increased by the lengthened day,
Until by's heat he drives all cold away.

My Subjects bare, my Brains are bad,
Or better Lines you should have had;
The first fell in so naturally,
I could not tell how to passe't by:
The last, though bad, I could not mend,
Accept therefore of what is penn'd,
And all the faults which you shall spy,
Shall at your feet for pardon cry.

Your dutifull Daughter.

A. B.

The

The Foure Monarchies,

the *Assyrian* being the first, begin-
ning under *Nimrod*, 131. yeares
after the Floud.

Hen Time was young, and World in in-
fancy,
Man did not strive for Soveraignty,
But each one thought his petty rule was
high,
If of his house he held the Monarchy:
This was the Golden Age, but after came
The boysterous Sons of *Cush*, Grand-child to *Ham*,
That mighty Hunter, who in his strong toyls,
Both Beasts and Men subjected to his spoyls.
The strong foundation of proud *Babel* laid,
Erech, Accad, and *Calneh* also made;
These were his first, all stood in *Shinar* land,
From thence he went *Assyria* to command;
And mighty *Ninivie*, he there begun,
Not finished, til he his race had run;
Resen, Caleh, and *Rehoboth* likewise,
By him, to Cities eminent did rise;
Of *Saturn*, he was the original,
Whom the succeeding times a god did call:

F

When

When thus with rule he had been dignified,
One hundred fourteen years, he after dyed.

Bellus.

GReat *Nimrod* dead, *Bellus* the next, his Son,
Confirmes the rule his Father had begun,
Whose acts, and power, is not for certainty,
Left to the world, by any History;
But yet this blot for ever on him lyes,
He taught the people first to Idolize;
Titles divine, he to himself did take,
Alive, and dead, a god they did him make;
This is that *Bell*, the *Chaldees* worshipped,
Whose Preists, in Stories, oft are mentioned;
This is that *Bell*, to whom the *Israelites*
So oft profanely offered sacred rites;
This is *Belzebub*, god of *Ekronites*,
Likewise *Bal-peor*, of the *Moabites*:
His reign was short, for as I calculate,
At twenty five, ended his regal date.

Ninus.

HIs father dead, *Ninus* begins his reign,
Transfers his Seat, to the *Assyrian* plain,
And mighty *Ninivie* more mighty made,
Whose foundation was by his Grand-fire laid;
Four hundred forty Furlongs, wall'd about,
On which stood fifteen hundred towers stout:

The

The walls one hundred fixty foot upright,,
So broad, three Chariots run abreft there might,
Upon the pleafant banks of *Tigris* flood,
This ftately feat of warlike *Ninus* ftood.
This *Ninus* for a god, his father canoniz'd,
To whom the fottifh people facrific'd ;
This Tyrant did his neighbours all oppreffe,
Where e're he warr'd he had too good fucceffe,
Barzanes, the great *Armenian* King,
By force, his tributary, he did bring.
The *Median* country, he did alfo gain,
Pharmus, their King, he caufed to be flain ;
An army of three Millions he led out,
Againft the *Bactrians* (but that I doubt)
Zoroafter, their King, he likewife flew,
And all the greater *Afia* did fubdue;
Semiramis from *Menon* he did take,
Then drown himfelf, did *Menon*, for her fake ;
Fifty two years he reign'd (as we are told)
The world then was two thoufand nineteen old.

Semiramis.

This great oppreffing *Ninus* dead, and gone,
His wife, *Semiramis*, ufurp'd the throne.
  She like a brave Virago, play'd the rex,
And was both fhame, and glory of her fex ;
Her birth-place was *Philiftius Afcalon*,
Her Mother *Decreta*, a Curtezan ;
Others report, fhe was a veftal Nun,
Adjudged to be drown'd, for what fhe'd done ;

F 2   Tranf-

Transform'd into a fish, by Venus will,
Her beautious face (they feign) retaining still.
Sure from this fiction, Dagon first began,
Changing his womans face, into a man.
But all agree, that from no lawfull bed ;
This great renowned Empresse, issued.
For which, she was obscurely nourished.
Whence rose that fable, she by birds was fed.
This gallant dame, unto the *Bactrian* war;
Accompaning her husband *Menon* far,
Taking a towne, such valour she did show,
That *Ninus* of her, amorous soon did grow;
And thought her fit, to make a Monarch's wife,
Which was the cause, poor *Menon* lost his life,
She flourishing with *Ninus*, long did reigne ;
Till her ambition, caus'd him to be slaine:
That having no compeer, she might rule all,
Or else she sought, revenge for *Menons* fall :
Some think the *Greeks*, this slander on her cast,
As of her life, licentious, and unchast.
And that her worth, deserved no such blame,
As their aspersions, cast upon the same.
But were her vertues, more, or lesse, or none,
She for her potency, must go alone.
Her wealth she shew'd, in building *Babylon*;
Admir'd of all, but equaliz'd of none.
The walls so strong, and curiously were wrought;
That after ages, skil, by them were taught.
With Towers, and Bulwarks made of costly stone
Quadrangle was the forme, it stood upon:
Each Square, was fifteen thousand paces long,
An hundred gates, it had, of mettall strong;

Three

Three hundred fixty foot, the walls in heighth:
Almoft incredible, they were in breadth.
Moft writers fay, fix chariots might a front,
With great facility, march fafe upon't.
About the wall, a ditch fo deep and wide,
That like a river, long it did abide.
Three hundred thoufand men, here day, by day;
Beftow'd their labour, and receiv'd their pay,
But that which did, all coft, and art excell,
The wondrous Temple was, fhe rear'd to *Bell*;
Which in the midft, of this brave Town was plac'd,
(Continuing, till *Xerxes* it defac'd)
Whofe ftately top, beyond the clouds did rife;
From whence, Aftrologers, oft view'd the skies.
This to difcribe, in each particular,
A ftructure rare, I fhould but rudely marre,
Her gardens, bridges, arches, mounts, and fpires;
All eyes that faw, or ears that hears, admires.
On *Shinar* plain, by the *Euphratan* flood,
This wonder of the world, this *Babell* ftood.
An expedition to the Eaft fhe made.
Great King *Staurobates*, for to invade.
Her Army of four Millions did confift,
(Each man beleive it, as his fancy lift)
Her Camells, Chariots, Gallyes in fuch number,
As puzzells beft hyftorians to remember :
But this is marvelous, of all thofe men,
(They fay) but twenty, ere came back agen.
The River *Indus* fwept them half away,
The reft *Staurobates* in fight did flay.
This was laft progreffe of this mighty Queen,
Who in her Country never more was feen.

The

The Poets feign her turn'd into a Dove,
Leaving the world, to *Venus*, soar'd above,
Which made the *Affyrians* many a day,
A Dove within their Enfigne to difplay.
Forty two years fhe reign'd, and then fhe dy'd,
But by what means, we are not certifi'd.

Ninias, or *Zamies*.

HIs Mother dead, *Ninias* obtains his right,
A Prince wedded to eafe, and to delight,
Or elfe was his obedience very great,
To fit, thus long (obfcure) wrong'd of his feat ;
Some write, his Mother put his habite on,
Which made the people think they ferv'd her Son ;
But much it is, in more then forty years,
This fraud, in war, nor peace, at all appears ;
It is more like, being with pleafures fed,
He fought no rule, til fhe was gone, and dead ;
What then he did, of worth, can no man tel,
But is fuppos'd to be that *Amraphel*,
Who warr'd with *Sodoms*, and *Gomorahs* King,
'Gainft whom his trained Bands *Abram* did bring.
Some may object, his Parents ruling all,
How he thus fuddenly fhould be thus fmall ?
This anfwer may fuffice, whom it wil pleafe,
He thus voluptuous, and given to eafe ;
Each wronged Prince, or childe that did remain,
Would now advantage take, their own to gain ;
So Province, after Province, rent away,
Until that potent Empire did decay.

                                        Again,

Again, the Country was left bare (there is no doubt)
Of men, and wealth, his mother carried out;
Which to her neighbours, when it was made known,
Did then incite, them to regain their own.
What e're he was, they did, or how it fel,
We may suggest our thoughts, but cannot tel;
For *Ninias*, and all his Race are left,
In deep oblivion, of acts bereft,
And eleav'n hundred of years in silence fir,
Save a few names anew, *Berofus* writ.
And such as care not, what befals their fames,
May feign as many acts, as he did names;
It is enough, if all be true that's paft,
T' *Sardanapalus* next we wil make hafte.

Sardanapalus.

SArdanapalus, (Son t' *Ocrazapes*)
Who wallowed in all voluptuousneffe,
   That palliardizing fot, that out of doores
Ne're fhew'd his face, but revell'd with his Whores.
Did wear their garb, their geftures imitate,
And their kind t' excel did emulate.
Knowing his bafeneffe, and the peoples hate,
Kept ever clofe, fearing fome difmal fate;
At laft *Arbaces* brave, unwarily,
His mafter like a Strumpet chanc'd to fpy,
His manly heart difdained, in the leaft,
Longer to ferve this Metamorphos'd beaft;
Unto *Belofus*, then he brake his minde,
Who fick of his difeafe, he foone did finde.

Thefe

These two rul'd *Media* and *Babylon,*
Both, for their King, held their dominion,
Belosus, promised *Arbaces* aide,
Arbaces him, fully to be repaid.
The last, the *Medes* and *Persians* doth invite.
Against their monstrous King to bring their might,
Belosus the *Chaldeans* doth require,
And the *Arabians,* to further his desire.
These all agree, and forty thousand make,
The rule from their unworthy Prince to take.
By prophesie, *Belosus* strength's their hands,
Arbaces must be master of their lands.
These Forces mustered, and in array,
Sardanapalus leaves his Apish play.
And though of wars, he did abhor the fight;
Fear of his diadem, did force him fight :
And either by his valour or his fate;
Arbaces courage he did sore abate :
That in dispaire, he left the field and fled :
But with fresh hopes *Belosus* succoured.
From *Bactaria* an Army was at hand,
Prest for this service, by the Kings command;
These with celerity, *Arbaces* meets,
And with all termes of amity, he greets,
Makes promises, their necks for to un-yoak,
And their Taxations sore, all to revoake,
T'infranchise them, to grant what they could crave,
To want no priviledge, Subjects should have,
Only intreats them, joyn their force with his,
And win the Crown, which was the way to blisse,
Won by his loving looks, more loving speech,
T' accept of what they could, they him beseech.

                                              Both

Both sides their hearts, their hands, their bands unite,
And set upon their Princes Camp that night ;
Who revelling in Cups, sung care away,
For victory obtain'd the other day ;
But all surpris'd, by this unlookt for fright,
Bereft of wits, were slaughtered down right.
The King his Brother leaves, all to sustaine,
And speeds himself to *Ninivie* amain ;
But *Salmeneus* slaine, his Army fals,
The King's pursu'd unto the City wals ;
But he once in, pursuers came too late,
The wals, and gates, their course did terminate ;
There with all store he was so wel provided,
That what *Arbaces* did, was but derided ;
Who there incamp'd two years, for little end,
But in the third, the River prov'd his friend,
Which through much rain, then swelling up so high,
Part of the wal it level caus'd to lye ;
Arbaces marches in, the town did take,
For few, or none, did there resistance make ;
And now they saw fulfill'd a Prophesie ;
That when the River prov'd their enemy,
Their strong wall'd town should suddenly be taken ;
By this accomplishment, their hearts were shaken :
Sardanapalus did not seek to fly,
This his inevitable destiny ;
But all his wealth, and friends, together gets,
Then on himself, and them, a fire he sets ;
This the last Monarch was, of *Ninus* race,
Which for twelve hundred years had held that place ;
Twenty he reign'd, same time, as Stories tel,
That *Amazia* was King of *Israel* ;

His

His Father was then King (as we suppose)
When *Jonah* for their sins denounc'd such woes ;
He did repent, therefore it was not done,
But was accomplished now, in his Son.
Arbaces thus, of all becomming Lord,
Ingeniously with each did keep his word ;
Of *Babylon*, *Belosus* he made King,
With over-plus of all treasures therein,
To *Bactrians*, he gave their liberty,
Of *Ninivites*, he caused none to dye,
But suffered, with goods to go elsewhere,
Yet would not let them to inhabite there ;
For he demolished that City great,
And then to *Media* transfer'd his seat.
Thus was the promise bound, since first he crav'd,
Of *Medes*, and *Persians*, their assisting aide ;
A while he, and his race, aside must stand,
Not pertinent to what we have in hand;
But *Belochus* in's progeny pursue,
Who did this Monarchy begin anew.

Belosus, or *Belochus*.

BElosus setled, in his new, old seat,
Not so content, but aiming to be great,
Incroached stil upon the bord'ring Lands,
Til *Mesopotamia* he got in's hands,
And either by compound, or else by strength,
Assyria he also gain'd at length ;
Then did rebuild destroyed *Ninivie*,
A costly work, which none could doe but he,

Who

Who own'd the treasures of proud *Babylon,*
And those which seem'd with *Sardanapal's* gone;
But though his Palace, did in ashes lye,
The fire, those Mettals could not damnifie;
From rubbish these, with diligence he rakes,
Arbaces suffers all, and all he takes.
He thus inricht, by this new tryed gold,
Raises a Phœnix new, from grave o'th old;
And from this heap did after Ages see,
As fair a Town, as the first *Ninivie.*
When this was built, and all matters in peace,
Molests poor *Israel,* his wealth t'encrease.
A thousand tallents of *Menahem* had,
Who to be rid of such a guest, was glad;
In sacred Writ, he's known by name of *Pul,*
Which makes the world of differences so ful,
That he, and *Belochus,* one could not be,
But circumstance, doth prove the verity;
And times of both computed, so fall our,
That those two made but one, we need not doubt:
What else he did, his Empire to advance,
To rest content we must, in ignorance.
Forty eight years he reign'd, his race then run,
He left his new got Kingdoms to his Son.

Tiglath Palasser.

BElosus dead, *Tiglath* his warlike Son
Next treads the steps, by which his Father won.
Damascus, ancient seat of famous Kings,
Under subjection by his sword he brings;

Resin

Refin their valiant King, he also flew,
And *Syria* t' obedience did subdue ;
Iuda's bad King occasioned this War,
When *Refins* force his borders fore did mar.
And divers Cities, by ftrong hand did feize,
To *Tiglath* then doth *Ahaz* fend for eafe.
The temple robes, fo to fulfill his ends,
And to *Affyria's* King a Prefent fends.
I am thy Servant, and thy Son (quoth he)
From *Rezin*, and from *Pekah* fet me free :
Gladly doth *Tiglath* this advantage take,
And fuccours *Ahaz*, yet for *Tiglath's* fake,
When *Rezin's* flain, his Army over-thrown,
Syria he makes a Province of his own.
Unto *Damafcus* then, comes *Iudah's* King,
His humble thankfulneffe (with haft) to bring,
Acknowledging th' *Affyrians* high defert,
To whom, he ought all loyalty of heart.
But *Tiglath*, having gain'd his wifhed end,
Proves unto *Ahaz* but a feigned friend ;
All *Ifraels* Land, beyond *Iordan*, he takes.
In *Galilee*, he woful havock makes ;
Through *Syria* now he marcht, none ftopt his way,
And *Ahaz* open, at his mercy lay,
Who ftil implor'd his love, but was diftreff'd,
(This was that *Ahaz*, which fo much tranfgreft.)
Thus *Tiglath* reign'd, and warr'd, twenty feven years,
Then by his death, releas'd, was *Ifraels* fears.

Salma-

Salmanaſſer, or *Nabonaſſer.*

TIglath deceas'd, *Salmanaſſer* is next,
He I*ſraelites,* more then his Father vext;
*Hoſhea,*their laſt King,he did invade,
And him ſix years his tributary made ;
But weary of his ſervitude, he ſought,
To *Ægypts* King, which did avail him nought ;
For *Salmanaſſer,* with a mighty Hoaſt,
Beſieg'd his regal town, and ſpoyl'd his Coaſt,
And did the people, nobles, and their King,
Into perpetual thraldome that time bring ;
Thoſe that from *Ioſhua's* time had been Eſtate,
Did Juſtice now, by him, eradicate :   [10 *years.*
This was that ſtrange degenerated brood,
On whom, nor threats, nor mercies could do good ;
Laden with honour, priſoners,and with ſpoyl,
Returns triumphant Victor to his ſoyl ;
Plac'd *Iſrael* in's Land, where he thought beſt,
Then ſent his Colonies, theirs to inveſt ;
Thus *Iacobs* Sons,in exile muſt remain,
And pleaſant *Canaan* ne're ſee again :
Where now thoſe ten Tribes are, can no man tel,
Or how they fare, rich, poor, or ill, or wel ;
Whether the *Indians* of the Eaſt, or Weſt,
Or wild *Tartarians,* as yet ne're bleſt,
Or elſe thoſe *Chinoes* rare, whoſe wealth, and Arts,
Hath bred more wonder, then beleeſe in hearts ;
But what, or where they are, yet know we this;
They ſhal return, and *Zion* ſee, with bliſſe.
                              Senacherib.

Senacherib.

SEnacherib *Salmanesèr* succeeds,
Whose haughty heart is shewn in works, and deeds;
His Wars none better then himself can boast,
On *Henah*, *Arpad*, and on *Ivah* least;
On *Hena's*, and on *Sepharuaim's* gods,
Twixt them and *Israels* he knew no odds.   {7 years.
Until the thundring hand of heaven he felt,
Which made his Army into nothing melt;
With shame then turn'd to *Ninivie* again,
And by his Sons in's Idols house was slain.

Essarhadon.

HIs Son, weak *Essarhadon* reign'd in's place,
The fifth, and last, of great *Belosus* race;
Brave *Merodach*, the Son of *Balladan*,
In *Babylon*, Leiutenant to this man,
Of opportunity advantage takes,
And on his Masters ruins, his house makes;
And *Belosus*, first, his did unthrone,
So he's now stil'd, the King of *Babylon*;
After twelve years did *Essarhadon* dye,
And *Merodach* assume the Monarchy.

Merodach

Merodach Baladan.

ALl yeelds to him, but *Ninivie* kept free,
  Until his Grand-childe made her bow the knee;
Embassadours to *Hezekiah* sent,   [21 *years.*
His health congratulates with complement.

Ben. Merodach.

BEn. *Merodach,* Successor to this King,
  Of whom is little said in any thing;   [22 *years.*
But by conjecture this, and none but he,
Led King *Manasseh,* to captivity.

Nebulassar.

BRave *Nebulassar* to this King was Sonne,
  The ancient *Niniveh* by him was won;
For fifty years, or more, it had been free,
Now yeelds her neck unto captivity :   [12 *years.*
A Vice-roy from her foe, she's glad t'accept,
By whom in firm obedience she's kept.

Nebuchadnezar, or *Nebopolassar.*

THe famous Wars, of this Heroyick King,
  Did neither *Homer, Hesiode, Virgil* sing ;

                                          Nor

Nor of his acts have we the certainty,
From some *Thucidides* grave History;
Nor's Metamorphosis from *Ovids* Book,
Nor his restoring from old legends took;
But by the Prophets, Pen-men most Divine,
This Prince in's magnitude doth ever shine;
This was of Monarchies that head of gold,
The richest, and the dreadfull'st to behold;
This was that tree, whose branches fill'd the earth,
Under whose shadow, birds, and beasts, had birth;
This was that King of Kings, did what he pleas'd,
Kild, sav'd, pull'd down, set up, or pain'd, or eas'd;
And this is he, who when he fear'd the least,
Was turned from a King, unto a Beast;
This Prince, the last year of his Fathers reign,
Against *Iehoiakim* marcht with his train;
Iudah's poor King besieg'd, who succourlesse,
Yeelds to his mercy, and the present stresse;
His Vassal is, gives pledges for his truth,
Children of Royal bloud, unblemish'd youth;
Wise *Daniel*, and his fellows 'mongst the rest,
By the victorious King to *Babel's* prest;
The temple of rich ornaments defac'd,
And in his Idols house the Vassal's plac'd.
The next year he, with unresisted hand,
Quite vanquish'd *Pharaoh Necho*, and his Band;
By great *Euphrates* did his Army fall,
Which was the losse of *Syria* withall;
Then into Ægypt, *Necho* did retire,
Which in few years proves the *Assyrians* hire;
A mighty Army next, he doth prepare,
And unto wealthy *Tyre* with hast repaire.

Such

Such was the scituation of this place,
As might not him, but all the world out-face;
That in her pride, she knew not which to boast,
Whether her wealth, or yet her strength was most ;
How in all Merchandise she did excell,
None but the true *Ezekiel* need to tell :
And for her strength, how hard she was to gain,
Can *Babels* tired Souldiers tell with pain ;
Within an Island had this City seat,
Divided from the maine, by channel great ;
Of costly Ships, and Gallies, she had store,
And Mariners, to handle sayle, and oare ;
But the *Chaldeans* had nor ships, nor skill,
Their shoulders must their Masters minde fulfill ;
Fetch rubbish from the opposite old town,
And in the channell throw each burden down ;
Where after many assayes, they make at last,
The Sea firm Land, whereon the Army past,
And took the wealthy town, but all the gain
Requited not the cost, the toyle, and pain.
Full thirteen yeares in this strange work he spent,
Before he could accomplish his intent ;
And though a Victor home his Army leads,
With peeled shoulders, and with balded heads,
When in the *Tyrian* wars, the King was hot,
Jehoiakim his Oath had clean forgot ;
Thinks this the fittest time to break his bands,
While *Babels* King thus deep ingaged stands ;
But he (alas) whose fortunes now i'th ebbe,
Had all his hopes like to a Spiders web ;
For this great King, with-drawes part of his force,
To *Judah* marches with a speedy course,

G   And

And unexpected findes the feeble Prince,
Whom he chastised for his proud offence;
Fast bound, intends at *Babel* he shal stay,
But chang'd his minde, and slew him by the way;
Thus cast him out, like to a naked Asse,
For this was he, for whom none said, Alas!
His Son three months he suffered to reign,
Then from his throne, he pull'd him down again:
Whom with his Mother, he to *Babel* led,
And more then thirty years in prison fed;
His Unckle, he established in's place,
Who was last King of holy *Davids* race;
But he, as perjur'd as *Ichoiakim*,
Iudah lost more (then e're they lost) by him;
Seven years he keeps his faith, and safe he dwels,
But in the eighth, against his Prince rebels;
The ninth, came *Nebuchadnezar* with power,
Besieg'd his City, Temple, *Zions* Tower;
And after eighteen months he took them all,
The wals so strong, that stood so long, now fall;
The cursed King, by flight could no wise free
His wel deserv'd, and fore-told misery;
But being caught, to *Babels* wrathful King,
With Children, Wives, and Nobles, all they bring,
Where to the sword, all but himself was put,
And with that woful sight his eyes close shut.
A haplesse man, whose darksome contemplation,
Was nothing, but such gastly meditation;
In mid'st of *Babel* now, til death he lyes,
Yet as was told, ne're saw it with his eyes;
The Temple's burnt, the Vessels had away,
The Towers, and Palaces, brought to decay;

Where

Where late, of Harp, and Lute, was heard the noyſe,
Now *Zim*, and *Sim*, lift up their ſhriking voyce ;
All now of worth, are captive led with tears,
There ſit bewailing *Zion* ſeventy years.
With all theſe Conqueſts, *Babels* King reſts not,
No, nor when *Moab*, *Edom* he had got.
Kedar, *Hazer*, the *Arabians* too,
All Vaſſals, at his hands, for grace muſt ſue ;
A totall Conqueſt of rich *Ægypt* makes,
All rule, he from the ancient *Pharoes* takes ;
Who had for ſixteen hundred years born ſway,
To *Babylons* proud King, now yeelds the day.
Then *Put*, and *Lud*, doe at his mercy ſtand,
Where e're he goes, he Conquers every Land ;
His ſumptuous buildings paſſes all conceit,
Which wealth, and ſtrong ambition made ſo great ;
His Image, *Iudahs* Captives worſhip not,
Although the Furnace be ſeven times more hot ;
His Dreams, wiſe *Daniel* doth expound ful wel,
And his unhappy change with grief fore-tel ;
Strange melancholly humours on him lay,
Which for ſeven years his reaſon took away ;
Which from no natural cauſes did proceed,
For by the Heavens above it was decreed :
The time expir'd, remains a Beaſt no more,
Reſumes his Government, as heretofore.
In ſplendor, and in Majeſty, he ſits,
Contemplating thoſe times he loſt his wits ;
And if by words, we may gueſſe at the heart,
This King among the righteous had a part :
Forty four years he reign'd, which being run,
He left his Wealth, and Conqueſt, to his Son.

Evilmerodach.

BAbels great Monarch, now laid in the duſt,
His ſon poſſeſſes wealth, and rule, as juſt;
    And in the firſt year of his royalty,
Eaſeth *Jehoiakims* captivity.
Poor forlorn Prince, that had all ſtate forgot,
In ſeven and thirty years, had ſeen no jot,
Among the Conquered Kings, that there did lye,
Is *Judah's* King, now lifted up on high.
But yet in *Babell*, he muſt ſtill remain :
And native *Canaan*, never ſee again,
Unlike his father, *Evilmerodach*,
Prudence, and magnanimity, did lack
Faire *Ægypt* is, by his remiſſeneſſe loſt ;
Arabia, and all the boardering coaſt.
Wars with the *Medes*, unhappily he wag'd,
(Within which broiles, rich *Crœſus* was engag'd,)
His Army routed, and himſelfe there ſlain,
His Kingdome to *Belſhazzar* did remain,

Belſhazzar.

UNworthy *Belſhazzar* next weares the Crown,
Whoſe prophane acts, a ſacred pen ſets down.
    His luſt, and cruelty, in books we find,
A Royall State, rul'd by a bruitiſh mind.
His life ſo baſe, and diſſolute, invites
The Noble *Perſians*, to invade his rights.

                                        Who

Who with his own, and Uncles power anon;
Layes fiedge to's regall feat, proud *Babylon*,
The coward King, whofe ftrength lay in his walls,
To banquetting, and revelling now falls,
To fhew his little dread, but greater ftore,
To chear his friends, and fcorn his foes the more.
The holy veffells, thither brought long fince,
Carous'd they in; and facrilegious Prince,
Did praife his gods of mettall, wood, and ftone,
Protectors of his Crown, and *Babylon*,
But he above, his doings did deride,
And with a hand, foon dafhed all his pride.
The King, upon the wall cafting his eye,
The fingers of his hand-writing did fpy.
Which horrid fight, he fears, muft needs portend,
Deftruction to his Crown, to's Perfon end.
With quaking knees, and heart appall'd, he crys,
For the Soothfayers, and Magicians wife;
This language ftrange, to read, and to unfold;
With guifts of Scarlet robe, and Chaines of gold,
And higheft dignity, next to the King,
To him that could interpret clear this thing:
But dumb the gazing Aftrologers ftand,
Amazed at the writing, and the hand.
None anfwers the affrighted Kings intent.
Who ftill expects fome fearfull fad event,
As thus amort he fits, as all undone:
In comes the Queen, to chear her heartleffe fon.
Of *Daniel* tells, who in his Grand-fires dayes,
Was held in more requeft, then now he was,
Daniel in hafte, is brought before the King,
Who doth not flatter, nor once cloake the thing.

G 3 Re-

Re-minds him of his Grand-fires height, and fall,
And of his own notorious fins, withall ;
His drunkenneffe, and his prophainneffe high,
His pride, and fottifh groffe Idolatry.
The guilty King, with colour pale, and dead,
There hears his *Mene*, and his *Tekel* read ;
And did one thing worthy a King (though late)
Perform'd his word, to him, that told his fate ;
That night victorious *Cyrus* took the town,
Who foone did terminate his Life, and Crown :
With him did end the race of *Baladan*,
And now the *Perfian* Monarchy began.

The end of the Affyrian *Monarchy.*

The

The Second Monarchy,

being the *Perſian*, begun under
Cyrus, Darius (being his Vnckle,
and his Father in Law) reign-
ing with him about two years.

Yrus Cambyſes, Son of *Perſia's* King,
Whom Lady *Mandana* did to him bring ;
She Daughter unto great *Aſtiages*,
He in deſcent the ſeventh from *Arbaces*.
Cambyſes was of *Achemenes* race,
Who had in *Perſia* the Lieutenants place.
When *Sardanapalus* was over-thrown,
And from that time, had held it as his own ;
Cyrus, Darius Daughter took to wife,
And ſo unites two Kingdoms, without ſtrife ;
Darius was unto *Mandana* brother,
Adopts her Son for his, having no other :
This is of *Cyrus* the true pedigree,
Whoſe Anceſtors, were royal in degree ;
His Mothers Dream, and Grand-ſires cruelty,
His preſervation in his miſery ;
His nouriſhment afforded by a Bitch,
Are fit for ſuch, whoſe eares for fables itch ;

G 4 He

He in his younger dayes an Army led,
Againſt great *Creſſus*, then of *Lidia* head ;
Who over-curious of wars event,
For information to *Apollo* went :
And the ambiguous Oracle did truſt,
So over-thrown of *Gyrus*, as was juſt ;
Who him purſues to *Sardis*, takes the town,
Where all that doe reſiſt, are ſlaughter'd down ;
Diſguiſed *Creſſus*, hop'd to ſcape i'th throng,
Who had no might to ſave himſelf from wrong ;
But as he paſt, his Son, who was born dumbe,
With preſſing grief, and ſorrow, over-come,
Amidſt the tumult, bloud-ſhed, and the ſtrife,
Brake his long ſilence, cry'd, ſpare *Creſſus* life :
Creſſus thus known, it was great *Cyrus* doome,
(A hard decree) to aſhes he conſume ;
Then on a Pike being ſet, where all might eye,
He *Solon, Solon, Solon*, thrice did cry.
Upon demand, his minde to *Cyrus* broke,
And told, how *Solon* in his hight had ſpoke.
With pitty *Cyrus* mov'd, knowing Kings ſtand,
Now up, now down, as fortune turnes her hand,
Weighing the age, and greatneſſe of the Prince,
(His Mothers Vnckle, ſtories doe evince :)
Gave him at once, his life, and Kingdom too,
And with the *Lidians*, had no more to doe.
Next war, the reſtleſſe *Cyrus* thought upon,
Was conqueſt of the ſtately *Babylon*,
Now trebble wall'd, and moated ſo about,
That all the world they neither feare, nor doubt ;
To drain this ditch, he many ſluces cut,
But till convenient time their heads kept ſhut ;

That

That night *Belſhazzar* feaſted all his rout,
He cuts thoſe banks, and let the river out ;
And to the walls ſecurely marches on,
Not finding a defendant thereupon ;
Enters the town, the ſottiſh King he ſlayes,
Upon earths richeſt ſpoyles his Souldiers preys ;
Here twenty yeares proviſion he found,
Forty five mile this City ſcarce could round ;
This head of Kingdoms, *Caldes* excellence,
For Owles, and Satyres, makes a reſidence ;
Yet wondrous Monuments this ſtately Queen,
Had after thouſand yeares faire to be ſeen.
Cyrus doth now the *Jewiſh* captives free,
An Edict makes, the Temple builded be,
He with his Vnckle *Daniel* ſets on high,
And cauſ'd his foes in Lions den to dye.
Long after this, he 'gainſt the *Sythians* goes,
And *Tomris* Son, an Army over-throwes ;
Which to revenge, ſhe hires a mighty power,
And ſets on *Cyrus*, in a fatall houre ;
There routs his Hoaſt, himſelf ſhe priſoner takes,
And at one blow, worlds head, ſhe headleſſe makes ;
The which ſhe bak'd within a But of bloud,
Uſing ſuch taunting words as ſhe thought good.
But *Zenophon* reports, he dy'd in's bed,
In honour, peace, and wealth, with a grey head,
And in his Town of *Paſargada* lyes,
Where *Alexander* ſought, in hope of prize,
But in this Tombe was only to be found
Two *Sythian* bowes, a ſword, and target round ;
Where that prond Conquerour could doe no leſſe,
Then at his Herſe great honours to expreſſe ;

Three

Three Daughters, and two Sons, he left behind,
Innobled more by birth, then by their mind ;
Some thirty years this potent Prince did reign,
Unto *Cambyses* then, all did remain.

Cambyses.

CAmbyses, no wayes like, his noble Sire,
   But to enlarge his state, had some desire ;
   His reign with Bloud, and Incest, first begins,
Then sends to finde a Law for these his sins ;
That Kings with Sisters match, no Law they finde,
But that the *Persian* King, may act his minde ;
Which Law includes all Lawes, though lawlesse stil,
And makes it lawful Law, if he but wil ;
He wages warre, the fifth year of his reign,
'Gainst *Ægypts* King, who there by him was slain,
And all of Royal bloud that came to hand,
He seized first of life, and then of Land ;
(But little *Marus*, scap'd that cruel fate,
Who grown a man, resum'd again his state)
He next to *Cyprus* sends his bloudy Hoast,
Who landed soon upon that fruitful coast,
Made *Evelthon* their King, with bended knee,
To hold his own, of his free courtesie ;
The Temples he destroyes not, for his zeal,
But he would be profest god of their Weal ;
Yea, in his pride, he ventured so farre,
To spoyl the Temple of great *Jupiter* ;
But as they marched o're those desart sands,
The stormed dust o'r-whelm'd his daring bands ;

But

But scorning thus by *Jove* to be out-brav'd,
A second Army there had almost grav'd ;
But vain he found, to fight with Elements,
So left his sacrilegious bold intents:
The Ægyptian *Apis* then he likewise slew,
Laughing to scorn that calvish, sottish crew.
If all his heat, had been for a good end,
Cambyses to the clouds, we might commend ;
But he that 'fore the gods, himself preferrs,
Is more prophane, then grosse *Idolaters* ;
And though no gods, if he esteem them some,
And contemn them, woful is his doome.
He after this, saw in a Vision,
His brother *Smerdis* sit upon his throne ;
He strait to rid himself of causlesse feats,
Complots the Princes death, in his green years,
Who for no wrong, poore innocent must dye,
Praraspes now must act this tragedy ;
Who into *Persia* with Commission sent,
Accomplished this wicked Kings intent ;
His sister, whom incestuously he wed,
Hearing her harmlesse brother thus was dead,
His woful fate with tears did so bemoane,
That by her Husbands charge, she caught her owne ;
She with her fruit was both at once undone,
Who would have born a Nephew, and a Son.
O hellish Husband, Brother, Vnckle, Sire,
Thy cruelty will Ages still admire.
This strange severity, one time he us'd,
Upon a Judge, for breach of Law accus'd ;
Flayd him alive, hung up his stuffed skin
Over his Seat, then plac'd his Son therein ;

To

To whom he gave this in rememberance,
Like fault must look, for the like recompence.
Praraspes, to *Cambyses* favourite,
Having one son, in whom he did delight,
His cruell Master, for all service done,
Shot through the heart of his beloved son:
And only for his fathers faithfullnesse,
Who said but what, the King bad him expresse.
'T would be no pleasant, but a tedious thing,
To tell the facts, of this most bloody King.
Fear'd of all, but lov'd of few, or none,
All thought his short reign long, till it was done.
At last, two of his Officers he hears,
Had set a *Smerdis* up, of the same years;
And like in feature, to the *Smerdis* dead,
Ruling as they thought good, under his head.
Toucht with this newes, to *Persia* he makes,
But in the way, his sword just vengeance takes.
Unsheathes, as he his horse mounted on high,
And with a *Mortall* thrust, wounds him ith' thigh,
Which ends before begun, the *Persian* Warre,
Yeelding to death, that dreadfull Conquerer.
Griefe for his brothers death, he did expresse,
And more, because he dyed issulesse.
The Male line, of great *Cyrus* now did end.
The Female many ages did extend,
A *Babylon* in *Egypt* did he make.
And built fair *Meroe*, for his sisters sake.
Eight years he reign'd, a short, yet too long time,
Cut off in's wickednesse, in's strength, and prime.

The

The inter Regnum between Cambyses, *and* Darius Hyslaspes.

CHildlesse *Cambyses,* on the sudden dead,
The Princes meet to chuse one in his stead,
Of which the cheife were seven, call'd *Satrapes,*
(Who like to Kings, rul'd Kingdomes as they please,)
Descended all, of *Achemenes* blood,
And kinsmen in account, to th'King they stood,
And first these noble *Magi* 'gree upon,
To thrust th'Imposter *Smerdis* out of throne,
Their Forces instantly they raise, and rout,
This King, with conspirators so stout,
Who little pleasure had, in his short reigne,
And now with his accomplyces lye slaine.
But yet, 'fore this was done, much blood was shed,
And two of these great Peers, in place lay dead:
Some write that sorely hurt, they 'scap'd away;
But so or no, sure tis, they won the day.
All things in peace, and Rebells throughly quel'd,
A Consultation by the States was held.
What forme of Government now to erect,
The old, or new, which best, in what respect,
The greater part, declin'd a Monarchy.
So late crusht by their Princes Tyranny;
And thought the people, would more happy be,
If governed by an Aristocracy.
But others thought (none of the dullest braine,)
But better one, then many Tyrants reigne.
What arguments they us'd, I know not well,
Too politicke (tis like) for me to tell,

But

But in conclusion they all agree,
That of the seven a Monarch chosen be ;
All envie to avoyd, this was thought on,
Upon a Green to meet, by rising Sun ;
And he whose Horse before the rest should neigh,
Of all the Peers should have precedency.
They all attend on the appointed houre,
Praying to Fortune, for a Kingly power ;
Then mounting on their snorting coursers proud,
Darius lusty stallion neighed full loud ;
The Nobles all alight, their King to greet,
And after *Persian* manner, kisse his feet.
His happy wishes now doth no man spare,
But acclamations ecchoes in the aire ;
A thousand times, God save the King, they cry,
Let tyranny now with *Cambyses* dye.
They then attend him, to his royall roome,
Thanks for all this to's crafty Stable-groome.

Darius Hystaspes.

Darius by election made a King,
His title to make strong omits no thing ;
He two of *Cyrus* Daughters now doth wed,
Two of his Neeces takes to nuptiall bed ;
By which he cuts their hopes (for future times)
That by such steps to Kingdoms often climbs.
And now a King, by marriage, choyce, and bloud,
Three strings to's bow, the least of which is good ;
Yet more the peoples hearts firmly to binde,
Made wholsome gentle Laws, which pleas'd each mind.

His

His affability, and milde aspect,
Did win him loyalty, and all respect;
Yet notwithstanding he did all so well,
The *Babylonians* 'gainst their Prince rebell;
An Hoast he rais'd, the City to reduce,
But strength against those walls was of no use;
For twice ten months before the town he lay,
And fear'd, he now with scorn must march away:
Then brave *Zopirus*, for his Masters good,
His manly face dis-figures, spares no bloud,
With his own hands cuts off his eares, and nose,
And with a faithfull fraud to' th' town he goes,
Tels them, how harshly the proud King had dealt,
That for their sakes, his cruelty he felt;
Desiring of the Prince to raise the siege,
This violence was done him by his Leige;
This told, for enterance he stood not long,
For they beleev'd his nose, more then his tongue;
With all the Cities strength they him betrust,
If he command, obey the greatest must:
When opportunity he saw was fit,
Delivers up the town, and all in it.
To loose a nose, to win a Town's no shame,
But who dare venture such a stake for th' game;
Then thy disgrace, thine honour's manifold,
Who doth deserve a Statue made of gold;
Nor can *Darius* in his Monarchy,
Scarse finde enough to thank thy loyalty;
But yet thou hast sufficient recompence,
In that thy fame shall sound whilst men have sence;
Yet o're thy glory we must cast this vaile,
Thy falshood, not thy valour did prevaile;

Thy

Thy wit was more then was thine honesty,
Thou lov'dst thy Master more then verity.
Darius in the second of his reign,
An Edict for the *Jews* publish'd again,
The temple to re-build, for that did rest
Since *Cyrus* time, *Cambyses* did molest ;
He like a King, now grants a Charter large,
Out of his owne revenues beares the charge ;
Gives sacrifices, wheat, wine, oyle, and salt,
Threats punishment to him, that through default
Shall let the work, or keep back any thing,
Of what is freely granted by the King ;
And on all Kings he poures out execrations,
That shall, but dare raze those firme foundations;
They thus backt of the King, in spight of foes,
Built on, and prosper'd, till their walls did close ;
And in the sixth yeare of his friendly reign
Set up a Temple (though, a lesse)again.
Darius on the *Sythians* made a war,
Entring that large and barren country far ;
A bridge he made, which serv'd for boat, and barge,
Over fair *Ister*, at a mighty charge ;
But in that Desart, 'mongst his barbarous foes,
Sharp wants, not swords, his vallour did oppose ;
His Army fought with Hunger, and with Cold,
Which two then to assaile, his Camp was bold .
By these alone his Hoast was pinch'd so sore,
He warr'd defensive, not offensive, more ;
The Salvages did laugh at his distresse,
Their minds by Hieroglyphicks they expresse;
A Frog, a Mouse, a Bird, an Arrow sent,
The King will needs interpret their intent ;

Posses-

Possession of water, earth, and aire,
But wise *Gobrias* reads not half so farre:
Quoth he, like Frogs, in water we must dive,
Or like to Mice, under the earth must live;
Or fly like birds, in unknown wayes full quick;
Or *Sythian* arrows in our sides must stick.
The King, seeing his men, and victuall spent,
His fruitlesse war, began late to repent;
Return'd with little honour, and lesse gaine,
His enemies scarce seen, then much lesse, slaine;
He after this, intends *Greece* to invade,
But troubles in lesse *Asia* him stay'd;
Which husht, he straight so orders his affaires;
For *Attica* an Army he prepares;
But as before, so now with ill successe,
Return'd with wondrous losse, and honour lesse:
Athens perceiving now their desperate state,
Arm'd all they could, which elev'n thousand make;
By brave *Miltiades* (their chief) being led,
Darius multitude before them fled;
At *Marathon* this bloudy field was fought,
Where *Grecians* prov'd themselves right Souldiers,
The *Persians* to their Gallies post with speed,   (stout;
Where an *Athenian* shew'd a valiant deed,
Pursues his flying-foes, and on the strand,
He stayes a landing Gally with his hand;
Which soon cut off, he with the left
Renews his hold; but when of that bereft,
His whetted teeth he sticks in the firm wood,
Off flyes his head, down showres his frolick bloud.
Go *Persians*, carry home that angry peece,
As the best trophie that ye won in *Greece.*

H

Darius

Darius light, he heavie, home returnes,
And for revenge his heart still restlesse burnes ;
His Queen *Attossa*, caused all this stir,
For *Grecian* Maids ('tis said) to wait on her;
She lost her aime; her Husband, he lost more,
His men, his coyn, his honour, and his store ;
And the ensuing yeare ended his life,
('Tis thought) through grief of his successesse strife.
Thirty six years this royall Prince did reign,
Unto his eldest Son, all did remain.

Xerxes.

XErxes, *Darius*, and *Attossa's* Son,
Grand-childe to *Cyrus*, now sits on the throne ;
The Father not so full of lenity,
As is the Son, of pride, and cruelty ;
He with his Crown, receives a double warre,
Th' *Ægyptians* to reduce, and *Greece* to marre ;
The first begun, and finish'd in such hast,
None write by whom, nor how, 'twas over-past ;
But for the last he made such preparation,
As if to dust he meant to grinde that Nation;
Yet all his men, and instruments of slaughter,
Produced but derision, and laughter ;
Sage *Artabanus* counsell, had he taken,
And's cousen, young *Mardonius* forsaken,
His Souldiers, credit, wealth, at home had stay'd,
And *Greece* such wondrous triumphs ne're had made.
The first deports, and layes before his eyes,
His Fathers ill successe in's enterprise,

Against

Against the *Sythians,* and *Grecians* too,
What infamy to's honour did accrue.
Flattering *Mardonius* on th' other side,
With certainty of *Europe* feeds his pride;
Vaine *Xerxes* thinks his counsell hath most wit,
That his ambitious humour best can fit;
And by this choyce, unwarily posts on,
To present losse, future subversion;
Although he hasted, yet foure yeares was spent,
In great provisions, for this great intent;
His Army of all Nations, was compounded,
That the large *Persian* government surrounded;
His Foot was seventeen hundred thousand strong;
Eight hundred thousand Horse to them belong;
His Camels, beasts, for carriage numberlesse,
For truth's asham'd how many to expresse;
The charge of all he severally commended,
To Princes of the *Persian* bloud descended,
But the command of these Commanders all,
To *Mardonius,* Captain Generall;
He was the Son of the fore-nam'd *Gobrias,*
Who married the sister of *Darius :*
These his Land Forces were, then next, a Fleet
Of two and twenty thousand Gallies meet,
Mann'd by *Phenisians,* and *Pamphilians,*
Cipriots, Dorians, and *Cilicians,*
Lycians, Carians, and *Ionians,*
Eolians, and the *Helispontines ;*
Besides, the Vessels for his transportation,
Three thousand (or more) by best relation,
Artemesia, Halicarna's Queene,
In person there, now for his help was seen ;

H 2　　　　　　　　Whose

Whose Gallies all the rest in neatnesse passe,
Save the *Zidonians*, where *Xerxes* was.
Hers she kept stil, seperate from the rest,
For to command alone, she thought was best.
O noble Queen, thy valour I commend,
But pitty 'twas, thine ayde that here did'st lend,
At *Sardis*, in *Lidia*, these all doe meet,
Whither rich *Pithyus* comes, *Xerxes* to greet;
Feasts all this multitude, of his own charge,
Then gives the King, a King-like gift, most large;
Three thousand Tallents of the purest gold;
Which mighty sum, all wondred to behold.
He humbly to the King then makes request,
One of his five Sons there, might be releast;
To be to's age a comfort, and a stay,
The other four he freely gave away:
The King cals for the Youth, who being brought,
Cuts him in twain, for whom his Sire besought.
O most inhumain incivility!
Nay, more then monstrous barb'rous cruelty!
For his great love, is this thy recompence?
Is this to doe like *Xerxes*, or a Prince?
Thou shame of Kings, of men the detestation,
I Rhethorick want, to poure out execration:
First thing, *Xerxes* did worthy recount,
A Sea passage cuts, behind *Orthos* Mount.
Next, o're the *Hellispont* a bridge he made,
Of Boats, together coupled, and there laid;
But winds, and waves, these couples soon dissever'd,
Yet *Xerxes* in his enterprise persever'd;
Seven thousand Gallies chain'd, by *Tyrians* skil,
Firmly at length, accomplished his wil;

Seven

Seven dayes and nights, his Hoaſt without leaſt ſtay,
Was marching o're this interrupting Bay ;
And in *Abidus* Plaines, muſtring his Forces,
He glories in his Squadrons, and his Horſes ;
Long viewing them, thought it great happineſſe,
One King, ſo many Subjects ſhould poſſeſſe ;
But yet this goodly ſight produced teares,
That none of theſe ſhould live a hundred yeares :
What after did enſue, had he fore-ſeen.
Of ſo long time, his thoughts had never been.
Of *Artabanus* he again demands,
How of this enterpriſe his thoughts now ſtands ;
His anſwer was, both Land and Sea he feared,
Which was not vaine, as it ſoon appeared :
But *Xerxes* reſolute, to *Thrace* goes firſt,
His Hoaſt, who *Liſſus* drinks to quench their thirſt,
And for his Cattell, all *Piſſirus* Lake
Was ſcarce enough, for each a draught to take.
Then marching to the ſtreight *Thermopyle*,
The *Spartan* meets him, brave Leonade,
This 'twixt the Mountains lyes (half Acre wide)
That pleaſant *Theſſaly*, from *Greece* divide ;
Two dayes and nights a fight they there maintain,
Till twenty thouſand *Perſians* falls down ſlain ;
And all that Army, then diſmay'd, had fled,
But that a Fugative diſcovered,
How parr, might o're the Mountains goe about,
And wound the backs of thoſe bold Warriours ſtout.
They thus behemm'd with multitude of foes,
Laid on more fiercely, their deep mortall blowes ;
None cryes for quarter, nor yet ſeeks to run,
But on their ground they dye, each Mothers Son.

O noble *Greeks*, how now, degenerate ?
Where is the valour, of your antient State ?
When as one thousand, could some Millions daunt ;
Alas, it is *Leonades* you want !
This shamefull Victory cost *Xerxes* deare,
Amongst the rest, two brothers he lost there ;
And as at Land, so he at Sea was crost,
Four hundred stately Ships by stormes was lost,
Of Vessels small almost innumerable,
Them to receive, the Harbour was not able ;
Yet thinking to out-match his foes at Sea,
Inclos'd their Fleet i'th' streights of *Eubea* ;
But they as valiant by Sea, as Land,
In this Streight, as the other, firmly stand.
And *Xerxes* mighty Gallies batter'd so,
That their split sides, witness'd his overthrow ;
Yet in the Streights of *Salamis* he try'd,
If that smal number his great force could bide ;
But he, in daring of his forward foe,
Received there, a shameful over-throw.
Twice beaten thus by Sea, he warr'd no more:
But *Phocians* Land, he then wasted sore :
They no way able to withstand his force,
That brave *Thymistocles* takes this wise course,
In secret manner word to *Xerxes* sends,
That *Greeks* to break his bridge shortly intends ;
And as a friend, warns him, what e're he doe,
For his retreat, to have an eye thereto :
He hearing this, his thoughts, and course home bended,
Much, that which never was intended !
Yet 'fore he went, to help out his expence,
Part of his Hoast to *Delphos* sent from thence,

To

To rob the wealthy Temple of *Apollo*,
But mischief, Sacriledge doth ever follow;
Two mighty Rocks, brake from *Parnassus* Hil,
And many thousands of these men did kil;
Which accident, the rest affrighted so,
With empty hands they to their Master go;
He seeing all thus tend unto decay,
Thought it his best, no longer for to stay;
Three hundred thousand yet he left behind,
With his *Mardon'us*, judex of his minde;
Who for his sake, he knew, would venture far,
(Chief instigater of this helpelesse War;)
He instantly to *Athens* sends for peace,
That all Hostility might thence-forth cease;
And that with *Xerxes* they would be at one,
So should all favour to their State be shown.
The *Spartans*, fearing *Athens* would agree,
As had *Macedon*, *Thebes*, and *Thessalie*,
And leave them out, the shock for to sustaine,
By their Ambassador they thus complain;
That *Xerxes* quarrel was 'gainst *Athens* State,
And they had helpt them, as confederate;
If now in need, they should thus fail their friends,
Their infamy would last till all things ends:
But the *Athenians*, this peace detest,
And thus reply'd unto *Mardon's* request;
That whilst the Sun did run his endlesse course,
Against the *Persians* they would use their force.
Nor could the brave Ambassador be sent,
With Rhetorick, t' gain better complement:
Though of this Nation borne a great Commander,
No lesse then Grand-sire to great *Alexander*.

H 4

Mardonius

Mardonius proud, hearing this anfwer ftout,
To adde unto his numbers, layes about,
And of thofe *Greeks*, which by his skil he'd won,
He fifty thoufand joynes unto his own ;
The other *Greeks*, which were confederate,
One hundred thoufand, and ten thoufand make.
The *Beotian* Fields, of war, the feats,
Where both fides exercis'd their manly feats ;
But all their controverfies to decide,
For one maine Battell fhortly, both provide ;
The *Athenians* could but forty thoufand arme,
For other Weapons, they had none would harme ;
But that which helpt defects, and made them bold,
Was Victory, by Oracle fore-told :
Ten dayes thefe Armies did each other face,
Mardonius finding victuals waft apace,
No longer dar'd, but fiercely on-fet gave,
The other not a hand, nor fword will wave,
Till in the entrails of their Sacrifice,
The fignall of their victory doth rife ;
Which found, like *Greeks* they fight, the *Perfians* fly,
And troublefome *Mardonius* now muft dye :
All's loft, and of three hundred thoufand men,
Three thoufand fcapes, for to run home agen ;
For pitty, let thofe few to *Xerxes* go,
To certifie this finall over-throw.
Same day, the fmall remainder of his Fleet,
The *Grecians* at *Myiale* in *Afia* meet,
And there fo utterly they wrack'd the fame,
Scarce one was left, to carry home the fame ;
Thus did the *Greeks* deftroy, confume, difperce,
That Army, which did fright the Univerfe ;

Scorn'd

Scorn'd *Xerxes*, hated for his cruelty.
Yet ceafes not to act his villany:
His brothers wife, follicites to his will;
The chafte, and beautious Dame, refufes ftill.
Some years by him in this vain fuit was fpent,
Yet words, nor guifts, could win him leaft content:
Nor matching of her daughter, to his fon :
But fhe was ftil, as when it firft begun.
When jealous Queen *Ameftris*, of this knew,
She *Harpy*-like, upon the Lady flew:
Cut off her lilly breafts, her nofe, and ears;
And leaves her thus, befmear'd with blood, and tears.
Straight comes her Lord, and finds his wife thus lie,
The forrow of his heart, did clofe his eye :
He dying to behold, that wounding fight;
Where he had fometime gaz'd with great delight.
To fee that face, where Rofe and Lilly ftood,
O're-flown with torrent of her ruby blood.
To fee thofe breafts, where chaftity did dwel,
Thus cut, and mangled by a hag of hell,
With loaden heart unto the King he goes,
Tels as he could, his unexpreffed woes,
But for his deep complaints; and fhowres of tears,
His brothers recompence was naught but jears:
The grieved Prince finding nor right, nor love,
To *Bactria* his houfhold did remove.
His wicked brother, after fent a crew,
Which him, and his, moft barbaroufly there flew,
Unto fuch height did grow his cruelty,
Of life, no man had leaft fecurity.
At laft his Uncle, did his death confpire,
And for that end, his Eunuch he did hire.

Which

Which wretch, him privately smother'd in's bed,
But yet by search, he was found murthered,
The *Artacanus* hirer of this deed,
That from suspition he might be freed,
Accus'd *Darius*, *Xerxes* eldest son,
To be the Authour of the deed was done,
And by his craft, ordered the matter so,
That the poor innocent, to death must go.
But in short time, this wickednesse was knowne,
For which he dyed, and not he alone.
But all his family was likewise slain,
Such Justice then, in *Persia* did remain,
The eldest son, thus immaturely dead,
The second was inthron'd, in's fathers stead.

Artaxerxes Longimanus.

A Mongst the Monarchs next, this Prince had place
The best that ever sprang of *Cyrus* race.
He first, war with revolting *Ægypt* made.
To whom the perjur'd *Grecians* lent their aide,
Although to *Xerxes*, they not long before,
A league of amity, had sworn before.
Which had they kept, *Greece* had more nobly done,
Then when the world, they after over-run:
Greeks and *Egyptians* both, he overthrows,
And payes them now, according as he owes,
Which done, a sumptuous feast; makes like a King
Where ninescore days, are spent in banquetting,
His Princes, Nobles, and his Captaines calls,
To be partakers in these festivalls.

His

His hangings, white, and green, and purple dye,
With gold and silver beds, most gorgiously.
The royall wine, in golden cups doth passe,
To drink more then he list, none bidden was.
Queen *Vashty* also feasts, but 'fore tis ended,
Alas, she from her Royalty's suspended.
And a more worthy, placed in her roome,
By *Memucan's* advice, this was the doome.
What *Hester* was, and did, her story reed,
And how her Country-men from spoile she freed.
Of *Hamans* fall, and *Mordica's* great rise;
The might o'th' Prince, the tribute on the Isles.
Unto this King *Thymistocles* did flye.
When under *Ostracisme* he did lye.
For such ingratitude, did *Athens* show
This valiant Knight, whom they so much did owe;
Such entertainment with this Prince he found,
That in all Loyalty his heart was bound;
The King not little joyfull of this chance,
Thinking his *Grecian* wars now to advance.
And for that end, great preparation made,
Fair *Attica*, a third time to invade.
His Grand-sires old disgrace, did vex him sore,
His father *Xerxes* losse, and shame, much more,
For punishment, their breach of oath did call,
The noble *Greek*, now fit for generall.
Who for his wrong, he could not chuse but deem,
His Country, nor his Kindred would esteem,
Provisions, and season now being fit,
T'*Thymistocles* he doth his war commit,
But he all injury, had soon forgate,
And to his Country-men could bear no hate.

Nor

Nor yet difloyall to his Prince would prove,
To whom oblig'd, by favour, and by love;
Either to wrong, did wound his heart fo fore,
To wrong himfelfe by death, he chofe before.
In this fad confli&t, marching on his ways,
Strong poyfon took, and put an end to's dayes.
The King this noble Captaine having loft,
Again difperfed, his new levyed hoaft.
'Reft of his time in peace he did remain;
And dy'd the two and fortieth of his reign.

Daryus Nothus.

THree fons great *Artaxerxes* left behind;
The eldeft to fucceed, that was his mind.
But he, with his next brother fell at ftrife,
That nought appeas'd him, but his brothers life.
Then the furviver is by *Nothus* flaine ;
Who now fole Monarch, doth of all remaine,
Thefe two lewd fons, are by hyftorians thought,
To be by *Hefter*, to her husband brought.
If they were hers, the greater was her moan ;
That for fuch gracelesse wretches fhe did groan,
Difquiet *Egypt*, 'gainft this King rebells,
Drives out his garifon that therein dwels.
Joynes with the *Greeks*, and fo maintains their right,
For fixty years maugre the *Perfians* might.
A fecond trouble, after this fucceeds.
Which from remiffenesse, in *Afia* proceeds
Amerges, whom their Vice-roy he ordain'd
Revolts, having treafure, and people gain'd:

In-

Invades the Country,and much trouble wrought,
Before to quietneffe things could be brought,
The King was glad, with *Sparta* to make peace,
So that he might, thefe tumults foon appeafe.
But they in *Afia*, muft firft reftore
All Townes, held by his Anceftors before.
The King much profit reapeth, by thefe leagues,
Re-gaines his own,and then the Rebell breaks:
Whofe forces by their helpe were overthrown,
And fo each man again poffeft his owne.
The King,his fifter, like *Cambyfes*, wed;
More by his pride, then luft, thereunto led.
(For *Perfian* Kings, did deem themfelves fo good,
No match was high enough, but their own blood,)
Two fons fhe bore, the youngeft *Cyrus* nam'd,
A hopefull Prince, whofe worth is ever fam'd.
His father would no notice of that take ;
Prefers his brother, for his birth-rights fake.
But *Cyrus* fcornes, his brothers feeble wit;
And takes more on him,then was judged fit.
The King provok'd, fends for him to the Court,
Meaning to chaftife him, in fharpeft fort,
But in his flow approach, ere he came there,
His fathers death, did put an end to's fear.
Nothus reign'd nineteen years, which run,
His large Dominions left, to's eldeft fon.

Artaxerxes Mnemon.

M*Nemon* now fits upon his fathers Throne,
Yet doubts, all he injoyes, is not his own.

Stil

Still on his brother, casts a jealous eye,
Judging all's actions, tends to's injury.
Cyrus o'th' other side, weighs in his mind,
What helps, in's enterprize he's like to find,
His interest, in the Kingdome, now next heir,
More deare to's mother, then his brother far.
His brothers litle love, like to be gone,
Held by his mothers intercession.
These and like motives, hurry him amain,
To win by force, what right could not obtain.
And thonght'it best, now in his mothers time,
By lesser steps, towards the top to climbe;
If in his enterprize he should fall short,
She to the King, would make a fair report:
He hop'd, if fraud, nor force the Crown could gaine;
Her prevailence, a pardon might obtain.
From the Lieutenant first, he takes away,
Some Townes commodious in lesse *Asia*,
Pretending still, the profit of the King,
Whose rents and customes, duly he sent in.
The King finding, revenues now amended;
For what was done, seemed no whit offended.
Then next, the *Lacedemons* he takes to pay;
(One *Greeke* could make ten *Persians* run away)
Great care was his pretence, those Souldiers stout,
The Rovers in *Pisidia*, should drive out.
But least some worser newes should fly to Court,
He meant himselfe to carry the report.
And for that end, five hundred Horse he chose,
With posting speed towards the King he goes;
But fame more quick, arrives ere he came there,
And fills the Court with tumult, and with fear.

The

The young Queen, and old, at bitter jars:
The one accus'd the other, for these wars:
The wife, against the mother, still doth cry
To be the Author of conspiracy.
The King dismay'd, a mighty Hoast doth raise;
Which *Cyrus* heares, and so sore-flowes his pace:
But as he goes, his Forces still augments,
Seven hundred *Greeks* now further his intents:
And others to be warm'd by this new sun,
In numbers from his brother daily run.
The fearfull King, at last, musters his Forces;
And counts nine hundred thousand foot and horses:
And yet with these, had neither heart, nor grace;
To look his manly brother in the face.
Three hundred thousand, yet to *Syria* sent;
To keep those streights, to hinder his intent.
Their Captain hearing, but of *Cyrus* name.
Ran back, and quite abandoned the same,
Abrocomes, was this base cowards name,
Not worthy to be known, but for his shame:
This place was made, by nature, and by art;
Few might have kept it, had they but a heart.
Cyrus dispair'd, a passage there to gain;
So hir'd a fleet, to waft him ore the Maine,
The mazed King, was now about to fly;
To th'utmost parts of *Bactr's*, and there lye.
Had not a Captain; sore against his will;
By reason, and by force, detain'd him still.
Up then with speed, a mighty trench he throwes,
For his security, against his foes.
Six yards the depth, and forty miles the length,
Some fifty, or else sixty foote in breadth.

Yet

Yet for his brothers comming, durſt not ſtay,
He ſureſt was, when furtheſt out o'th' way.
Cyrus finding his campe, and no man there;
Rejoyced not a little at his ſeare.
On this, he and his Souldiers careleſſe grow,
And here, and there, in carts their Armes they throw,
When ſuddenly their Scouts come in and cry,
Arme, arme, the King is now approaching nigh;
In this confuſion, each man as he might,
Gets on his armes, arayes himſelfe for fight;
And ranged ſtood, by great *Euphrates* ſide,
The brunt of that huge multitude to bide.
Of whoſe great numbers, their intelligence,
Was gather'd by the duſt that roſe from thence :
Which like a mighty cloud darkned the skye;
And black and blacker grew, as they drew nigh
But when their order, and ſilence they ſaw ;
That, more then multitudes, their hearts did awe :
For tumult and confuſion they expeſted,
And all good diſcipline to be negleſted.
But long under their ſears, they did not ſtay,
For at firſt charge the *Perſians* ran away.
Which did ſuch courage to the *Grecians* bring,
They ſtraight adored *Cyrus* for their King,
So had he been, and got the victory,
Had not his too much valour put him by.
He with ſix hundred, on a ſquadron ſet,
Of ſix thouſand, wherein the King was yet;
And brought his Souldiers on ſo gallantly,
They were about to leave their King and fly,
Whom *Cyrus* ſpi'd, cries out, I ſee the man,
And with a full career, at him he ran.

But

But in his speed a Dart hit him i'th' eye,
Down *Cyrus* fals, and yeelds to destiny;
His Host in chase, knowes not of his disaster,
But treads down all, for to advance their Master;
At last his head they spy upon a Launce,
Who knowes the sudden change made by this chance;
Sencelesse and mute they stand, yet breath out groans,
Nor *Gorgons* like to this, transform'd to stones.
After this trance, revenge, new spirits blew,
And now more eagerly their foes pursue,
And heaps on heaps, such multitudes they laid,
Their armes grew weake, through slaughters that they
The King unto a country Village flyes,   (made.
And for a while unkingly there he lyes;
At last, displayes his Ensigne on a Hil,
Hoping with that to make the *Greeks* stand stil,
But was deceiv'd; to it they make amain,
The King upon the spur, runs back again;
But they too faint, still to pursue their game,
Being Victors oft, now to their Camp they came;
Nor lackt they any of their number small,
Nor wound receiv'd, but one among them all:
The King with his dispers'd also incampt.
With infamy upon each fore-head stampt;
After a while his thoughts he re-collects,
Of this dayes cowardize, he feares the effects;
If *Greeks* unto their Country-men declare,
What dastards in the field the *Persians* are;
They soone may come, and place one in his Throne,
And rob him both of Scepter, and of Crown;
That their return be stopt, he judg'd was best,
That so *Europians* might no more molest;

I   Forth

Forth-with he fends to's Tent, they ftraight addreffe,
And there all wait his mercy, weaponleffe ;
The *Greeks* with fcorn reject his proud commands;
Asking no favour, where they fear'd no bands.
The troubled King, his Herauld fends again,
And fues for peace, that they his friends remain ;
The fmiling *Greeks* reply, they firft muft bait,
They were too hungry to capitulate ;
The King great ftore of all provifion fends,
And courtefie to th' utmoft he pretends ;
Such terrour on the *Perfians* then did fall,
They quak'd, to heare them, to each other call.
The King's perplext, there dares not let them ftay,
And feares as much to let them march away ;
But Kings ne're want fuch as can ferve their will,
Fit inftruments t' accomplifh what is ill ;
As *Tyffaphern*, knowing his Mafters minde,
Invites their chief Commander, as moft kinde ;
And with all Oathes, and deepeft flattery,
Gets them to treat with him in privacy,
But violates his honour, and his word,
And Villaine-like, there puts them to the fword.
The *Greeks*, having their valiant Captaines flaine,
Chofe *Xenophon*, to lead them home again ;
But *Tyffaphern* did what he could devife,
To ftop the way in this their enterprife ;
But when through difficulties ftill they brake,
He fought all fuftinance from them to take,
Before them burnt the country as they went,
So to deprive them of all nourifhment ;
But on they march, through hunger, and through cold,
O're mountains, rocks, and hils, as Lions bold ;

Nor

Nor rivers course, nor *Persians* force could stay,
But on to *Trabezond* they kept their way;
There was of *Greeks*, setled a Colony,
These after all, receiv'd them joyfully:
There for some time they were, but whilst they staid,
Into *Bithynia* often in-rodes made;
The King afraid what further they might doe,
Unto the *Spartan* Admirall did sue,
Straight to transport them to the other side,
For these incursions he durst not abide;
So after all their travell, danger, pain,
In peace they saw their Native soyl again.
The *Greeks* now (as the *Persian* King suspects)
The *Asiatiques*, cowardize detects;
The many victories themselves did gain,
The many thousand *Persians* they had slain;
And now their Nation with facility,
Might win the universall Monarchy;
They then *Dercilladas*, send with an Hoast,
Who with his *Spartans* on the *Asian* coast;
Town after town, with small resistance take,
Which rumor makes great *Artaxerxes* quake;
The *Greeks* by this successe, incourag'd so,
Agesilaus himself doth over-goe,
By th' Kings Lieutenant is encountered,
But *Tyssaphernes* with his Army fled;
Which over-throw incens'd the King so sore,
That *Tyssapherne* must be Vice-roy no more;
Tythraustes now is placed in his stead,
And hath command, to take the others head,
Of that false perjur'd wretch, this was the last,
Who of his cruelty made many tast,

I 2   *Tythraustes*

Tythraustes trusts more to his wit then Arms,
And hopes by craft to quit his Masters harmes ;
He knows that many towns in *Greece* envies
The *Spartans* height, which now apace doth rise ;
To these he thirty thousand Tallents sent,
With suit, their force, against his foes be bent ;
They to their discontent, receiving hire,
With broyls, and quarrels, sets all *Greece* on fire.
Agesilaus is called home with speed,
To defend, more then offend, he had need.
They now lost all, and were a peace to make,
The Kings conditions they are forc't to take ;
Dissention in *Greece* continued long,
Til many a Captain fel, both wise, and strong,
Whose courage nought but death could ever tame,
'Mongst these *Epimanondas* wants no fame ;
Who had (as noble *Raleigh* doth evince)
All the peculiar vertues of a Prince :
But let us leave these *Greeks*, to discord bent,
And turne to *Persia*, as is pertinent ;
The King from forraign foes, and all at ease,
His home-bred troubles seeketh to appease ;
The two Queens, by his means, 'gin to abate
Their former envie, and inveterate hate ;
Then in voluptuousnesse he leads his life,
And weds his Daughter for a second wife ;
His Mothers wicked counsell was the cause,
Who sooths him up, his owne desires are Lawes :
But yet for all his greatnesse, and long reign,
He must leave all, and in the pit remain ;
Forty three years he rules, then turns to dust,
As all the mighty ones, have done, and must :

But

But this of him is worth the memory,
He was the Master of good *Nehemie.*

Darius Ochus.

GReat *Artaxerxes* dead, *Ochus* succeeds,
Of whom no Record's extant of his deeds ;
Was it because the *Grecians* now at war,
Made Writers work at home, they sought not far ?
Or dealing with the *Persian,* now no more
Their Acts recorded not, as heretofore ?
Or else, perhaps the deeds of *Persian* Kings
In after wars were burnt, 'mongst other things ?
That three and twenty years he reign'd, I finde,
The rest is but conjecture of my minde.

Arsames, or *Arses.*

WHy *Arsames* his brother should succeed,
I can no reason give, cause none I read ;
It may be thought, surely he had no Son,
So fell to him, which else it had not done :
What Acts he did, time hath not now left pend,
But as 'tis thought, in him had *Cyrus* end :
Whose race long time had worn the Diadem,
But now's divolved, to another Stem.
Three years he reign'd, as Chronicles expresse,
Then Natures debt he paid, quite Issue-lesse.

Darius

Darius Codomanus.

HOw this *Darius* did attain the Crown,
By favour, force, or fraud, is not set down:
If not (as is before) of *Cyrus* race,
By one of these, he must obtain the place.
Some writers say, that he was *Arses* son,
And that great *Cyrus* line, yet was not run,
That *Ochus* unto *Arsames* was father,
Which by some probabilities (seems rather;)
That son, and father, both were murthered
By one *Bagoas*, an Eunuch (as is sed.)
Thus learned *Pemble*, whom we may not slight,
But as before doth (well read) *Raleigh* write,
Antd he that story reads, shall often find;
That severall men, will have their severall mind;
Yet in these differences, we may behold;
With our judicious learned Knight to hold.
And this 'mongst all's no controverted thing,
That this *Darius* was last *Persian* King,
Whose warres and losses we may better tell;
In *Alexanders* reign who did him quell,
How from the top of worlds felicity;
He fell to depth of greatest misery,
Whose honours, treasures, pleasures, had short stay;
One deluge came, and swept them all away;
And in the sixt year of his haplesse reigne,
Of all, did scarce his winding sheet retaine.
And last; a sad catastrophe to end,
Him, to the grave, did Traytor *Bessus* send.

           The end of the Persian *Monarchy.*

                                        The

The third Monarchy was the *Grecian,* beginning un= der *Alexander* the Great, in the 112 *Olimpiad.*

Reat *Alexander,* was wise *Phillips* son,
He, to *Amintas,* Kings of *Macedon* ;
The cruell, proud, *Olimpias,* was his mo-
ther,
Shee to the rich *Molossians* King, was
daughter.
This Prince (his father by *Pausanias* slain)
The twenty first of 's age, began to reign.
Great were the guifts of nature, which he had ;
His Education, much to these did adde.
By Art, and Nature both, he was made fit,
T' accomplish that, which long before was writ.
The very day of his nativity,
To th' ground was burnt, *Diana's* Temple high,
An Omen, to their near approaching woe;
Whose glory to the Earth, this Prince did throw,
His rule to *Greece,* he scorn'd should be confin'd.
The universe, scarce bounds his large vast minde;

I 4   This

This is the hee-goat, which from *Grecia* came,
Who ran in fury, on the *Persian* Ram,
That broke his hornes, that threw him on the ground,
To save him from his might, no man was found.
Phillip, on this great conquest had an eye ;
But death did terminate, those thoughts so high.
The *Greeks* had chose him Captain Generall,
Which honour to his son, now did befall.
(For as worlds Monarch, now we speak not on,
But as the King of little *Macedon.*)
Restlesse both day and night, his heart now was,
His high resolves which way to bring to passe :
Yet for a while, in *Greece* is forc'd to stay,
Which makes each moment seem, more then a day:
Thebes, and old *Athens*, both 'gainst him rebell,
But he their mutinies, full soon doth quell.
This done, against all right, and natures laws,
His kinsmen puts to death without least cause ;
That no combustion in his absence be,
In seeking after Soveraignity :
And many more, whom he suspects will climbe,
Now taste of death, (least they deserv't in time)
Nor wonder is't, if he in blood begin,
For cruelty, was his parentall sin.
Thus eased now, of troubles, and of fears;
His course to *Asia*, next Spring he steers.
Leaves sage *Antipater* at home to sway,
And through the *Hellispont*, his ships make way.
Comming to land, his dart on shoar he throwes,
Then with alacrity he after goes:
Thirty two thousand made up his foot force,
To these were joyn'd, five thousand goodly horse.

Then

Then on he march'd, in's way he veiw'd old *Troy*;
And on *Achillis* Tombe, with wondrous joy,
He offer'd, and for good successe did pray
To him, his mothers Ancestor (men say.)
When newes of *Alexander*, came to th' Court,
To scorn at him, *Darius* had good sport:
Sends him a frothy, and contemptuous letter,
Stiles him disloyall servant, and no better;
Reproves him, for his proud audacity;
To lift his hand, 'gainst such a Monarchy.
Then to his Lieutenant, in *Asia* sends,
That he be tane alive, (for he intends)
To whip him well with rods, and then to bring,
That boy so mallepart, before the King.
Ah! fond vaine man, whose pen was taught ere while,
In lower termes to write a higher stile,
To th' river *Granicke*, *Alexander* hyes,
Which twixt *Phrigia*, and *Propontis* lyes.
The *Persians* for encounter ready stand,
And think to keep his men from off the land,
Those banks so steep, the *Greeks*, now scramble up
And beat the coward *Persians* from the top,
And twenty thousand, of their lives bereave,
Who in their backs did all their wounds receive
This Victory did *Alexander* gain;
With losse of thirty four, of his there slaine:
Sardis, then he, and *Ephesus*, did gaine,
Where stood of late *Diana's*, wondrous *Phane*,
And by *Parmenio* (of renowned fame)
Miletus, and *Pamphilia* overcame,
Hallicarnassus and *Pisidia*
He for his master takes, with *Lycia.*

Next:

Next *Alexander* marcht, t'wards the black sea ;
And easily takes old *Gordium* in his way ;
(Of Asse-eard)*Midas*, once the regall seat,
Whose touch turn'd all to gold,yea even his meat:
There the Prophetick knot, he cuts in twain;
Which who so did, must Lord of all remain,
Now newes, of *Memnons* death (the Kings Vice-roy)
To *Alexanders* heart's no little joy.
For in that Peer, more valour did abide;
Then in *Darius* multitudes beside :
There *Arsemes* was plac'd ,yet durst not stay;
But sets one in his roome, and ran away.
His substitute, as fearfull as his master,
Goes after too, and leaves all to disaster.
Now *Alexander* all *Cilicia* takes:
No stroake for it he struck, their hearts so quakes.
To *Greece* he thirty thousand talents sends ;
To raise more force, for what he yet intends.
And on he goes *Darius* for to meet:
Who came with thousand thousands at his feet,
Though some there be, and that more likely,write;
He but four hundred thousand had to fight,
The rest attendants, which made up no lesse;
(Both sexes there) was almost numberlesse.
For this wise King, had brought to see the sport;
Along with him, the Ladyes of the Court.
His mother old,beautious wife,and daughters,
It seemes to see the *Macedonians* slaughters.
Sure its beyond my time, and little Art ;
To shew,how great *Darius* plaid his part:
The splendor, and the pompe, he marched in,
For since the world,was no such Pageant seen.

Oh

Oh 'twas a goodly fight, there to behold;
The *Perfians* clad in filk, and glitt'ring gold;
The ftately Horfes trapt, the launces guilt;
As if they were, now all to run at tilt:
The Holy fire, was borne before the Hoft:
(For Sun and Fire the *Perfians* worfhip moft)
The Priefts in their ftrange habit follow after;
An object not fo much of fear, as laughter.
The King fat in a chariot made of gold,
With Robes and Crowne, moft glorious to behold.
And o're his head, his golden gods on high;
Support a party coloured canopy.
A number of fpare horfes next were led,
Leaft he fhould need them, in his chariots ftead.
But they that faw him in this ftate to lye;
Would think he neither thought to fight nor fly,
He fifteen hundred had like women dreft,
For fo to fright the *Greekes* he judg'd was beft,
Their golden Ornaments fo to fet forth,
Would afke more time, then were their bodys worth.
Great *Sifigambis*, fhe brought up the Reare ;
Then fuch a world of Wagons did appear,
Like feverall houfes moving upon wheeles:
As if fhe'd drawne, whole *Sufhan* at her heeles.
This brave Virago, to the King was mother;
And as much good fhe did, as any other.
Now leaft this Gold, and all this goodly ftuffe,
Had not been fpoile, and booty rich enough,
A thoufand Mules, and Camells ready wait.
Loaden with gold, with Jewels and with Plate,
For fure *Darius* thought, at the firft fight,
The *Greekes* would all adore, and would nane fight.

But

But when both Armies met, he might behold,
That valour was more worth then Pearls, or gold,
And how his wealth serv'd but for baits t'allure,
Which made his over-throw more fierce, and sure.
The *Greeks* come on, and with a gallant grace,
Let fly their Arrowes, in the *Persians* face ;
The cowards feeling this sharp stinging charge,
Most basely run, and left their King at large,
Who from his golden Coach is glad t'alight,
And cast away his Crown, for swifter flight ;
Of late, like some immovable he lay,
Now finds both leggs, and Horse, to run away ;
Two hundred thousand men that day were slaine,
And forty thousand Prisoners also tane ;
Besides, the Queens, and Ladies of the Court,
If *Curtius* be true, in his report.
The Regall ornaments now lost, the treasure
Divided at the *Macedonians* pleasure.
Yet all this grief, this losse, this over-throw,
Was but beginning of his future woe ;
The Royall Captives, brought to *Alexander*,
T'ward them, demean'd himself like a Commander ;
For though their beauties were unparalled
Conquer'd himself (now he had conquered)
Preserv'd their honour, us'd them courteously,
Commands, no man should doe them injury,
And this to *Alexander* is more a fame,
Then that the *Persian* King he over-came ;
Two hundred eighty *Greeks* he lost in fight,
By too much heat, not wounds (as Authors write.)
No sooner had this Captaine won the field,
But all *Phenicia* to his pleasures yeeld ;

Of

Of which, the Government he doth commit
Unto *Parmenio*, of all, most fit ;
Darius now, more humble then before,
Writes unto *Alexander*, to restore
Those mournfull Ladies, from captivity,
For whom he offers him a ransome high ;
But down his haughty stomach could not bring,
To give this Conquerour, the stile of King ;
His Letter *Alexander* doth disdaine,
And in short termes, sends this reply againe ;
A King he was, and that not only so,
But of *Darius* King, as he should know.
Now *Alexander* unto *Tyre* doth goe,
(His valour, and his victories they know)
To gain his love, the *Tyrians* do intend,
Therefore a Crown, and great provisions send ;
Their present he receives with thankfulnesse,
Desires to offer unto *Hercules*,
Protector of their Town ; by whom defended,
And from whom also, lineally descended :
But they accept not this, in any wise,
Least he intend more fraud, then sacrifice ,
Sent word, that *Hercules* his Temple stood,
In the old town (which now lay like a wood)
With this reply, he was so sore enrag'd,
To win their town, his honour he engag'd ;
And now, as *Babels* King did once before,
He leaves not, till he makes the sea firme shoar ;
But far lesse cost, and time, he doth expend,
The former ruines, help to him now lend ;
Besides, he had a Navie at command,
The other by his men fetcht all by Land ;

In

In seven months space he takes this lofty town,
Whose glory, now a second time's brought down;
Two thousand of the cheif he crucifi'd,
Eight thousand by the sword now also dy'd,
And thirteen thousand Gally-slaves he made,
And thus the *Tyrians* for mistrust were paid,
The rule of this he to *Philotas* gave,
Who was the Son of that *Parmenio* brave;
Cilicia he to *Socrates* doth give,
For now's the time, Captains like Kings may live;
For that which easily comes, as freely goes;
Zidon he on *Ephestion* bestowes:
He scorns to have one worse then had the other,
And therefore gives this Lord-ship to another.
Ephestion now, hath the command o' th' Fleet,
And must at *Gaza*, *Alexander* meet;
Darius finding troubles still increase,
By his Embassadours now sues for peace:
And layes before great *Alexanders* eyes,
The dangers, difficulties, like to rise;
First, at *Euphrates*, what he's like to abide,
And then at *Tigris*, and *Araxis* side:
These he may scape, and if he so desire,
A league of friendship make, firm, and entire;
His eldest Daughter, (him) in marriage offers,
And a most Princely Dowry with her proffers;
All those rich Kingdoms large, which doe abide
Betwixt the *Hellespont*, and *Hallis* side;
But he with scorn, his courtesie rejects,
And the distressed King no way respects;
Tels him, these proffers great (in truth were none)
For all he offered now, was but his owne:

                                    But

But, quoth *Parmenio*, (that brave Commander)
Was I as great, as is great *Alexander*,
Darius offers I would not reject,
But th' Kingdoms, and the Ladies, foone accept ;
To which, brave *Alexander* did reply,
And fo if I *Parmenio* were, would I.
He now to *Gaza* goes, and there doth meet
His favourite *Epheſtion*, with his fleet ;
Where valiant *Betis*, doth defend the town,
(A loyall Subject to *Darius* Crown)
For more repulfe, the *Grecians* here abide,
Then in the *Perſian* Monarchy befide ;
And by thefe walls, fo many men were flaine,
That *Greece* muſt yeeld a freſh fupply againe ;
But yet, this well defended town is taken,
(For 'twas decreed, that Empire fhould be fhaken)
The Captaine tane, had holes bor'd through his feet,
And by command was drawn through every ſtreet,
To imitate *Achilles* (in his ſhame)
Who did the like to *Hector* (of more fame)
What, haſt thou loſt thy late magnanimity ?
Can *Alexander* deale thus cruelly ?
Sith valour, with Heroyicks is renown'd,
Though in an enemy it ſhould be found ;
If of thy future fame thou hadſt regard,
Why didſt not heap up honour, and reward ?
From *Gaza*, to *Jeruſalem* he goes,
But in no hoſtile way (as I fuppofe)
Him in his Prieſtly Robes, high *Jaddus* meets,
Whom with great reverence *Alexander* greets ;
The Prieſt ſhews him good *Daniels* Prophefie,
How he ſhould over-throw this Monarchy ;

By

By which he was so much incouraged,
No future dangers he did ever dread:
From thence, to fruitfull *Ægypt* marcht with speed,
Where happily in's wars he did succeed;
To see how fast he gain'd, is no small wonder,
For in few dayes he brought that Kingdom under.
Then to the *Phane* of *Jupiter*, he went,
For to be call'd a god, was his intent;
The Pagan Priest through hire, or else mistake,
The Son of *Jupiter* did straight him make:
He Diabolicall must needs remaine,
That his humanity will not retaine;
Now back to *Ægypt* goes, and in few dayes,
Faire *Alexandria* from the ground doth raise;
Then setling all things in lesse *Asia*,
In *Syria*, *Ægypt*, and *Phœnicia*;
Unto *Euphrates* marcht, and over goes,
For no man to resist his valour showes;
Had *Betis* now been there, but with his Band,
Great *Alexander* had been kept from Land;
But as the King is, so's the multitude,
And now of valour both were destitute;
Yet he (poore Prince) another Hoast doth muster,
Of *Persians*, *Scithians*, *Indians*, in a cluster;
Men but in shape, and name, of valour none,
Fit for to blunt the swords of *Macedon* ,
Two hundred fifty thousand by account,
Of Horse, and Foot, this Army did amount;
For in his multitudes his trust still lay,
But on their fortitude he had small stay;
Yet had some hope, that on that eeven plain,
His numbers might the victory obtaine.

                                    About

About this time, *Darius* beauteous Queen,
Who had long travaile, and much forrow feen,
Now bids the world adieu, her time being fpent,
And leaves her wofull Lord for to lament.
Great *Alexander* mourns, as well as he,
For this loft Queen (though in captivity)
When this fad newes (at firft) *Darius* heares,
Some injury was offered, he feares ;
But when inform'd, how royally the King
Had ufed her, and hers, in every thing,
He prayes the immortall gods, for to reward
Great *Alexander*, for this good regard ;
And if they down, his Monarchy wil throw,
Let them on him, that dignity beftow :
And now for peace he fues, as once before,
And offers all he did, and Kingdoms more ;
His eldeft Daughter, for his Princely Bride,
(Nor was fuch match, in all the world befide)
And all thofe Countries, which (betwixt) did lye,
Phenifian Sea, and great *Euphrates* high,
With fertile *Ægypt*, and rich *Syria*,
And all thofe Kingdoms in leffe *Afia* ;
With thirty thoufand Tallents, to be paid
For his Queen-Mother, and the royall Maid ;
And till all this be wel perform'd, and fure,
Ochus his Son a hoftage fhall endure.
To this, ftout *Alexander*, gives no eare,
No, though *Parmenio* plead, he will not heare ;
Which had he done (perhaps) his fame had kept,
Nor infamy had wak'd, when he had flept ;
For his unlimited profperity,
Him boundleffe made, in vice, and cruelty ;

K   Thus

Thus to *Darius* he writes back again,
The Firmament two Suns cannot contain;
Two Monarchies on Earth cannot abide,
Nor yet two Monarchs in one World reside;
The afflicted King, finding him set to jar,
Prepares against to morrow for the war;
Parmenio, Alexander wisht, that night,
To force his Camp, so put them all to flight;
For tumult in the dark doth cause most dread,
And weaknesse of a foe is covered;
But he disdain'd to steale a victorie,
The Sun should witnesse of his valour be:
Both Armies meet, *Greeks* fight, the *Persians* run,
So make an end, before they well begun;
Forty five thousand *Alexander* had,
But 'tis not known what slaughters here they made.
Some write, th' other had a million, some more,
But *Quintus Curtius*, as was said before.
At *Arbela*, this victory was gain'd,
And now with it, the town also obtain'd.
Darius stript of all, to *Media* came,
Accompani'd with sorrow, fear, and shame;
At *Arbela* left, his ornaments, and treasure,
Which *Alexander* deals, as suits his pleasure.
This Conquerour now goes to *Babylon*,
Is entertain'd with joy, and pompous train,
With showres of Flowers, the streets along are strown,
And Insence burnt, the silver Altars on;
The glory of the Castle he admires,
The firme foundations, and the lofty spires;
In this a masse of gold, and treasure lay,
Which in few hours was carried all away;

With

With greedy eyes, he views this City round,
Whose fame throughout the world, was so renown'd;
And to possesse, he counts no little blisse,
The Towers, and Bowers, of proud *Semiramis*:
Though worn by time, and raz'd by foes full sore,
Yet old foundations shew'd, and somewhat more;
With all the pleasures that on earth was found,
This City did abundantly abound;
Where four and thirty dayes he now doth stay,
And gives himself to banqueting, and play:
He, and his Souldiers, wax effeminate,
And former Discipline begins to hate;
Whilst revelling at *Babylon*, he lyes,
Antipater, from *Greece*, sends great supplyes;
He then to *Sushan* goes, with his fresh bands,
But needs no force, 'tis rendred to his hands;
He likewise here a world of treasure found,
For 'twas the seat of *Persian* Kings renown'd;
Here stood the Royall houses of delight,
Where Kings have shown their glory, wealth, and might;
The sumptuous Palace of Queen *Hester* here,
And of good *Mordecai*, her Kinsman dear;
Those purple hangings, mixt with green, and white,
Those beds of gold, and couches of delight,
And furniture, the richest of all Lands,
Now falls into the *Macedonians* hands.
From *Sushan*, to *Persapolis* he goes,
Which newes doth still augment *Darius* woes;
In his approach, the Governour sends word,
For his receit with joy, they all accord;
With open Gates, the wealthy town did stand,
And all in it was at his high command;

Of all the Cities, that on Earth was found;
None like to this in riches did abound.
Though *Babylon* was rich, and *Sufhan* too;
Yet to compare with this, they might not do.
Here lay the bulk, of all those precious things;
Which did pertain unto the *Perfian* Kings.
For when the Souldiers, had rifled their pleasure,
And taken mony, plate, and golden treasure;
Statues of gold, and silver numberlesse,
Yet after all, as stories do expresse.
The share of *Alexander* did amount,
To a hundred thousand Tallents by account.
Here of his own, he sets a Garrison,
(As first at *Sufhan*, and at *Babylon*)
On their old Governours, titles he laid;
But on their faithfullnesse, he never staid:
Their charge, gave to his Captains (as most just)
For such revolters false, what Prince will trust:
The pleasures and the riches of this town,
Now makes this King, his vertues all to drown.
He walloweth now, in all licenciousnesse,
In pride, and cruelty, to th'highest excesse.
Being inflam'd with wine upon a season,
(Filled with madnesse, and quite void of reason)
He at a bold, base Strumpets, lewd desire;
Commands to set this goodly town on fire.
Parmenio wise, intreats him to desift,
And layes before his eyes, if he persist
His names dishonour, losse unto his State.
And just procuring of the *Perfians* hate.
But deafe to reason, (bent to have his will;)
Those stately streets with raging flames doth fil.

                                                    Now

Now to *Darius*, he directs his way,
Who was retir'd, and gone to *Media.*
(And there with forrows, fears, and cares furrounded)
Had now his fourth, and laft Army compounded,
Which forty thoufand made ; but his intent,
Was ftraight in *Baftria* thefe to augment,
But hearing, *Alexander* was fo near ;
Thought now this once, to try his fortunes here,
Chufing rather an honorable death :
Then ftill with infamy, to draw his breath.
But *Beffus* falfe, who was his cheife Commander;
Perfwades him not to fight, with *Alexander.*
With fage advice, he layes before his eyes,
The little hope, of profit like to rife.
If when he'd multitudes, the day he loft;
Then with fo few, how likely to be croft.
This counfell, for his fafety, he pretended,
But to deliver him to's foes, intended.
Next day this treafon, to *Darius* known,
Tranfported fore, with griefe and paffion ;
Grinding his teeth, and plucking off his haire,
Sate down o'rewhelm'd, with forrow, and defpair,
Bidding his fervant *Artabaffus* true;
Look to himfelfe, and leave him to that crew;
Who was of hopes, and comfort quite bereft ;
And of his Guard, and Servitors now left.
Straight *Beffus* comes, and with his traiterous hands,
Lays hold on's Lord, and binding him with bands.
Into a cart him throwes, covered with hides ;
Who wanting means t' refift, thefe wrongs abides.
Then draws the Cart along, with chaines of gold;
In more difpight, the thrawled Prince to hold.

And

And thus to *Alexander*, on he goes,
Great recompence, in's thoughts, he did propose ;
But some detesting, this his wicked fact,
To *Alexander* fly, and told this act ;
Who doubling of his march, posts on amain,
Darius from those Traitors hands to gain ;
Bessus gets knowledge, his disloyalty,
Had *Alexanders* wrath incensed high ;
Whose Army now, was almost within sight,
His hopes being dasht, prepares himself for flight :
Unto *Darius*, first he brings a Horse,
And bids him, save himself, by speedy course :
This wofull King, his courtesie refuses,
Whom thus the execrable wretch abuses:
By throwing Darts, gives him his mortall wound,
Then slew his servants, that were faithfull found ;
Yea, wounds the beasts (that drew him) unto death,
And leaves him thus, to gaspe out his last breath.
(*Bessus*, his Partner in this Tragedy,
Was the false Governour of *Media*)
This done, they with their Hoast, soon speed away,
To hide themselves, remote, in *Bactria* ;
Darius bath'd in bloud, sends out his groanes,
Invokes the heavens, and earth, to heare his moanes ;
His lost felicity did greive him sore,
But this unheard of injury much more ;
Yea, above all, that neither eare, nor eye,
Should heare, nor see, his groans, and misery :
As thus he lay, *Polistratus* a *Greeke*,
Wearied with his long march, did water seek,
So chanc'd these bloudy Horses to espy,
Whose wounds had made their skins of purple dye ;

To

To them he goes, and looking in the Cart,
Findes poore *Darius*, peirced to the heart ;
Who not a little chear'd, to have some eye,
The witnesse of his dying misery :
Prayes him, to *Alexander* to commend,
The just revenge of this his wofull end ;
And not to pardon such disloyalty,
Of treason, murther, and base cruelty.
If not, because *Darius* thus did pray,
Yet that succeeding Kings in safety may
Their lives enjoy, their crowns, and dignity,
And not by Traitors hands untimely dye.
He also sends his humble thankfulnesse,
For all that Kingly Grace he did expresse,
To's Mother, Children deare, and Wife now gone,
Which made their long restraint, seeme to be none ;
Praying the immortall gods, that Sea, and Land,
Might be subjected to his royall hand ;
And that his rule as farre extended be,
As men, the rising, setting Sun shall see.
This said, the *Greek* for water doth intreat,
To quench his thirst, and to allay his heat ;
Of all good things (quoth he) once in my power,
I've nothing left, at this my dying houre ;
Thy pitty, and compassion to reward,
Wherefore the gods requite thy kinde regard.
This said, his fainting breath did fleet away,
And though a Monarch once, now lyes like clay ;
Yea, thus must every Son of *Adam* lye,
Though gods on earth, like Sons of men shall dye.
Now to the East great *Alexander* goes,
To see if any dare his might oppose ;

(For

(For scarce the world, or any bounds thereon,
Could bound his boundlesse, fond ambition)
Such as submits, he doth againe restore,
And makes their riches, and their honours more ;
On *Artabasus* more then all bestow'd,
For his fidelity to 's Master show'd ;
Thalestris, Queen of th' *Amazons*, now brought
Her traine to *Alexander* (as 'tis thought)
Though some of reading best, and soundest minde,
Such country there, nor yet such people finde.
Then tell her errand, we had better spare
To th' ignorant, her title may declare.
As *Alexander* in his greatnesse growes,
So daily of his vertues doth he lose ;
He basenesse counts his former clemency,
And not beseeming such a dignity ;
His past sobriety doth also hate,
As most incompatible to his state ;
His temperance, is but a sordid thing,
No wayes becomming such a mighty King ;
His greatnesse now he takes, to represent,
His fancied gods, above the firmament,
And such as shew'd but reverence before,
Are strictly now commanded to adore ;
With *Persian* Robes, himselfe doth dignifie,
Charging the same on his Nobility ;
His manners, habit, gestures, now doth fashion,
After that conquer'd, and luxurious Nation ;
His Captains, that were vertuously enclin'd,
Griev'd at this change of manners, and of minde ;
The ruder sort, did openly deride
His fained Deity, and foolish pride :

The

The certainty of both comes to his eares,
But yet no notice takes, of what he hears;
With those of worth, he still desires esteem,
So heaps up gifts, his credit to redeem;
And for the rest new wars, and travels findes,
That other matters may take up their minds.
Then hearing, *Bessus* makes himselfe a King,
Intends with speed, that Traitor down to bring;
Now that his Hoast from luggage might be free,
And no man with his burden, burdened be,
Commands forth-with, each man his fardle bring,
Into the Market-place, before the King;
Which done, sets fire upon those costly spoyls
The recompence of travels, wars, and toyls;
And thus unwisely, in one raging fume,
The wealth of many Cities doth consume:
But marvell 'tis, that without muteny,
The Souldiers should let passe this injury;
Nor wonder lesse, to Readers may it bring,
For to observe the rashnesse of the King.
Now with his Army, doth he hast away,
False *Bessus* to finde out, in *Bactria*;
But sore distrest for water, in their march,
The drought, and heat, their bodies much doth parch;
At length, they came to th' River *Oxus* brink,
Where most immoderatly these thirsty drink;
This more mortality to them did bring,
Then did their wars, against the *Persian* King.
Here *Alexander*'s almost at a stand,
How to passe over, and gaine the other Land;
For Boats here's none, nor neare it any wood,
To make them rafts, to waft them o're the floud;

But

But he that was resolved in his minde,
Would by some means a transportation finde;
So from his carriages the Hides he takes,
And stuffing them with straw, he bundles makes;
On these, together ty'd, in six dayes space,
They all passe over, to the other place;
Had *Bessus* had but valour to his wil,
He easily might have made them stay there stil;
But coward, durst not fight, nor could he fly,
Hated of all, for's former treachery,
Is by his owne, now bound in Iron chaines,
(A coller of the same his neck containes)
And in this sort, they rather drag, then bring,
This Malefactor vild, before the King,
Who to *Darius* Brother gives the wretch,
With wracks, and tortures, every limbe to stretch.
Here was of *Greeks*, a town in *Bactria*,
Whom *Xerxes* from their country led away;
These not a little joy'd, this day to see,
Wherein their own had soveraignity.
And now reviv'd with hopes, held up their head,
From bondage, long to be infranchised;
But *Alexander* puts them to the sword,
Without cause, given by them, in deed, or word:
Nor sex, nor age, nor one, nor other spar'd,
But in his cruelty alike they shar'd;
Nor could he reason give, for this great wrong,
But that they had forgot their Mother-tongue.
Whilst thus he spent some time in *Bactria*,
And in his Camp strong, and securely lay,
Down from the mountains twenty thousand came,
And there most fiercely set upon the same;

Repelling

Repelling thefe two marks of honour got,
Imprinted deep in's legg, by Arrowes fhot;
And now the *Bactrians* 'gainft him rebel,
But he their ftubbornneffe full foone doth quel;
From hence he to *Jaxartis* river goes,
Where *Scithians* rude, his valour doth oppofe,
And with their out-cries, in a hideous fort,
Befets his Camp, or Military Court;
Of Darts, and Arrowes, made fo little fpare,
They flew fo thick they feem'd to dark the aire:
But foone the *Grecians* forc'd them to a flight,
Whofe nakedneffe could not endure their might;
Upon this Rivers banck in feventeen dayes,
A goodly City doth compleatly raife;
Which *Alexandria* he doth alfo name,
And furlongs fixty could not round the fame.
His third fupply, *Antipater* now fent,
Which did his former Army much augment,
And being an hundred twenty thoufand ftrong,
He enters now the *Indian* Kings among;
Thofe that fubmit, he doth reftore again.
Thofe that doe not, both they, and theirs, are flain;
To age, nor fex, no pitty doth expreffe,
But all fall by his fword, moft mercileffe.
He t' *Nifa* goes, by *Bacchus* built long fince,
Whofe feafts are celebrated by this Prince;
Nor had that drunken god, one that would take
His liquors more devoutly in, for's fake.
When thus, ten dayes, his brain with wine he'd foak'd,
And with delicious meats, his Pallat choak'd,
To th' river *Indus* next, his courfe he bends,
Boats to prepare, *Epheftion* firft he fends,

Who

Who comming thither, long before his Lord;
Had to his mind, made all things now accord :
The Veffells ready were, at his command ;
And *Omphis*, King of that part of the land:
Through his perfwafion *Alexander* meets;
And as his Sovereign Lord, him humbly greets.
Fifty fix Elephants he brings to's hands:
And tenders him the ftrength of all his lands,
Prefents himfelfe, there with a golden Crowne,
And eighty Tallents to his Captaines down.
But *Alexander*, caus'd him to behold;
He glory fought, no filver, nor yet gold ;
His Prefents all, with thanks he doth reftore;
And of his own, a thoufand Tallents more.
Thus all the *Indian* Kings, to him fubmit ;
But *Porus* ftout, who will not yeeld as yet ;
To him doth *Alexander* thus declare,
His pleafure is, that forthwith he repaire
Unto his Kingdoms borders, and as due,
His Homage unto him as Soveraigne doe.
But Kingly *Porus* this brave anfwer fent,
That to attend him there, was his intent ;
And come as well provided as he could,
But for the reft, his fword advife him fhould.
Great *Alexander* vext at this reply,
Did more his valour then his Crown envie ;
Is now refolv'd to paffe *Hidafpes* floud,
And there his Soveraignty for to make good ;
But on the banks doth *Porus* ready ftand,
For to receive him, when he comes to land ;
A potent Army with him, like a King,
And ninety Elephants for war did bring ;

Had

Had *Alexander* such resistance seen,
On *Tygris* side, here now he had not been;
Within this spacious river, deep, and wide,
Did here, and there, Isles full of trees abide;
His Army *Alexander* doth divide,
With *Ptolomy*, sends part o' th' tother side.
Porus encounters them, thinking all's there,
Then covertly, the rest gets o're else where;
But whilst the first he valiantly assayl'd,
The last set on his back, and so prevail'd:
Yet work enough, here *Alexander* found,
For to the last, stout *Porus* kept his ground.
Nor was't dishonour, at the length to yeeld;
When *Alexander* strives to win the field,
His fortitude his Kingly foe commends;
Restores him, and his bounds further extends;
East-ward, now *Alexander* would goe still,
But so to doe, his Souldiers had no will;
Long with excessive travailes wearied,
Could by no means be further drawn, or led:
Yet that his fame might to posterity,
Be had in everlasting memory,
Doth for his Camp a greater circuit take,
And for his Souldiers larger Cabins make;
His Maungers he erected up so high,
As never Horse his Provender could eye;
Huge Bridles made, which here, and there, he left,
Which might be found, and so for wonders kept:
Twelve Altars, he for Monuments then rears,
Whereon his acts, and travels, long appears;
But doubting, wearing Time would these decay,
And so his memory might fade away,

He

He on the faire *Hidaspis* pleasant side,
Two Cities built, his fame might there abide ;
The first *Nicea*, the next *Bucephalon*,
Where he entomb'd his stately stallion.
His fourth, and last supply, was hither sent,
Then down t' *Hidaspis* with his Fleet he went ;
Some time he after spent upon that shore,
Where one hundred Embassadours, or more,
Came with submission, from the *Indian* Kings
Bringing their Presents, rare, and precious things :
These, all he feasts in state, on beds of gold,
His furniture most sumptuous to behold ;
The meat, and drink, attendants, every thing,
To th' utmost shew'd, the glory of a King ;
With rich rewards, he sent them home again,
Acknowledg'd for their Masters Soveraigne ;
Then sayling South, and comming to the shore,
These obscure Nations yeelded as before ;
A City here he built, cal'd by his name,
Which could not sound too oft, with too much fame ;
Hence sayling down by th' mouth of *Indus* floud,
His Gallies stuck upon the sand, and mud ;
Which the stout *Macedonians* mazed sore
Depriv'd at once, the use of Saile, and Oare ;
But well observing th' nature of the tide,
Upon those Flats they did not long abide ;
Passing faire *Indus* mouth, his course he stear'd,
To th' coast which by *Euphrates* mouth appear'd ;
Whose inlets neare unto, he winter spent,
Unto his starved Souldiers small content ;
By hunger, and by cold, so many slaine,
That of them all, the fourth did scarce remaine.

Thus

Thus Winter, Souldiers, and proviſion ſpent,
From hence he to *Gedroſia* went,
And thence he marcht into *Carmania*,
So he at length drew neare to *Perſia*;
Now through theſe goodly countries as he paſt,
Much time in feaſts, and ryoting doth waſt;
Then viſits *Cyrus* Sepulcher in's way,
Who now obſcure at *Paſſagardis* lay;
Upon his Monument his Robes he ſpread,
And ſet his Crown on his ſuppoſed head;
From hence to *Babylon*, ſome time there ſpent,
He at the laſt to royall *Suſhan* went;
A Wedding Feaſt to's Nobles then he makes,
And *Statirah*, *Darius* daughter takes,
Her Siſter gives to his *Epheſtion* deare,
That by this match he might be yet more neare.
He fourſcore *Perſian* Ladies alſo gave,
At the ſame time, unto his Captains brave;
Six thouſand Gueſts he to this feaſt invites,
Whoſe Sences all, were glutted with delights;
It far exceeds my meane abilities,
To ſhadow forth theſe ſhort felicities:
Spectators here, could ſcarce relate the ſtory,
They were ſo wrapt with this externall glory.
If an Ideall Paradiſe, a man ſhould frame,
He might this feaſt imagine by the ſame.
To every Gueſt, a cup of gold he ſends,
So after many dayes this Banquet ends.
Now, *Alexanders* conqueſts, all are done,
And his long travells paſt, and over-gone;
His vertues dead, buried, and all forgot,
But vice remaines, to his eternall blot.

'Mongſt

'Mongſt thoſe, that of his cruelty did taſte,
Philotas was not leaſt, nor yet the laſt ;
Accus'd, becauſe he did not certifie
The King of treaſon, and conſpiracy ;
Upon ſuſpicion being apprehended,
Nothing was found, wherein he had offended ;
His ſilence, guilt was, of ſuch conſequence,
He death deſerv'd, for this ſo high offence ;
But for his Fathers great deſerts, the King,
His Royall pardon gave, for this ſame thing ;
Yet is Philotas unto Judgement brought,
Muſt ſuffer, not for what he did, but thought :
His Maſter is Accuſer, Judge, and King,
Who to the height doth aggravate each thing ;
Enveighs againſt his Father, now abſent,
And's Brethren, whom for him their lives had ſpent ;
But Philotas, his unpardonable crime,
Which no merit could obliterate, or time :
He did the Oracle of Iupiter deride,
By which his Majeſty was deifi'd.
Philotas thus o're-charg'd, with wrong, and greif,
Sunk in deſpair, without hope of releif ;
Faine would have ſpoke, and made his owne defence,
The King would give no eare, but went from thence ;
To his malicious foes delivers him,
To wreak their ſpight, and hate, on every limbe.
Philotas after him ſends out this cry,
Oh, Alexander, thy free clemency,
My foes exceeds in malice, and their hate,
Thy Kingly word can eaſily terminate ;
Such torments great, as wit could firſt invent,
Or fleſh, or life could bear, till both were ſpent,

                                                    Are

Are now inflicted on *Parmenio's* Son,
For to accuse himself, as they had done ;
At last he did : So they were justified,
And told the world, that for desert he dyed.
But how these Captaines should, or yet their Master,
Look on *Parmenio*, after this disaster,
They knew not ; wherefore, best now to be done,
Was to dispatch the Father, as the Son.
This sound advice, at heart, pleas'd *Alexander*,
Who was so much engag'd, to this Commander,
As he would ne're confesse, nor could reward,
Nor could his Captaines bear so great regard ;
Wherefore at once all these to satisfie,
It was decreed *Parmenio* should dye :
Polidamus, who seem'd *Parmenio's* friend,
To doe this deed, they into *Media* send ;
He walking in his Garden, too and fro,
Thinking no harme, because he none did owe,
Most wickedly was slaine, without least crime,
(The most renowned Captaine of his time)
This is *Parmenio*, which so much had done,
For *Philip* dead, and his surviving Son,
Who from a petty King of *Macedon*,
By him was set upon the *Persian* Throne :
This that *Parmenio*, who still over-came,
Yet gave his Master the immortall fame ;
Who for his prudence, valour, care, and trust,
Had this reward most cruel, and unjust.
The next that in untimely death had part,
Was one of more esteem, but lesse desart ;
Clitus, belov'd next to *Epheftion*,
And in his cups, his chief Companion ;

L.   When

When both were drunk, *Clitus* was wont to jeere ;
Alexander, to rage, to kill, and sweare,
Nothing more pleasing to mad *Clitus* tongue,
Then's Masters god-head, to defie, and wrong ;
Nothing toucht *Alexander* to the quick
Like this, against his deity to kick :
Upon a time, when both had drunken well,
Upon this dangerous theam fond *Clitus* fell ;
From jeast, to earnest, and at last so bold,
That of *Parmenio's* death him plainly told.
Alexander now no longer could containe,
But instantly commands him to be slaine ;
Next day, he tore his face, for what he'd done,
And would have slaine himself, for *Clitus* gone ,
This pot companion he did more bemoan,
Then all the wrong to brave *Parmenio* done.
The next of worth, that suffered after these,
Was vertuous, learned, wise *Calisthines*,
Who lov'd his Master more then did the rest,
As did appeare, in flattering him the least :
In his esteem, a God he could not be,
Nor would adore him for a Deity :
For this alone, and for no other cause,
Against his Soveraigne, or against his Lawes,
He on the wrack, his limbs in peeces rent,
Thus was he tortur'd, till his life was spent.
Of this unkingly deed, doth *Seneca*
This censure passe, and not unwisely, say,
Of *Alexander*, this th'eternall crime,
Which shall not be obliterate by time,
Which vertues fame can ne're redeem by farre,
Nor all felicity, of his in war ;

When

When e're 'tis said, he thousand thousands slew,
Yea, and *Calisthines* to death he drew,
The mighty *Persian* King he over-came,
Yea, and he kild *Calisthines* by name ;
All Kingdoms, Countries, Provinces, he won,
From *Hellispont*, to th' furthest Ocean ;
All this he did, who knows not to be true,
But yet withall, *Calisthines* he slew ;
From *Macedon* his Empire did extend,
Unto the furthest bounds of th' orient ;
All this he did, yea, and much more, 'tis true,
But yet withall, *Calisthines* he slew.
Now *Alexander* goes to *Media*,
Findes there the want of wise *Parmenio*,
Here his cheif favourite *Ephestion* dyes,
He celebrates his mournfull obsequies ;
For him erects a stately Monument,
Twelve thousand Tallents on it franckly spent ;
Hangs his Phisitian, the reason why,
Because he let *Ephestion* to dye.
This act (me thinks) his god-head should ashame ;
To punish, where himself deserved blame :
Or of necessity, he must imply,
The other was the greatest Deity.
From *Media* to *Babylon* he went,
To meet him there, t' *Antipater* had sent,
That he might next now act upon the Stage,
And in a Tragedy there end his age.
The Queen *Olimpias*, bears him deadly hate,
(Not suffering her to meddle in the State)
And by her Letters did her Son incite,
This great indignity for to requite.

His

His doing so, no whit displeas'd the King,
Though to his Mother he disprov'd the thing;
But now, *Antipater* had liv'd thus long,
He might well dye, though he had done no wrong;
His service great now's suddenly forgot,
Or if remembred, yet regarded not;
The King doth intimate 'twas his intent,
His honours, and his riches, to augment
Of larger Provinces, the rule to give,
And for his Counsell, ne're the King to live.
So to be caught, *Antipater's* too wise,
Parmenio's death's too fresh before his eyes;
He was too subtile for his crafty foe,
Nor by his baits could be ensnared so:
But his excuse with humble thanks he sends,
His age, and journey long, he now pretends;
And pardon craves, for his unwilling stay,
He shewes his grief, he's forc'd to disobey:
Before his answer came to *Babylon*,
The thread of *Alexanders* life was spun;
Poyson had put an end to's dayes 'twas thought,
By *Philip*, and *Cassander*, to him brought,
Sons to *Antipater*, bearers of his Cup,
Least of such like, their Father chance to sup:
By others thought, and that more generally,
That through excessive drinking he did dye.
The thirty third of 's age doe all agree,
This Conquerour did yeeld to destiny;
Whose famous Acts must last, whilst world shall stand,
And Conquests be talkt of, whilst there is Land;
His Princely qualities, had he retain'd
Unparalel'd, for ever had remain'd;

                                    But

But with the world his vertues overcame,
And so with black,be-clouded all his fame.
Wise *Aristotle,* tutour to his youth,
Had so instructed him in morall truth.
The principles of what he then had learn'd
Might to the last (when sober) be discern'd.
Learning,and learned men,he much regarded,
And curious Artists evermore rewarded.
The Illiads of *Homer* he still kept,
And under's pillow laid them when he slept.
Achille's happinesse he did envy,
'Cause *Homer* kept his Acts to memory ;
Profusely bountifull, without desert,
For those that pleas'd him ; had both wealth and heart :
Cruell by nature,and by custome too,
As oft his Acts throughout his reigne did shew :
More boundles in ambition then the skie,
Vain thirsting after immortality :
Still fearing that his Name might hap to die,
And fame not last unto Eternity :
This conquerour did oft lament ('tis sed)
There was no worlds, more, to be conquered:
This folly great *Augustus* did deride,
For had he had but wisdome to his pride,
He would have found enough for to be done,
To govern that he had already won :
His thoughts are perish'd he aspires no more,
Nor can he kill, or save as heretofore,
A God alive him all must Idolize ;
Now like a mortall helplesse man he lies ;
Of all those kingdomes large which he had got,
To his posterity remain'd no jot,

For

For by that hand, which still revengeth bloud,
None of his Kindred, or his Race, long stood ;
And as he took delight, much bloud to spill,
So the same cup to his, did others fill.
Four of his Captains, all doe now divide,
As *Daniel*, before had Prophesied ;
The Leopard down, his four wings 'gan to rise,
The great Horn broke, the lesse did tyrannize ;
What troubles, and contentions did ensue,
We may hereafter shew, in season due.

Aridæns.

GReat *Alexander* dead, his Army's left,
Like to that Giant, of his eye bereft ;
When of his monstrous bulk it was the guide,
His matchlesse force no Creature could abide ;
But by *Ulysses*, having lost his sight,
Each man began for to contemn his might ;
For ayming still amisse, his dreadfull blowes
Did harm himself, but never reacht his foes :
Now Court, and Camp, all in confusion be,
A King they'l have, but who, none can agree :
Each Captain wisht this prize to beare away,
Yet none so hardy found as so durst say.
Great *Alexander* had left issue none,
Except by *Artabasus* daughter one ;
And *Roxan* faire, whom late he married,
Was neare her time to be delivered ;
By Natures right, these had enough to claime,
But meannesse of their Mothers bard the same :

Alleadg'd

Alleadg'd by thofe, which by their fubtill plea
Had hope themfelves, to beare the Crown away;
A Sifter *Alexander* had, but fhe
Claim'd not, perhaps her Sex might hindrance be.
After much tumult, they at laft proclaim'd
His bafe born Brother, *Aridæus* nam'd,
That fo under his feeble wit, and reign,
Their ends they might the better ftill attain.
This choyfe *Perdicas*, vehemently difclaim'd,
And th' unborn babe of *Roxan* he proclaim'd;
Some wifhed him, to take the ftile of King,
Becaufe his Mafter gave to him his Ring,
And had to him, ftill fince *Epheftion* dyed,
More then to th'reft, his favour teftified:
But he refus'd, with fained modefty,
Hoping to be elect more generally;
He hold of this occafion fhould have laid,
For fecond offers there were never made;
'Mongft thefe contentions, tumults, jealoufies,
Seven dayes the Corps of their great Mafter lyes
Untoucht, uncovered, flighted, and neglected,
So much thefe Princes their owne ends refpected.
A contemplation to aftonifh Kings,
That he, who late, poffeft all earthly things,
And yet not fo content, unleffe that he
Might be efteemed for a Deity;
Now lay a fpectacle, to teftifie
The wretchedneffe of mans mortality.
After this time, when ftirs began to calme,
The *Egyptians*, his body did enbalme;
On which, no figne of poyfon could be found,
But all his bowels, coloured well, and found.

Perdicas

Perdicas, seeing *Aridaus* must be King,
Under his name begins to rule each thing.
His chief opponents who kept off the Crown,
Was stiffe *Meleager*, whom he would take down,
Him by a wile he got within his power,
And took his life unworthily that houre :
Using the name, and the command o'th' King
To authorize his Acts in every thing.
The Princes seeing *Perdica's* power and Pride,
Thought timely for themselves, now to provide.
Antigonus, for his share *Asia* takes,
And *Ptolomy*, next sure of *Egypt* makes.
Seleuchus afterward held *Babylon*;
Antipater, had long rul'd *Macedon*,
These now to govern for the King pretends,
But nothing lesse : each one himself intends.
Perdicas took no Province, like the rest,
But held command o'th' Armies which was best ;
And had a higher project in his head,
Which was his Masters sister for to wed :
So, to the Lady secretly he sent,
That none might know, to frustrate his intent ;
But *Cleopatra*, this suitour did deny,
For *Leonatus*, more lovely in her eye,
To whom she sent a message of her mind,
That if he came, good welcome he should find :
In these tumultuous dayes, the thralled *Greeks*
Their ancient liberty, afresh now seeks,
Shakes off the yoke, sometimes before laid on
By warlike *Philip*, and his conquering son.
The *Athenians*, force *Antipater* to fly
To *Lamia*, where he shut up doth ly ;

To

To brave *Craterus*, then, he sends with speed,
To come and to release him in his need,
The like of *Leonatus*, he requires,
(Which at this time well suited his desires)
For to *Antipater* he now might go,
His Lady take i'th' way, and no man know.
Antiphilus the *Athenian* Generall,
With speed his forces doth together call,
Striving to stop *Leonatus*, that so
He joyn not with *Antipater*, that foe.
The *Athenian* Army was the greater far,
(Which did his match with *Cleopatra* mar)
For fighting still, whilst there did hope remain,
The valiant Chief, amidst his foes was slain,
'Mongst all the Captains of great *Alexander*,
For personage, none was like this Commander :
Now to *Antipater*, *Craterus* goes,
Blockt up in *Lamia*, still by his foes ;
Long marches through *Cilicia* he makes,
And the remains of *Leonatus* takes ;
With them and his, he into *Grecia* went,
Antipater releas'd from's prisonment,
After this time, the *Greeks* did never more
Act any thing of worth, as heretofore,
But under servitude, their necks remain'd,
Nor former liberty, or glory gain'd ;
Now dy'd (about the end of th' *Lamian* warre)
Demosthenes, that sweet tongu'd oratour.
Craterus, and *Antipater* now joyn
In love, and in affinity combine:
Craterus doth his daughter *Phisa* wed,
Their friendship may the more be strengthened :
Whilst

Whilst they in *Macedon* doe thus agree,
In *Asia* they all asunder be.
Perdicas griev'd, to see the Princes bold,
So many Kingdoms in their power to hold,
Yet to regain them, how he did not know,
For's Souldiers 'gainst those Captains would not goe;
To suffer them goe on, as they begun,
Was to give way, himself might be undone;
With *Antipater* t' joyn, sometimes he thought,
That by his help, the rest might low be brought:
But this again dislikes, and would remain,
If not in word, in deed a Soveraigne.
Desires the King, to goe to *Macedon*,
Which of his Ancestors was once the throne,
And by his presence there, to nullifie
The Acts of his Vice-royes, now grown so high:
Antigonus of Treason first attaints.
And summons him, to answer these complaints;
This he avoyds, and ships himself, and's Son,
Goes to *Antipater*, and tels what's done;
He, and *Craterus*, both with him now joyn,
And 'gainst *Perdicas*, all their strength combine.
Brave *Ptolomy*, to make a fourth now sent,
To save himself from dangers eminent;
In midst of these, *Garboyles*, with wondrous state,
His Masters Funerals doth celebrate;
At *Alexandria*, in Ægypt Land,
His sumptuous monument long time did stand;
Two years and more since, Natures debt he paid,
And yet till now, at quiet was not laid.
Great love did *Ptolomy* by this act gain.
And made the Souldiers on his side remain;

Perdicas

Perdicas hears, his foes are now combin'd,
('Gainst which to goe, is troubled in his minde ;)
With Ptolomy for to begin was best,
Near'st unto him, and farthest from the rest.
Leaves Eumenes, the Afian coast to free,
From the invasions of the other three ;
And with his Army into Ægypt goes,
Brave Ptolomy to th'utmost to oppose.
Perdicas surly carriage, and his pride,
Did alienate the Souldiers from his side ;
But Ptolomy by affability,
His sweet demeanour, and his courtesie,
Did make his owne firme to his cause remaine,
And from the other, daily some did gaine.
Pithon, next Perdicas, a Captaine high,
Being entreated by him scornfully,
Some of the Souldiers enters Perdica's tent,
Knocks out his braines, to Ptolomy then went,
And offers him his Honours, and his place,
With stile of the Protector, would him grace ;
Next day into the Camp comes Ptolomy,
And is of all received joyfully ;
Their proffers he refus'd, with modesty
Confers them Pithon on, for's courtesie ;
With what he held, he now was well content,
Then by more trouble to grow eminent.
Now comes there newes of a great victory,
That Eumenes got of the other three,
Had it but in Perdicas life arriv'd,
With greater joy it would have been receiv'd ;
Thus Ptolomy rich Ægypt did retaine,
And Pithon turn'd to Afia againe.

Whilst

Whilft *Perdicas* thus ftaid in *Africa*,
Antigonus did enter *Afia*,
And fain would draw *Eumenes* to their fide,
But he alone now faithfull did abide :
The other all, had kingdomes in their eye,
But he was true to's mafters family,
Nor could *Craterus* (whom he much did love)
From his fidelity make him once move.
Two battells now he fought, and had the beft,
And brave *Craterus* flew, amongft the reft,
For this great ftrife, he pours out his complaints,
And his beloved foe, full fore laments.
I fhould but fnip a ftory into verfe,
And much eclipfe his glory to rehearfe
The difficulties *Eumenes* befell,
His ftratagems, wherein he did excel,
His policies, how he did extricate
Himfelf from out of labyrinths intricate.
For all that fhould be faid, let this fuffice,
He was both valiant, faithfull, patient, wife.
Python now chofe protector of the State,
His rule Queen *Euridice* begins to hate,
Perceives *Aridæus* muft not king it long,
If once young *Alexander* grow more ftrong,
But that her Husband ferve for fupplement,
To warm the feat, was never her intent,
She knew her birthright gave her *Macedon*,
Grandchild to him, who once fat on that throne,
Who was *Perdicas*, *Philips* elder brother,
She daughter to his fon, who had no other;
Her mother *Cyna* fifter to *Alexander*,
Who had an Army, like a great Commander.

Ceria

Ceria the *Phrigian* Queen for to withstand,
And in a Battell slew her hand to hand;
Her Daughter she instructed in that Art,
Which made her now begin to play her part;
Pithons commands, She ever countermands
What he appoints, She purposely withstands:
He wearied out, at last, would needs be gone,
Resign'd his place, and so let all alone;
In's stead, the Souldiers chose *Antipater*,
Who vext the Queen more then the other farre;
He plac'd, displac'd, controld, rul'd, as he list,
And this no man durst question, or resist;
For all the Princes of great *Alexander*
Acknowledged for chief, this old Commander:
After a while, to *Macedon* he makes;
The King, and Queen, along with him he takes.
Two Sons of *Alexander*, and the rest,
All to be order'd there as he thought best:
The Army with *Antigonus* did leave,
And government of *Asia* to him gave;
And thus *Antipater* the ground-work layes,
On which *Antigonus* his height doth raise:
Who in few years the rest so over-tops,
For universall Monarchy he hopes;
With *Eumenes* he divers Battels fought,
And by his sleights to circumvent him sought;
But vaine it was to use his policy,
'Gainst him, that all deceits could scan, and try:
In this Epitomy, too long to tell
How neatly *Eumenes* did here excell,
That by the selfe-same traps the other laid,
He to his cost was righteously repaid.

Now

Now great *Antipater*, the world doth leave
To *Polisperchon*, then his place he gave,
Fearing his Son *Caßander* was unstay'd,
Too young to beare that charge, if on him lay'd;
Antigonus hearing of his decease,
On most part of *Aßyria* doth seize,
And *Ptolomy*, now to encroach begins,
All *Syria*, and, *Phenicia* he wins;
Now *Polisperchon* 'gins to act in's place,
Recals *Olimpias*, the Court to grace;
Antipater had banisht her from thence,
Into *Epire*, for her great turbulence;
This new Protector's of another minde,
Thinks by her Majesty much help to finde;
Caßander could not (like his father) see
This *Polisperchons* great ability,
Slights his commands, his actions he disclaimes;
And to be great himselfe now bends his aymes;
Such as his father had advanc'd to place,
Or by his favour any way did grace,
Are now at the devotion of the Son,
Prest to accomplish what he would have done;
Besides, he was the young Queens favourite,
On whom ('twas thought) she set her chief delight;
Unto these helps, in *Greece*, he seeks out more,
Goes to *Antigonus*, and doth implore,
By all the Bonds 'twixt him and's father past,
And for that great gift, which he gave him last;
By these, and all, to grant him some supply,
To take down *Polisperchon* grown so high;
For this *Antigonus* needed no spurs.
Hoping still more to gaine by these new stirs;

                                    Straight

Straight furnisht him with a sufficient aide,
Cassander for return all speed now made :
Polisperchon, knowing he did relye
Upon those friends, his father rais'd on high,
Those absent, banished, or else he slew
All such as he suspected to him true.
Cassander with his Hoast to *Grecia* goes,
Whom *Polisperchon* labours to oppose,
But had the worst at Sea, as well as Land,
And his opponent still got upper hand,
Athens, with many Townes in *Greece* besides,
Firme to *Cassander* at this time abides :
Whilst hot in wars these two in *Greece* remaine,
Antigonus doth all in *Asia* gaine ;
Still labours *Eumenes* might with him side,
But to the last he faithfull did abide ;
Nor could Mother, nor Sons of *Alexander*,
Put trust in any, but in this Commander ;
The great ones now began to shew their minde,
And act, as opportunity they finde :
Aridæus the scorn'd, and simple King,
More then he bidden was, could act no thing ;
Polisperchon hoping for's office long,
Thinks to enthrone the Prince when riper grown ;
Euridice this injury disdaines,
And to *Cassander* of this wrong complaines;
Hatefull the Name, and House of *Alexander*,
Was to this proud, vindicative *Cassander*,
He still kept fresh within his memory,
His Fathers danger, with his Family ;
Nor counts he that indignity but small,
When *Alexander* knockt his head to th' wall :

These

These, with his love, unto the amorous Queen
Did make him vow her servant to be seen.
Olimpias, Aridæus deadly hates,
As all her Husbands children by his Mates ;
She gave him poyson formerly ('tis thought)
Which damage both to minde and body brought ;
She now with *Polisperchon* doth combine,
To make the King by force his seat resigne ;
And her young Nephew in his stead t' inthrone,
That under him she might rule all alone.
For ayde goes to *Epire,* among her friends,
The better to accomplish these her ends ;
Euridice hearing what she intends,
In hast unto her deare *Cassander* sends,
To leave his Seige at *Tagra,* and with speed
To come and succour her, in this great need ;
Then by intreaties, promises, and coyne,
Some Forces did procure, with her to joyne.
Olimpias now enters *Macedon,*
The Queen to meet her, bravely marched on ;
But when her Souldiers saw their ancient Queen,
Remembring what sometime she had been,
The Wife, and Mother, of their famous Kings,
Nor Darts, nor Arrowes now, none shoots, nor flings ;
Then King, and Queen, to *Amphipolis* doe fly,
But soone are brought into captivity ;
The King by extreame torments had his end,
And to the Queen, these presents she doth send ;
A Halter, cup of Poyson, and a Sword,
Bids chuse her death, such kindnesse she'l afford :
The Queen with many a curse, and bitter check,
At length yeelds to the Halter, her faire neck ;

                                          Praying,

Praying, that fatall day might quickly haste,
On which *Olimpias* of the like might taste.
This done, the cruell Queen rests not content,
Till all that lov'd *Caffander* was nigh fpent ;
His Brethren, Kinsfolk, and his chiefeft friends,
That were within her reach, came to their ends ;
Digg'd up his brother dead, 'gainft natures right,
And throwes his bones about, to fhew her fpight.
The Courtiers wondring at her furious minde,
Wifht in *Epire* fhe ftill had been confin'd ;
In *Pelioponefus* then *Caffander* lay,
Where hearing of this newes he fpeeds away,
With rage, and with revenge, he's hurried on,
So goes to finde this Queen in *Macedon* ;
But being ftopt, at Straight *Tharmipoley*
Sea paffage gets, and lands in *Theffaly* ;
His Army he divides, fends part away,
Polifperchon to hold a while in play,
And with the reft *Olimpias* purfues,
To give her for all cruelties her dues :
She with the flow'r o'th Court to *Pidna* flyes,
Well fortified, and on the Sea it lies ;
There by *Caffander* fhe's block'd up, fo long,
Untill the Famine growes exceeding ftrong.
Her Coufen of *Epire* did what he might,
To raife the Seige, and put her foes to flight ;
Caffander is refolv'd, there to remaine,
So fuccours, and endeavours proves but vaine .
Faine would fhe come now to capitulate,
Caffander will not heare, fuch is his hate.
The Souldiers pinched with this fcarcity,
By ftealth unto *Caffander* daily fly ;

M

Olimpias

Olimpias wills to keep it, to the laſt,
Expecting nothing, but of death to taſte ;
But he unwilling longer there to ſtay,
Gives promiſe for her life, and wins the day :
No ſooner had he got her in his hands,
But made in Judgement her Accuſers ſtand,
And plead the blood of their deare Kindred ſpilt,
Deſiring Juſtice might be done for guilt ;
And ſo was he acquitted of his word,
For Juſtice ſake ſhe being put to th' ſword.
This was the end of this moſt cruell Queen,
Whoſe fury yet unparalleld hath been ;
The Daughter, Siſter, Mother, Wiſe to Kings,
But Royalty no good conditions brings ;
So boundleſſe was her pride, and cruelty,
She oft forgot bounds of Humanity.
To Husbands death ('twas thought) ſhe gave conſent,
The Authours death ſhe did ſo much lament,
With Garlands crown'd his head, bemoan'd his Fates,
His ſword unto *Apollo* conſecrates :
Her out-rages too tedious to relate,
How for no cauſe, but her inveterate hate ;
Her Husbands Wife, and Children, after's death
Some ſlew, ſome fry'd, of others, ſtopt the breath ;
Now in her age ſhe's forc't to taſte that Cup,
Which ſhe had often made others to ſup :
Now many Townes in *Macedon* ſuppreſt,
And *Pellas* faine to yeeld amongſt the reſt ;
The Funeralls *Caſſandra* celebrates,
Of *Arideus*, and his Queen, with ſtate ;
Among their Anceſtors by him there laid,
And ſhewes of lamentation for them made.

Old *Thebes* he then re-built (so much of fame)
And rais'd *Caffandria* after his name,
But leave him building, others in their urn,
And for a while, let's into *Afia* turn,
True *Eumenes* endeavours by all skill,
To keep *Antigonus* from *Sufha* still,
Having Command o'th treasure he can hire,
Such as nor threats, nor favour could acquire;
In divers battels, he had good succeffe,
Antigonus came off still honourlesse,
When victor oft had been, and so might still,
Penceftas did betray him by a wile,
Antigonus, then takes his life unjust,
Because he never would let go his trust:
Thus lost he all for his fidelity,
Striving t'uphold his Masters family,
But as that to a period did haste,
So *Eumenes* of destiny must taste.
Antigonus, all *Perfia* now gains,
And Master of the treasure he remains;
Then with *Seleushus* straight at ods doth fall,
But he for aid to *Ptolomy* doth call.
The Princes all begin now to envie
Antigonus, his growing up so hye,
Fearing their state, and what might hap ere long,
Enter into a combination strong:
Seleuchus, *Ptolomy*, *Caffander* joynes,
Lyfimachus to make a fourth combines:
Antigonus, defirous of the *Greeks*,
To make *Caffander* odious to them, feeks,
Sends forth his declaration from a farre,
And shews what cause they had to take up warre.

M 2   The

The Mother of their King to death he'd put,
His Wife, and Son, in prison close had shut ;
And how he aymes to make himselfe a King,
And that some title he might seeme to bring,
Theffalonica he had newly wed,
Daughter to *Phillip*, their renowned head ;
Had built, and call'd a City by his name,
Which none e're did but those of royall fame ;
And in despight of their two famous Kings,
Th' hatefull *Olinthians* to *Greece* re-brings ;
Rebellious *Thebs* he had re-edified,
Which their late King in dust had damnified ;
Requires them therefore to take up their Armes,
And to requite this Traytor for those harmes :
Now *Ptolomy* would gaine the *Greeks* likewise,
For he declares against his injuries ;
First, how he held the Empire in his hands,
Seleuchus drove from government, and lands ;
Had valiant *Eumenes* unjustly slaine,
And Lord o'th' City *Susha* did remain.
So therefore craves their help to take him down,
Before he weare the universall Crown ;
Antigonus at Sea soone had a fight,
Where *Ptolomy*, and the rest put him to flight ;
His Son at *Gaza* likewise lost the field,
So *Syria* to *Ptolomy* did yeeld ;
And *Seleuchus* recovers *Babylon*,
Still gaining Coumtries East-ward goes he on.
Demetrius againe with *Ptolomy* did fight,
And comming unawares put him to flight ;
But bravely sends the Prisoners back againe,
And all the spoyle and booty they had tane ;

Curtious

Curtius, as noble *Ptolomy*, or more,
Who at *Gaza* did th' like to him before.
Antigonus did much rejoyce his son,
His loft repute with victorie had won ;
At laft thefe Princes tired out with warres,
Sought for a peace, and laid afide their jarres :
The terms of their agreement thus expreffe,
That each fhall hold what he doth now poffeffe,
Till *Alexander* unto age was grown,
Who then fhall be inftalled in the throne :
This touch'd *Caffander* fore, for what he'd done,
Imprifoning both the mother, and her fon,
He fees the *Greeks* now favour their young Prince,
Whom he in durance held, now and long fince,
That in few years he muft be forc'd or glad
To render up fuch kingdomes as he had
Refolves to quit his fears by one deed done,
And put to death, the mother and her fon,
This *Roxane* for her beautie all commend,
But for one act fhe did, juft was her end,
No fooner was great *Alexander* dead,
But fhe *Darius's* daughters murthered,
Both thrown into a well to hide her blot,
Perdicas was her partner in this plot :
The Heavens feem'd flow in paying her the fame,
But yet at laft the hand of vengeance came,
And for that double fact which fhe had done,
The life of her muft go, and of her fon
Perdicas had before, for his amiffe,
But from their hands, who thought not once of this.
Caffander's dead, the Princes all deteft,
But 'twas in fhew, in heart it pleas'd them beft.

That

That he was odious to the world, they'r glad,
And now they are free Lords, of what they had,
When this foul tragedy was past, and done,
Polisperchon brings up the other son,
Call'd *Hercules*, and elder then his brother,
(But, *Olympias*, thought to preferre th' other:)
The *Greeks* touch'd with the murther done so late,
This Prince began for to compassionate.
Begin to mutter much 'gainst proud *Cassander*,
And place their hopes o'th heire of *Alexander*,
Cassander fear'd what might of this insue,
So *Polisperchon* to his Counsell drew,
Gives *Peloponesus* unto him for hire,
Who slew the prince according to desire:
Thus was the race, and house of *Alexander*
Extinct, by this inhumane wretch *Cassander*,
Antigonus for all this doth not mourn,
He knows to's profit, all i'th end will turn,
But that some title he might now pretend,
For marriage to *Cleopatra*, doth send
Lysimachus and *Ptolomy*, the same,
And vile *Cassander* too, sticks not for shame;
She now in *Lydia* at *Sardis* lay,
Where, by Embassage, all these Princes pray,
Choise above all, of *Ptolomy* she makes
With his Embassadour, her journey takes,
Antigonu's Lieutenant stayes her still,
Untill he further know his Masters will;
To let her go, or hold her still, he fears,
Antigonus thus had a wolf by th' ears,
Resolves at last the Princesse shou'd be slain,
So hinders him of her, he could not gain.

Her

Her women are appointed to this deed,
They for their great reward no better speed,
For ſtraight way by command they'r put to death,
As vile conſpiratours that took her breath,
And now he thinks, he's ordered all ſo well,
The world muſt needs believe what he doth tell :
Thus *Philips* houſe was quite extinguiſhed,
Except *Caſſanders* wife, who yet not dead,
And by their means, who thought of nothing leſſe
Then vengeance juſt, againſt the ſame t'expreſſe ;
Now blood was paid with blood, for what was done
By cruell father, mother, cruell ſon,
Who did erect their cruelty in guilt,
And wronging innocents whoſe blood they ſpilt,
Philip and *Olympias* both were ſlain,
Aridæus and his Queen by ſlaughters ta'ne ;
Two other children by *Olympias* kill'd,
And *Cleopatra's* blood, now likewiſe ſpill'd,
If *Alexander* was not poyſoned,
Yet in the flower of's age, he muſt lie dead,
His wife and ſons then ſlain by this *Caſſander*,
And's kingdomes rent away by each Commander :
Thus may we hear, and fear, and ever ſay,
That hand is righteous ſtill which doth repay :
Theſe Captains now, the ſtile of Kings do take,
For to their Crowns, there's none can title make.
Demetrius is firſt, that ſo aſſumes,
To do as he, the reſt full ſoon preſumes,
To *Athens* then he goes, is entertain'd,
Not like a King, but like ſome God they fain'd ;
Moſt groſſely baſe, was this great adulation,
Who incenſe burnt, and offered oblation.

Theſe

These Kings fall now afresh to warres again,
Demetrius of Ptolomy doth gain ;
'Twould be an endlesse story to relate
Their severall battells, and their severall fate,
Antigonus and Seleuchus, now fight
Near Ephesus, each bringing all their might,
And he that conquerour shall now remain,
Of Asia the Lordship shall retain.
This day twixt these two foes ends all the strife,
For here Antigonus lost rule, and life,
Nor to his son did there one foot remain,
Of those dominions he did sometimes gain,
Demetrius with his troops to Athens flies,
Hoping to find succour in miseries.
But they adoring in prosperity,
Now shut their gates in his adversity,
He sorely griev'd at this his desperate state,
Tries foes, since friends will not compassionate,
His peace he then with old Seleuchus makes,
Who his fair daughter Stratonica takes,
Antiochus, Seleuchus dear lov'd son,
Is for this fresh young Lady half undone,
Falls so extreamly sick, all fear his life,
Yet dares not say, he loves his fathers wife ;
When his disease the skilfull Physician found,
He wittily his fathers mind did sound,
Who did no sooner understand the same,
But willingly resign'd the beauteous dame :
Cassander now must die, his race is run,
And leaves the ill got kingdomes he had won,
Two sons he left, born of King Philips daughter,
Who had an end put to their dayes by slaughter.
                                              Which

Which fhould fucceed, at variance they fell,
The mother would the youngeft fhould excell,
The eld'ft enrag'd did play the vipers part,
And with his Sword did pierce his mothers heart,
(Rather then *Philips* child muft longer live)
He, whom fhe gave his life, her death muft give)
This by *Lyfimachus* foon after flain,
(Whofe daughter unto wife, he'd newly ta'n)
The youngeft by *Demetrius* kill'd in fight,
Who took away his now pretended right :
Thus *Philips*, and *Caffander's* race is gone,
And fo falls out to be extinct in one,
Yea though *Caffander* died in his bed,
His feed to be extirpt, was deftined,
For blood which was decreed, that he fhould fpill,
Yet muft his children pay for fathers ill.
Jehu in killing *Ahabs* houfe did well,
Yet be aveng'd, muft th' blood of *Jefreel*.
Demetrius, *Caffanders* kingdomes gains,
And now as King, in *Macedon* he reigns ;
Seleuchus, *Afia* holds, that grieves him fore,
Thofe Countries large, his father got before,
Thefe to recover, mufters all his might,
And with his fon in law, will needs go fight :
There was he taken and imprifoned
Within an Ifle that was with pleafures fed,
Injoy'd what fo befeem'd his Royalty,
Onely reftrained of his liberty ;
After three years he dyed, left what he'd won
In *Greece*, unto *Amigonus*, his fon,
For his pofterity unto this day,
Did ne'r regain one foot in *Afia*.

Now

Now dyed the brave and noble *Ptolomy*,
Renown'd for bounty, valour, clemency,
Rich Ægypt left, and what elfe he had won
To *Philadelphus*, his more worthy Son.
Of the old Heroes, now but two remaine,
Seleuchus, and *Lyfimachus*; those twaine
Must needs goe try their fortune, and their might,
And fo *Lyfimachus* was flaine in fight.
'Twas no fmall joy, unto *Seleuchus* breaft,
That now he had out-lived all the reft:
Poffeffion he of *Europe* thinks to take,
And fo himfelfe the only Monarch make;
Whilft with thefe hopes, in *Greece* he did remaine,
He was by *Ptolomy Cerannus* flaine.
The fecond Son of the firft *Ptolomy*,
Who for rebellion unto him did fly,
Seleuchus was as Father, and a friend,
Yet by him had this moft unworthy end.
Thus with thefe Kingly Captaines have we done,
A little now, how the Succeffion run:
Antigonus, Seleuchus, and *Caffander,*
With *Ptolomy*, reign'd after *Alexander*;
Caffanders Sons, foone after's death were flaine,
So three Succeffors only did remaine;
Antigonus his Kingdoms loft, and's life,
Unto *Seleuchus*, author of that ftrife.
His Son *Demetrius*, all *Caffanders* gaines,
And his pofterity, the fame retaines,
Demetrius Son was call'd *Antigonus*,
And his againe, alfo *Demetrius*.
I muft let paffe thofe many battels fought,
Between thofe Kings, and noble *Pyrrus* ftout,

And

And his son *Alexander* of *Epire*,
Whereby immortall honour they acquire.
Demetrius had *Philip* to his son,
He *Perseus*, from him the kingdom's won,
Emillius the *Roman* Generall,
Did take his rule, his sons, himself and all.
This of *Antigonus*, his seed's the fate,
Whose kingdomes were subdu'd by th' *Roman* state.
Longer *Seleuchus* held the Royalty
In *Syria* by his posterity,
Antiochus Soter his son was nam'd,
To whom Ancient *Berosus* (so much fam'd)
His book of *Assurs* Monarchs dedicates,
Tells of their warres, their names, their riches, fates;
But this is perished with many more,
Which we oft wish were extant as before.
Antiochus Theos was *Soters* son,
Who a long warre with *Egypts* King begun.
The affinities and warres *Daniel* set forth,
And calls them there, the Kings of South, and North;
This *Theos* he was murthered by his wife,
Seleuchus reign'd, when he had lost his life,
A third *Seleuchus* next sits on the seat,
And then *Antiochus* surnam'd the great,
Seleuchus next *Antiochus* succeeds,
And then *Epiphanes*, whose wicked deeds,
Horrid massacres, murders, cruelties,
Against the Jewes, we read in *Macchabees*,
By him was set up the abomination
I'th' holy place, which caused desolation;
Antiochus Eupator was the next,
By Rebells and imposters daily vext;

So

So many Princes still were murthered,
The Royall blood was quite extinguished.
That *Tygranes* the great *Armenian* King,
To take the government was called in,
Him *Lucullus*, the *Romane* Generall
Vanquish'd in fight, and took those kingdomes all,
Of *Greece*, and *Syria* thus the rule did end,
In *Egypt* now a little time we'l spend.
First *Ptolomy* being dead, his famous son,
Cal'd *Philadelphus*, next sat on the throne,
The Library at *Alexandria* built,
With seven hundred thousand volumes fill'd,
The seventy two interpreters did seek,
They might translate the Bible into *Greek*,
His son was *Evergetes* the last Prince
That valour shew'd, vertue or excellence.
Philopater was *Evergete's* son,
After *Epiphanes*, sat on the Throne
Philometer : then *Evergetes* again.
And next to him, did false *Lathurus* reigne,
Alexander, then *Lathurus* in's stead,
Next *Auletes*, who cut off *Pompey's* head :
To all these names we *Ptolomy* must adde,
For since the first, that title still they had,
Fair *Cleopatra* next, last of that race,
Whom *Julius Cæsar* set in Royall place,
Her brother by him, lost his trayterous head
For *Pompey's* life, then plac'd her in his stead,
She with her Paramour *Mark Antony*,
Held for a time the *Egyptian* Monarchy :
Till great *Augustus* had with him a fight,
At *Actium* slain, his Navy put to flight .

                                           Then

Then poyſonous Aſpes ſhe ſets unto her Armes,
To take her life, and quit her from all harmes ;
For 'twas not death, nor danger, ſhe did dread,
But ſome diſgrace, in triumph to be led.
Here ends at laſt the *Grecian* Monarchy,
Which by the *Romans* had its deſtiny.
Thus Kings, and Kingdoms, have their times, and dates,
Their ſtandings, over-turnings, bounds, and fates ;
Now up, now down, now chief, and then brought under,
The Heavens thus rule, to fill the earth with wonder.
The *Aſſyrian* Monarchy long time did ſtand,
But yet the *Perſian* got the upper hand ;
The *Grecian*, them did utterly ſubdue,
And Millions were ſubjected unto few :
The *Grecian* longer then the *Perſian* ſtood,
Then came the *Romane*, like a raging flood,
And with the torrent of his rapid courſe,
Their Crownes, their Titles, riches beares by force.
The firſt, was likened to a head of gold,
Next, armes and breaſt, of ſilver to behold ;
The third, belly and thighs of braſſe in ſight,
And laſt was Iron, which breaketh all with might.
The Stone out of the Mountaine then did riſe,
And ſmote thoſe feet, thoſe legs, thoſe arms and thighs;
Then gold, ſilver, braſſe, iron, and all that ſtore,
Became like chaffe upon the threſhing floor ;
The firſt a Lion, ſecond was a Beare,
The third a Leopard, which four wings did rear ;
The laſt more ſtrong, and dreadfull, then the reſt,
Whoſe Iron teeth devoured every beaſt ;
And when he had no appetite to eate,
The reſidue he ſtamped under's feet :

But

But yet this Lion, Bear, this Leopard, Ram,
All trembling stand, before that powerfull Lambe.
With these three Monarchies, now have I done,
But how the fourth, their Kingdoms from them won;
And how from small beginnings it did grow,
To fill the world with terrour, and with woe:
My tired braine, leaves to a better pen,
This taske befits not women, like to men:
For what is past I blush, excuse to make,
But humbly stand, some grave reproof to take:
Pardon to crave, for errours, is but vaine,
The Subject was too high, beyond my straine;
To frame Apologie for some offence,
Converts our boldnesse, into impudence.
This my presumption (some now) to requite,
Ne sutor ultra crepidum, may write.

*After some dayes of rest, my restlesse heart,
To finish what begun, new thoughts impart
And maugre all resolves, my fancy wrought
This fourth to th' other three, now might be brought.
Shortnesse of time, and inability,
Will force me to a confus'd brevity;
Yet in this Chaos, one shall easily spy,
The vast limbs of a mighty Monarchy.
What e're is found amisse, take in best part,
As faults proceeding from my head, not heart.*

The

The *Roman* Monarchy,
being the Fourth, and laſt,
beginning, *Anno Mundi,*
3 2 1 3.

Tout *Romulus, Romes* Founder, and firſt
King,
Whom veſtall *Rhea,* into th' world did
bring
His Father was not *Mars,* as ſome devis'd,
But *Æmulus,* in Armour all diſguis'd.
Thus he deceiv'd his Neece, ſhe might not know
The double injury, he then did doe :
Where Shepheards once had Coats, and Sheep their
Folds,
Where Swaines, and ruſtick Peaſants made their
Holds.
A Citty faire did *Romulvs* erect:
The Miſtris of the World, in each reſpect.
His Brother *Remus* there, by him was ſlaine,
For leaping o're the Walls with ſome diſdaine ;
The Stones at firſt was cimented with bloud,
And bloudy hath it prov'd, ſince firſt it ſtood :

This City built, and Sacrifices done,
A forme of Government he next begun ;
A hundred Senators he likewise chose,
And with the stile of *Patres* honour'd those ;
His City to replenish, men he wants,
Great priviledges then, to all he grants,
That wil within these strong built walls reside,
And this new gentle Government abide :
Of Wives there was so great a scarsity,
They to their neighbours sue, for a supply ;
But all disdaine alliance then to make,
So *Romulus* was forc'd this course to take.
Great shewes he makes at Tilt, and Turnament,
To see these sports, the *Sabins* all are bent ;
Their Daughters by the *Romans* then were caught,
For to recover them, a Feild was fought ;
But in the end, to finall peace they come,
And *Sabins*, as one people, dwelt in *Rome*.
The *Romans* now more potent 'gin to grow,
And *Fedinates* they wholly over-throw :
But *Romulus* then comes unto his end,
Some faining say, to heav'n he did ascend ;
Others, the seven and thirtyeth of his reigne
Affirme, that by the Senate he was slaine.

Numa Pompilius.

NVma *Pompilius*, is next chosen King,
Held for his Piety, some sacred thing ;
To *Janus*, he that famous Temple built,
Kept shut in peace, but ope when bloud was spilt ;

Religious

Religious Rites, and Cuſtoms inſtituted,
And Prieſts, and Flamines likewiſe he deputed ;
Their Augurs ſtrange, their habit, and attire,
And veſtall Maids to keep the holy fire.
Goddeſſe *Ægeria* this to him told,
So to delude the people he was bold :
Forty three yeares he rul'd with generall praiſe,
Accounted for ſome god in after dayes.

Tullus Hoſtilius.

TUllus *Hoſtilius*, was third *Roman* King,
  Who Martiall Diſcipline in uſe did bring ;
  War with the antient *Albans* he doth wage,
The ſtrife to end, ſix Brothers doe ingage ;
Three call'd *Horatii*, on *Romans* ſide,
And *Curiatii*, three *Albans* provide ;
The *Romans* Conquereth, others yeeld the day,
Yet for their compact, after falſe they play :
The *Romans* ſore incens'd, their Generall ſlay,
And from old *Alba* fetch the wealth away ;
Of *Latine* Kings this was long ſince the Seat,
But now demoliſhed, to make *Rome* great.
Thirty two years doth *Tullus* reigne, then dye,
Leaves *Rome*, in wealth and power, ſtill growing high.

Aneus Martius.

NExt, *Aneus Martius* ſits upon the Throne,
  Nephew unto *Pomphilius* dead, and gone ;

N

Rome

Rome he inlarg'd, new built againe the wall,
Much stronger, and more beautifull withall;
A stately Bridge he over *Tyber* made,
Of Boats, and Oares, no more they need the aide;
Faire *Ostia* he built, this Town, it stood,
Close by the mouth of famous *Tyber* flood:
Twenty foure yeare, th' time of his royall race,
Then unto death unwillingly gives place.

Tarquinius Priscus.

TArquin, a Greek, at *Corinth* borne, and bred;
    Who for sedition from his Country fled;
        Is entertain'd at *Rome*, and in short time,
By wealth, and favour, doth to honour climbe;
He after *Martius* death the Kingdome had,
A hundred Senatours he more did adde;
Warres with the *Latins* he againe renewes,
And Nations twelve, of *Tuscany* subdues.
To such rude triumphs, as young *Rome* then had,
Much state, and glory, did this *Priscus* adde:
Thirty eight yeares (this Stranger borne) did reigne,
And after all, by *Aneus* Sons was slaine.

Servius Tullius.

NExt, *Servius Tullius* sits upon the Throne,
    Ascends not up, by merits of his owne,
        But by the favour, and the speciall grace
Of *Tanaquil*, late Queen, obtaines the place;

He

He ranks the people, into each degree,
As wealth had made them of abilitie ;
A generall Muſter takes, which by account,
To eighty thouſand ſoules then did amount :
Forty foure yeares did *Servius Tullius* reigne,
And then by *Tarquin, Priſcus* Son, was ſlaine.

Tarquinius Superbus, the laſt *Roman* King.

TArquin the proud, from manners called ſo,
Sate on the Throne, when he had ſlaine his foe ;
Sextus his Son, doth (moſt unworthily)
Lucretia force , mirrour of chaſtety ;
She loathed ſo the fact, ſhe loath'd her life,
And ſhed her guiltleſſe blood, with guilty knife .
Her Husband ſore incens'd,to quit this wrong,
With *Junius Brutus* roſe, and being ſtrong,
The *Tarquins* they from *Rome* with ſpeed expell,
In baniſhment perpetuall, to dwell ;
The Government they change, a new one bring,
And people ſweare, ne're to accept of King.

The end of the Roman *Monarchy,*
being the fourth and laſt.

A

A Dialogue between Old *England* and New, concerning their prefent troubles.
Anno 1642.

New England.

ALas, deare Mother, faireſt Queen, and beſt,
With honour, wealth, and peace, happy and
bleſt;
What ayles thee hang thy head, and croſſe
thine armes?
And ſit i'th duſt, to ſigh theſe ſad alarms?
What deluge of new woes thus over-whelme
The glories of thy ever famous Realme?
What meanes this wailing tone, this mourning guiſe?
Ah, tell thy Daughter, ſhe may ſimpathize.

Old England.

Art ignorant indeed, of theſe my woes?
Or muſt my forced tongue theſe griefes diſcloſe?

And

And muſt my ſelfe diſſect my tatter'd ſtate,
Which 'maz ed Chriſtendome ſtands wondring at ?
And thou a childe, a Limbe, and doſt not feele
My weakned fainting body now to reele ?
This Phiſick-purging-potion I have taken,
Will bring Conſumption, or an Ague quaking,
Unleſſe ſome Cordial thou fetch from high,
Which preſent help may eaſe this malady.
If I deceaſe, doſt think thou ſhalt ſurvive ?
Or by my waſting ſtate, doſt think to thrive ?
Then weigh our caſe, if 't be not juſtly ſad,
Let me lament alone, while thou art glad.

New England.

And thus, alas, your ſtate you much deplore,
In generall terms, but will not ſay wherefore :
What Medicine ſhall I ſeek to cure this woe,
If th' wound's ſo dangerous I may not know ?
But you perhaps would have me gueſſe it out,
What, hath ſome *Hengiſt*, like that *Saxon* ſtout,
By fraud, and force, uſurp'd thy flowring crown,
And by tempeſtuous Wars thy fields trod down ?
Or hath *Canutus*, that brave valiant *Dane*,
The regall, peacefull Scepter from thee tane ?
Or is't a *Norman*, whoſe victorious hand
With *Engliſh* blood bedews thy conquered Land ?
Or is't inteſtine Wars that thus offend ?
Doe *Maud*, and *Stephen* for the Crown contend ?
Doe Barons riſe, and ſide againſt their King ?
And call in Forreign ayde, to help the thing ?

N 3   Muſt

Muſt *Edward* be depos'd, or is't the houre
That ſecond *Richard* muſt be clapt i'th' Tower ?
Or is the fatall jarre againe begun,
That from the red, white pricking Roſes ſprung ?
Muſt *Richmonds* ayd, the Nobles now implore,
To come, and break the tuſhes of the Boar ?
If none of theſe, deare Mother, what's your woe ?
Pray, doe not feare *Spaines* bragging Armado ?
Doth your Allye, faire *France*, conſpire your wrack?
Or, doth the *Scots* play falſe behind your back ?
Doth *Holland* quit you ill, for all your love ?
Whence is this ſtorme, from Earth, or Heaven above ?
Is't Drought, is't Famine, or is't Peſtilence ?
Doſt feele the ſmart, or feare the conſequence ?
Your humble Childe intreats you, ſhew your grief,
Though Armes, nor Purſe ſhe hath, for your releif :
Such is her poverty, yet ſhall be found
A ſupplyant for your help, as ſhe is bound.

Old England.

I muſt confeſſe, ſome of thoſe Sores you name,
My beauteous Body at this preſent maime ;
But forraigne Foe, nor fained friend I feare,
For they have work enough (thou knowſt)elſewhere ;
Nor is it *Alcies* Son, and *Henries* Daughter,
Whoſe proud contention cauſe this ſlaughter ;
Nor Nobles ſiding, to make *John* no King
French *Lewis* unjuſtly to the Crown to bring ;
No *Edward*, *Richard*, to loſe rule, and life,
Nor no *Lancaſtrians*, to renew old ſtrife ;

No

No Crook-backt Tyrant, now ufurps the Seat,
Whofe tearing tusks did wound, and kill, and threat:
No Duke of *Tork*, nor Earle of *March*, to foyle
Their hands in Kindreds blood, whom they did foyle:
No need of *Teder*, Rofes to unite,
None knowes which is the Red, or which the White:
Spaines braving Fleet a fecond time is funke,
France knowes, how of my fury fhe hath drunk;
By *Edward* third, and *Henry* fifth of fame,
Her Lillies in mine Armes avouch the fame.
My Sifter *Scotland* hurts me now no more,
Though fhe hath bin injurious heretofore.
What *Holland* is, I am in fome fufpence,
But truft not much unto his Excellence;
For wants, fure fome I feele, but more I feare,
And for the Peftilence, who knowes how neare?
Famine, and Plague, two fifters of the Sword,
Deftruction to a Land doth foone afford;
They're for my punifhments ordain'd on high,
Unleffe thy teares prevent it fpeedily.
But yet, I anfwer not what you demand,
To fhew the grievance of my troubled Land;
Before I tell the effect, ile fhew the caufe,
Which are my Sins, the breach of facred Lawes;
Idolatry, fupplanter of a Nation,
With foolifh fuperftitious adoration;
And lik'd, and countenanc'd by men of might,
The Gofpel is trod down, and hath no right;
Church Offices are fold, and bought, for gaine,
That Pope, had hope, to finde *Rome* here againe;
For Oathes, and Blafphemies did ever eare
From *Beelzebub* himfelf, fuch language heare?

N 4   What

What scorning of the Saints of the most high,
What injuries did daily on them lye;
What false reports, what nick-names did they take,
Not for their owne, but for their Masters sake;
And thou, poore soule, wast jeer'd among the rest,
Thy flying for the Truth I made a jeast;
For Sabbath-breaking, and for Drunkennesse,
Did ever Land prophannesse more expresse?
From crying bloods, yet cleansed am not I,
Martyrs, and others, dying causelesly:
How many Princely heads on blocks laid down,
For nought, but title to a fading Crown?
'Mongst all the cruelties which I have done,
 Oh, *Edwards* Babes, and *Clarence* haplesse Son,
O *Jane*, why didst thou dye in flowring prime,
Because of Royall Stem, that was thy crime;
For Bribery, *Adultery*, for Thefts, and Lyes,
Where is the Nation, I cann't paralize;
With Usury, Extortion, and Oppression,
These be the *Hydra's* of my stout transgression;
These be the bitter fountains, heads, and roots,
Whence flow'd the source, the sprigs, the boughs, and
Of more then thou canst heare, or I relate,   (fruits;
That with high hand I still did perpetrate;
For these, were threatned the wofull day,
I mock'd the Preachers, put it faire away;
The Sermons yet upon record doe stand,
That cry'd, destruction to my wicked Land:
These Prophets mouthes (alls the while) was stopt,
Unworthily, some backs whipt, and eares crept;
Their reverent cheeks, did beare the glorious markes
Of stinking, stigmatizing, Romish Clerkes;

                                    Some

Some lost their livings, some in prison pent,
Some grossely fin'd, from friends to exile went:
Their silent tongues to heaven did vengeance cry,
Who heard their cause, and wrongs judg'd righteously,
And will repay it sevenfold in my lap,
This is fore-runner of my after-clap,
Nor took I warning by my neighbours falls,
I saw sad *Germanie's* dismantled walls.
I saw her people famish'd, Nobles slain,
Her fruitfull land, a barren heath remain.
I saw (unmov'd) her Armies foil'd and fled,
Wives forc'd, babes toss'd, her houses calcined,
I saw strong *Rochel* yeelding to her foe,
Thousands of starved Christians there also.
I saw poore *Ireland* bleeding out her last, }
Such cruelty as all reports have past.   }
My heart obdurate, stood not yet agast.   }
Now sip I of that cup, and just 't may be,
The bottome dregs reserved are for me.

New England.

To all you've said, sad mother, I assent
Your fearfull sinnes, great cause there's to lament,
My guilty hands(in part)hold up with you,
A sharer in your punishment 's my due,
But all you say, amounts to this effect,
Not what you feel, but what you do expect.
Pray in plain termes, what is your present grief,
Then let's join heads, and hands for your relief.

                                        Old

Old England.

Well, to the matter then, there's grown of late,
'Twixt King and Peeres a question of state,
Which is the chief, the law, or else the King,
One saith its he, the other no such thing.
My better part in Court of Parliament,
To ease my groaning land shew their intent,
To crush the proud, and right to each man deal.
To help the Church, and stay the Common-Weal,
So many obstacles comes in their way,
As puts me to a stand what I should say,
Old customes, new Prerogatives stood on,
Had they not held law fast, all had been gone,
Which by their prudence stood them in such stead,
They took high *Strafford* lower by the head,
And to their *Laud* be't spoke, they held i'th' Tower,
All *Englands* Metropolitane that houre,
This done, an Act they would have passed fain,
No prelate should his Bishoprick retain ;
Here tugg'd they hard indeed, for all men saw,
This must be done by Gospel, not by law.
Next the *Militia* they urged sore,
This was deny'd, I need not say wherefore.
The King displeas'd, at *York* himself absents,
They humbly beg return, shew their intents,
The writing, printing, posting to and fro,
Shews all was done, I'll therefore let it go.
But now I come to speak of my disaster,
Contention's grown 'twixt Subjects and their Master :

They

They worded it so long, they fell to blows,
That thousands lay on heaps, here bleeds my woes.
I that no warres, so many yeares have known,
Am now destroy'd, and slaughter'd by mine own,
But could the field alone this cause decide,
One battell, two or three I might abide,
But these may be beginnings of more woe,
Who knows, the worst, the best may overthrow;
Religion, Gospell, here lies at the stake,
Pray now dear child, for sacred *Zions* sake,
Oh pity me, in this sad perturbation,
My plundered *Townes*, my houses devastation,
My ravisht virgins, and my young men slain,
My wealthy trading faln, my dearth of grain,
The seed time's come, but Ploughman hath no hope,
Because he knows not, who shall inn his crop:
The poore they want their pay, their children bread,
Their wofull mother's tears unpitied.
If any pity in thy heart remain,
Or any child-like love thou dost retain,
For my relief now use thy utmost skill,
And recompence me good, for all my ill.

New England.

Dear mother cease complaints, and wipe your eyes,
Shake off your dust, chear up, and now arise,
You are my mother, nurse, I once your flesh,
Your sunken bowels gladly would refresh:
Your griefs I pity much, but should do wrong,
To weep for that we both have pray'd for long,

To

To see these latter dayes of hop'd for good,
That Right may have its right, though't be with blood;
After dark Popery the day did clear,
But now the Sun in's brightnesse shall appear,
Blest be the Nobles of thy Noble Land,
With (ventur'd lives) for truths defence that stand,
Blest be thy Commons, who for Common good,
And thine infringed Lawes have boldly stood.
Blest be thy Counties which do aid thee still
With hearts and states, to testifie their will.
Blest be thy Preachers, who do chear thee on,
O cry: the sword of God, and *Gideon*:
And shall I not on those wish *Mero's* curse,
That help thee not with prayers, arms, and purse,
And for my self, let miseries abound,
If mindlesse of thy state I e'r be found.
These are the dayes, the Churches foes to crush,
To root out Prelates, head, tail, branch, and rush.
Let's bring *Baals* vestments out, to make a fire,
Their Myters, Surplices, and all their tire,
Copes, Rochets, Crossiers, and such trash,
And let their names consume, but let the flash
Light Christendome, and all the world to see,
We hate *Romes* Whore, with all her trumperie.
Go on brave *Essex*, shew whose son thou art,
Not false to King, nor Countrey in thy heart,
But those that hurt his people and his Crown,
By force expell, destroy, and tread them down :
Let Gaoles be fill'd with th' remnant of that pack,
And sturdy *Tyburn* loaded till it crack,
And yee brave Nobles, chase away all fear,
And to this blessed Cause closely adhere

O

O mother, can you weep, and have such Peeres.
When they are gone, then drown your self in teares.
If now you weep so much, that then no more,
The briny Ocean will o'rflow your shore,
These, these, are they (I trust) with *Charles* our King,
Out of all mists, such glorious dayes will bring,
That dazzled eyes beholding much shall wonder
At that thy setled Peace, thy wealth and splendour,
Thy Church and Weal, establish'd in such manner,
That all shall joy that thou display'dst thy banner,
And discipline erected, so I trust,
That nursing Kings, shall come and lick thy dust :
Then Justice shall in all thy Courts take place,
Without respect of persons, or of case,
Then bribes shall cease, and suits shall not stick long,
Patience, and purse of Clients for to wrong :
Then High Commissions shall fall to decay,
And Pursevants and Catchpoles want their pay,
So shall thy happy Nation ever flourish,
When truth and righteousnesse they thus shall nourish.
When thus in Peace : thine Armies brave send out,
To sack proud *Rome*, and all her vassalls rout :
There let thy name, thy fame, thy valour shine,
As did thine Ancestours in *Palestine*,
And let her spoils, full pay, with int'rest be,
Of what unjustly once she poll'd from thee,
Of all the woes thou canst let her be sped,
Execute toth' full the vengeance threatned.
Bring forth the beast that rul'd the world with's beek,
And tear his flesh, and set your feet on's neck,
And make his filthy den so desolate,
To th' 'stonishment of all that knew his state.

This

This done, with brandish'd swords, to *Turky* go,
(For then what is't, but English blades dare do)
And lay her waft, for fo's the facred doom,
And do to *Gog,* as thou haft done to *Rome.*
Oh *Abrahams* feed lift up your heads on high.
For fure the day of your redemption's nigh ;
The fcales fhall fall from your long blinded eyes,
And him you fhall adore, who now defpife,
Then fulnes of the Nations in fhall flow,
And Jew and Gentile, to one worfhip go,
Then follows dayes of happineffe and reft,
Whofe lot doth fall to live therein is bleft :
No Canaanite fhall then be found ith' land,
And holineffe, on horfes bells fhall ftand,
If this make way thereto, then figh no more,
But if at all, thou didft not fee't before.
Farewell dear mother, Parliament, prevail,
And in a while you'l tell another tale.

An

An Elegie upon that Ho-nourable and renowned Knight,

Sir *Philip Sidney*, who was untime-ly slaine at the Seige of *Zutpbon*, Anno 1 5 8 6.

By *A. B.* in the yeare, 1638.

Hen *England* did injoy her Halsion
dayes,
Her noble *Sidney* wore the Crown of
Bayes;
No lesse an Honour to our *Britiſh* Land,
Then ſhe that ſway'd the Scepter with her hand:
Mars and *Minerva* did in one agree,
Of Armes, and Arts, thou ſhould'ſt a patterne be.
Calliope with *Terpſecher* did ſing,
Of Poeſie, and of Muſick thou wert King;
Thy Rhethorick it ſtruck *Polimnia* dead,
Thine Eloquence made *Mercury* wax red;
Thy Logick from *Euterpe* won the Crown,
More worth was thine, then *Clio* could ſet down.
Thalia and *Melpomene*, ſay th' truth,
(Witneſſe *Arcadia*, penn'd in his youth)

Are

Are not his Tragick Comedies so acted,
As if your nine-fold wit had been compacted ;
To shew the world, they never saw before,
That this one Volumne should exhaust your store.
I praise thee not for this, it is unfit,
This was thy shame, O miracle of wit:
Yet doth thy shame (with all) purchase renown,
What doe thy vertues then ? Oh, honours crown !
In all records, thy Name I ever see,
Put with an Epithet of dignity ;
Which shewes, thy worth was great, thine honour such,
The love thy Country ought thee, was as much .
Let then, none dis-allow of these my straines,
Which have the self-same blood yet in my veines ;
Who honours thee for what was honourable,
But leaves the rest, as most unprofitable :
Thy wiser dayes, condemn'd thy witty works,
Who knowes the Spels that in thy Rethorick lurks ?
But some infatuate fooles soone caught therein,
Found *Cupids* Dam, had never such a Gin ;
Which makes severer eyes but scorn thy Story,
And modest Maids, and Wives, blush at thy glory ;
Yet, he's a beetle head, that cann't discry
A world of treasure, in that rubbish lye ;
And doth thy selfe, thy worke, and honour wrong,
(O brave Refiner of our *Brittish* Tongue ;)
That sees not learning, valour, and morality,
Justice, friendship, and kind hospitality ;
Yea, and Divinity within thy Book,
Such were prejudicate, and did not look :
But to say truth, thy worth I shall but staine,
Thy fame, and praise, is farre beyond my straine ;

Yet

Yet great *Augustus* was content (we know)
To be saluted by a silly Crow ;
Then let such Crowes as I, thy praises sing,
A Crow's a Crow, and *Cæsar* is a King.
O brave *Achilles*, I wish some *Homer* would
Engrave on Marble, in characters of Gold,
What famous feats thou didst, on *Flanders* coast,
Of which, this day, faire *Belgia* doth boast.
O *Zutphon*, *Zutphon*, that most fatall City,
Made famous by thy fall, much more's the pitty;
Ah, in his blooming prime, death pluckt this Rose,
E're he was ripe ; his thred cut *Atropos*.
Thus man is borne to dye, and dead is he;
Brave *Hector* by the walls of *Troy*, we see :
Oh, who was neare thee, but did sore repine ;
He rescued not with life, that life of thine,
But yet impartiall Death this Boone did give,
Though *Sidney* dy'd, his valiant name should live ;
And live it doth, in spight of death, through fame,
Thus being over-come, he over-came.
Where is that envious tongue, but can afford,
Of this our noble *Scipio* some good word ?
Noble *Bartas*, this to thy praise adds more,
In sad, sweet verse, thou didst his death deplore;
Illustrious *Stella*, thou didst thine full well,
If thine aspect was milde to *Astrophell* ;
I feare thou wert a Commet, did portend
Such prince as he, his race should shortly end :
If such Stars as these, sad presages be,
I wish no more such Blazers we may see;
But thou art gone, such Meteors never last,
And as thy beauty, so thy name would wast.

O   But

But that it is record by *Philips* hand,
That such an omen once was in our land ,
O Princely *Philip*, rather *Alexander*,
Who wert of honours band, the chief Commander.
How could that *Stella*, so confine thy will ?
To wait till she, her influence distill,
I rather judg'd thee of his mind that wept,
To be within the bounds of one world kept,
But *Omphala*, set *Hercules* to spin,
And *Mars* himself was ta'n by *Venus* gin ;
Then wonder lesse, if warlike *Philip* yield,
When such a *Hero* shoots him out o'th' field,
Yet this preheminence thou hast above,
That thine was true, but theirs adult'rate love.
Fain would I shew, how thou fame's path didst tread,
But now into such Lab'rinths am I led
With endlesse turnes, the way I find not out,
For to persist, my muse is more in doubt:
Calls me ambitious fool, that durst aspire,
Enough for me to look, and so admire.
And makes me now with *Sylvester* confesse,
But *Sydney's* Muse, can sing his worthinesse.
Too late my errour see, that durst presume
To fix my faltring lines upon his tomb:
Which are in worth, as far short of his due,
As *Vulcan* is, of *Venus* native hue.
Goodwill, did make my head-long pen to run,
Like unwise *Phaeton* his ill guided sonne,
Till taught to's cost , for his too hasty hand,
He left that charge by *Phœbus* to be man'd :
So proudly foolish I, with *Phaeton* strive,
Fame's flaming Chariot for to drive.

Till

Till terrour-struck for my too weighty charge.
I leave't in brief, *Apollo* do't at large.
Apollo laught to patch up what's begun,
He bad me drive, and he would hold the Sun ;
Better my hap, then was his darlings fate,
For dear regard he had of *Sydney's* state,
Who in his Deity, had so deep share,
That those that name his fame, he needs must spare,
He promis'd much, but th' muses had no will,
To give to their detractor any quill.
With high disdain, they said they gave no more,
Since *Sydney* had exhausted all their store,
That this contempt it did the more perplex,
In being done by one of their own sex ;
They took from me, the scribling pen I had,
I to be eas'd of such a task was glad.
For to revenge his wrong, themselves ingage,
And drave me from *Parnassus* in a rage,
Not because, sweet *Sydney's* fame was not dear,
But I had blemish'd theirs, to make 't appear :
I pensive for my fault, sat down, and then,
Errata, through their leave threw me my pen,
For to conclude my poem two lines they daigne,
Which writ, she bad return't to them again.
So *Sydney's* fame, I leave to *England's* Rolls,
His bones do lie interr'd in stately *Pauls.*

His Epitaph.

Here lies intomb'd in fame, under this stone,
Philip *and* Alexander both in one.

Heir

Heire to the *Muses*, the Son of Mars *in truth*,
Learning, *valour, beauty, all in vertuous youth:*
His *praise is much, this shall suffice my pen,*
That Sidney *dy'd the quintessence of men.*

In honour of *Du Bartas.*
1 6 4 1.

A. B.

Amongst the happy wits this Age hath showne,
Great, deare, sweet *Bartas,* thou art matchlesse
    knowne ;
My ravisht eyes, and heart, with faltering tongue,
In humble wise have vow'd their service long ;
But knowing th' taske so great, and strength but small,
Gave o're the work, before begun withall :
My dazled sight of late, review'd thy lines,
Where Art, and more then Art in Nature shines ;
Reflection from their beaming altitude,
Did thaw my frozen hearts ingratitude ;
Which Rayes, darting upon some richer ground,
Had caused flowers, and fruits, soone to abound ;
But barren I, my Daysey here doe bring,
A homely flower in this my latter spring ;
If Summer, or my Autumne age, doe yeeld
Flowers, fruits, in garden, orchard, or in field ;

They

They shall be consecrated in my Verse,
And prostrate off'red at great *Bartas* Herse.
My Muse unto a Childe, I sitly may compare,
Who sees the riches of some famous Fayre;
He feeds his eyes, but understanding lacks,
To comprehend the worth of all those knacks;
The glittering Plate, and Jewels, he admires,
The Hats, and Fans, the Plumes, and Ladies tires,
And thousand times his mazed minde doth wish
Some part, at least, of that brave wealth was his;
But seeing empty wishes nought obtaine,
At night turnes to his Mothers cot againe,
And tells her tales; (his full heart over-glad)
Of all the glorious sights his eyes have had :
But findes too soone his want of Eloquence,
The silly Pratler speakes no word of sence;
And seeing utterance fayle his great desires,
Sits down in silence, deeply he admires :
Thus weake brain'd I, reading thy lofty stile,
Thy profound Learning; viewing other while
Thy Art, in Naturall Philosophy:
Thy Saint-like minde in grave Divinity,
Thy peircing skill in high Astronomy,
And curious in-sight in Anatomy;
Thy Phisick, Musick, and State policy,
Valour in War, in Peace good Husbandry.
Sure liberall Nature, did with Art not small,
In all the Arts make thee most liberall;
A thousand thousand times my senslesse Sences,
Movelesse, stand charm'd by thy sweet influences,
More sencelesse then the Stones to *Amphions* Lute,
Mine eyes are sightlesse, and my tongue is mute;

My

My full aſtoniſh'd heart doth pant to break,
Through grief it wants a faculty to ſpeak,
Vollies of praiſes could I eccho then,
Had I an Angels voice, or *Barta's* pen,
But wiſhes cann't accompliſh my deſire,
Pardon, if I adore, when I admire.
O *France*, in him thou didſt more glory gain,
Then in thy *Pippin, Martell, Charlemain.*
Then in Saint *Lewis*, or thy laſt *Henry* great,
Who tam'd his foes, in bloud, in ſkarres and ſweat,
Thy fame is ſpread as farre, I dare be bold,
In all the Zones, the temp'rate, hot and cold,
Their trophies were but heaps of wounded ſlain,
Thine the quinteſſence of an Heroick brain.
The Oaken garland ought to deck their browes,
Immortall bayes, all men to thee allows.
Who in thy tryumphs (never won by wrongs)
Leadſt millions chaind by eyes, by eares, by tongues,
Oft have I wondred at the hand of heaven,
In giving one, what would have ſerved ſeven.
If e'r this golden gift was ſhowr'd on any,
Thy double portion would have ſerved many.
Unto each man his riches are aſſign'd,
Of names, of ſtate, of body, or of mind,
Thou haſt thy part of all, but of the laſt.
Oh pregnant brain, Oh comprehenſion vaſt:
Thy haughty ſtile, and rapted wit ſublime,
All ages wondring at, ſhall never clime.
Thy ſacred works are not for imitation,
But monuments for future admiration :
Thus *Bartas* fame ſhall laſt while ſtarres do ſtand,
And whilſt there's aire, or fire, or ſea or land.

But

But left my ignorance fhould doe thee wrong,
To celebrate thy merits in my Song,
Ile leave thy praife, to thofe fhall doe thee right,
Good will, not skill, did caufe me bring my mite.

His Epitaph.

HEre lyes the pearle of France, Parnaſſus glory,
  The world rejoyc'd at's birth, at's death was ſorry;
Art and Nature joyn'd, by heavens high decree,
Now ſhew'd what once they ought, Humanity,
And Natures Law; had it been revocable,
To reſcue him from death, Art had been able:
But Nature vanquiſh'd Art, ſo Bartas dy'd,
But Fame, out-living both, he is reviv'd.

In honour of that High and Mighty Princeſs, Queen ELIZABETH, of moſt happy memory.

The Proem.

ALthough great Queen, thou now in ſilence lye,
  Yet thy loud Herauld Fame, doth to the sky
  Thy wondrous worth proclaime, in every clime,
And ſo has vow'd, whilſt there is world, or time;

So great's thy glory, and thine excellence,
The found thereof raps every humane fence ;
That men account it no impiety,
To fay, thou wert a flefhly Deity :
Thoufands bring off'rings, (though out of date)
Thy world of honours to accumulate,
Mongft hundred Hecatombs of roaring Verfe,
'Mine bleating ftands before thy royall Herfe :
Thou never didft, nor canft thou now difdaine,
T' accept the tribute of a loyall Braine ;
Thy clemency did yerft efteeme as much
The acclamations of the poore, as rich ;
Which makes me deeme, my rudeneffe is no wrong,
Though I refound thy greatneffe 'mongft the throng.

The Poem.

NO *Phœnix* Pen, nor *Spencers* Poetry,
    No *Speeds*, nor *Chamdens* learned Hiftory;
Eliza's works, wars, praife, can e're compact,
The World's the Theater where fhe did act;
No memories, nor volumes can containe,
The nine *Olimp'ades* of her happy reigne ;
Who was fo good, fo juft, fo learn'd, fo wife,
From all the Kings on earth fhe won the prize ;
Nor fay I more then duly is her due,
Millions will teftifie that this is true ;
She hath wip'd off th' afperfion of her Sex,
That women wifdome lack to play the Rex ;
Spaines Monarch fa's not fo; not yet his Hoaft,
She taught them better manners to their coft.

                                            The

The *Salique* Law had not in force now been,
If *France* had ever hop'd for such a Queen ;
But can you Doctors now this point dispute,
She's argument enough to make you mute ;
Since first the Sun did run, his ne'r runn'd race,
And earth had twice a yeare, a new old face :
Since time was time, and man unmanly man,
Come shew me such a Phœnix if you can ;
Was ever people better rul'd then hers ?
Was ever Land more happy, freed from stirs ?
Did ever wealth in *England* so abound ?
Her Victories in forraigne Coasts resound ?
Ships more invincible then *Spaines*, her foe
She ract, she sackt, she sunk his Armadoe ;
Her stately Troops advanc'd to *Lisbons* wall,
Don Anthony in's right for to install ;
She frankly help'd *Franks* (brave) distressed King,
The *States* united now her fame doe sing ;
She their Protectrix was, they well doe know.
Unto our dread Virago, what they owe :
Her Nobles sacrific'd their noble blood,
Nor men, nor coyne she spar'd, to doe them good ;
The rude untamed *Irish* she did quell,
And *Tiron* bound, before her picture fell.
Had ever Prince such Counsellors as she ?
Her selfe *Minerva*, caus'd them so to be ;
Such Souldiers, and such Captaines never seen,
As were the subjects of our (*Pallas*) Queen :
Her Sea-men through all straights the world did round,
Terra incognitæ might know her sound ;
Her *Drake* came laded home with *Spanish* gold,
Her *Essex* took *Cades*, their *Herculean* hold :

But

But time would faile me, so my wit would to,
To tell of halfe she did, or she could doe ;
Semiramis to her is but obscure,
More infamie then fame she did procure ;
She plac'd her glory but on *Babels* walls,
Worlds wonder for a time, but yet it falls ;
Feirce *Tomris* (*Cirus* Heads-man, *Sythians* Queen)
Had put her Harnesse off, had she but seen
Our *Amazon* i' th' Camp at *Tilberry*:
(Judging all valour, and all Majesty)
Within that Princesse to have residence,
And prostrate yeelded to her Excellence :
Dido first Foundresse of proud *Carthage* walls,
(Who living consummates her Funerals)
A great *Eliza*, but compar'd with ours,
How vanisheth her glory, wealth, and powers ;
Proud profuse *Cleopatra*, whose wrong name,
Instead of glory prov'd her Countries shame :
Of her what worth in Story's to be seen,
But that she was a rich *Ægyptian* Queen :
Zenobia, potent Empresse of the East,
And of all these without compare the best ;
(Whom none but great *Aurelius* could quell)
Yet for our Queen is no fit parallel :
She was a Phœnix Queen, so shall she be,
Her ashes not reviv'd more Phœnix she ;
Her personall perfections, who would tell,
Must dip his Pen i' th' Heliconian Well ;
Which I may not, my pride doth but aspire,
To read what others write, and then admire.
Now say, have women worth, or have they none ?
Or had they some, but with our Queen ist gone ?

                                                Nay

Nay Masculines, you have thus tax'd us long,
But she though dead, will vindicate our wrong.
Let such, as say our sex is void of reason,
Know 'tis a slander now, but once was treason.
But happy *England*, which had such a Queen,
O happy, happy, had those dayes still been,
But happinesse, lies in a higher sphere,
Then wonder not, *Eliza* moves not here.
Full fraught with honour, riches, and with dayes :
She set, she set, like *Titan* in his rayes,
No more shall rise or set such glorious Sun,
Untill the heavens great revolution :
If then new things, their old form must retain,
Eliza shall rule *Albian* once again.

Her Epitaph.

Here sleeps T H E *Queen, this is the royall bed*
O'th' Damask Rose, sprung from the white and red,
Whose sweet perfume fills the all-filling aire,
This Rose is withered, once so lovely faire,
On neither tree did grow such Rose before,
The greater was our gain, our losse the more.

Another.

Here lies the pride of Queens, pattern of Kings,
So blaze it fame, here's feathers for thy wings,
Here lies the envy'd, yet unparralell'd Prince,
Whose living vertues speak (though dead long since)
If many worlds, as that fantastick framed,
In every one, be her great glory famed.

1 6 4 3.   *Davids*

Davids Lamentation for Saul, and Jonathan, 2 Sam. 1. 19.

ALas, flaine is the head of *Ifrael*,
Illuftrious *Saul*, whofe beauty did excell
Upon thy places, mountan'ous and high,
How did the mighty fall, and falling dye?
In *Gath*, let not this thing be fpoken on,
Nor publifhed in ftreets of *Afkelon*,
Left Daughters of the *Philiftins* rejoyce,
Left the uncircumcis'd lift up their voyce:
O! *Gilbo* Mounts, let never pearled dew,
Nor fruitfull fhowres your barren tops beftrew,
Nor fields of offerings e're on you grow,
Nor any pleafant thing e're may you show;
For the mighty ones did foone decay,
The Shield of *Saul* was vilely caft away;
There had his dignity fo fore a foyle,
As if his head ne're felt the facred Oyle:
Sometimes from crimfon blood of gaftly ftaine,
The bow of *Jonathan* ne're turn'd in vaine,
Nor from the fat, and fpoyles, of mighty men,
Did *Saul* with bloodleffe Sword turne back agen.

Pleafant

Pleasant and lovely were they both in life,
And in their deaths was found no parting strife;
Swifter then swiftest Eagles, so were they,
Stronger then Lions, ramping for their prey.
O *Israels* Dames, o're-flow your beauteous eyes,
For valiant *Saul*, who on Mount *Gilbo* lyes;
Who cloathed you in cloath of richest dye,
And choyse delights, full of variety.
On your array put ornaments of gold,
Which made you yet more beauteous to behold.
O! how in battell did the mighty fall,
In mid'st of strength not succoured at all:
O! lovely *Ionathan*, how wert thou slaine,
In places high, full low thou dost remaine;
Distrest I am, for thee, deare *Ionathan*,
Thy love was wonderfull, passing a man;
Exceeding all the Love that's Feminine,
So pleasant hast thou been, deare brother mine:
How are the mighty falne into decay,
And war-like weapons perished away.

Of

Of the vanity of all worldly creatures.

AS he said vanity, so vain say I,
O vanity, O vain all under skie,
Where is the man can say, lo, I have found
On brittle earth, a consolation sound?
What is 't in honour, to be set on high?
No, they like beasts, and sonnes of men shall die,
And whilst they live, how oft doth turn their State?
He 's now a slave, that was a Prince of late.
What is't in wealth, great treasures for to gain?
No, that's but labour anxious, care and pain.
He heaps up riches, and he heaps up sorrow,
Its his to day, but who 's his heire to morrow?
What then? content in pleasures canst thou find?
More vain then all, that's but to grasp the wind.
The sensuall senses for a time they please,
Mean while the conscience rage, who shall appease?
What is't in beauty? no, that's but a snare,
They'r foul enough to day, that once was fair,
What, Is't in flowring youth, or manly age?
The first is prone to vice, the last to rage.
Where is it then? in wisdome, learning, arts?
Sure if on earth, it must be in those parts;
Yet these, the wisest man of men did find,
But vanity, vexation of the mind,
And he that knows the most doth still bemoan,
He knows not all, that here is to be known,
What is it then? to do as Stoicks tell,
Nor laugh, nor weep, let things go ill or well:

                                                    Such

Such ſtoicks are but ſtocks, ſuch teaching vain:
While man is man, he ſhall have eaſe or pain.
If not in honour, beauty, age, nor treaſure,
Nor yet in learning, wiſdome, youth nor pleaſure?
Where ſhall I climbe, ſound, ſeek, ſearch or find,
That *ſummum Bonum* which may ſtay my mind?
There is a path, no vultures eye hath ſeen.
Where lions fierce, nor lions whelps hath been,
Which leads unto that living Chriſtall fount,
Who drinks thereof, the world doth naught account.
The depth, and ſea, hath ſaid its not in me,
With pearl and gold it ſhall not valued be:
For *Saphyre, Onix, Topas,* who will change,
Its hid from eyes of men, they count it ſtrange,
Death and deſtruction, the fame hath heard,
But where, and what it is, from heaven's declar'd,
It brings to honour, which ſhall not decay,
It ſteeres with wealth, which time cann't wear away.
It yeeldeth pleaſures, farre beyond conceit,
And truly beautifies without deceit.
Nor ſtrength nor wiſdome, nor freſh youth ſhall fade,
Nor death ſhall ſee, but are immortall made,
This pearl of price, this tree of life, this ſpring,
Who is poſſeſſed of, ſhall reign a King.
Nor change of ſtate, nor cares ſhall ever ſee,
But wear his Crown unto eternitie,
This ſatiates the ſoul, this ſtayes the mind,
The reſt's but vanity, and vain we find.

F I N I S.

MANUSCRIPTS

For my deare Sonne
Simon Brads

Parents perpetuate their liues
in their posterity, and their
maners, in their imitation
children do naturkally rather
follow the failings then the ver
tues of their predecessors, but
am perswaded better things of you
you once desired me to leaue some
thing for you in writing that
you might look vpon, when you
should see me no more, I could
think of nothing more fit for you
nor of more ease to my self then
these short meditations followi
ing such as they are I bequeath
to you, small legacys are accepti
by true friends much more by
dutyfull children, I haue avoyded
in touching vpon others conceptions
because I would leaue you nothing

2

que my owne, though in value
they fall short of all in this kinde
yet I presume they will be
better prised by you, for the
Authors sake. the lord blesse
you with grace heer and Crown
you with glory heereafter, that I
may meet you with reioyceing
at that great day of appear-
ing, which is the Continuall pray
er, of
                    your affectionate
                    mother AB

March 20
1664

Meditations Divine 3
and morall

There is no object that we see
no action that we doe, no good
that we injoy, no evill that we
feele, or feare, but we may make
some spirituall advantage of all
and he that makes such improve-
ment is wise as well as pious

2

Many can speak well, but few
can do well, we are better scho-
lars in the Theory, then the
practique part, but he is a true
Christian that is a proficient
in both

3

youth is the time of getting
middle age of improuing, and old
age of spending, a negligent youth
is usually attended by an ignorant
middle age, and both by an empty
old age, he that hath nothing to
feed on but vanity and lyes

4

... ... lye down in the
Bed of ... ...

4

... that beares much saile &
... or no ballast, is easily over
... that man whose head hath
great abilities and his heart lit
tle or no grace is in danger of
foundering.

5

It is reported of the peacock
that prideing himself in his gay
feathers he ruffles them up, but spying
his black feet, he soon lets fall his
plumes, so he that glorys in his
gifts and adornings, should look
upon his corruptions, and 'will
damp his high thoughts

6

The finest bread hath the least bran
the purest hony the least wax
and the sincerest christian the
least self love

Jonathan ...

The hireling that labours and in
comforts himself, that when night coms
he shall both take his rest and receiue
his reward, the painfull christian
that hath wrought hard in gods vine
yeard and hath born the heat and
drought of the day, when he per-
ceiues his sun apace to decline
and the shadowes of his euening
to be stretched out; lifts vp his
head wth joy, knowing his refresh
ing is at hand

8

Downny beds make drosey persons
but hard lodging, keeps the eyes open
a prosperous state makes a secure
christian, but aduersity makes him
consider

9

Sweet words are like hony, a little
may refresh, but too much gluts
the stomach .

Jonathan Loby Hob

10

Diverse children, have their differ
ent natures, some are like flesh
w'ch nothing but salt will keep from
putrefaction, some again like ten
der fruits that are best preserued
w'th sugar, those parents are wise
that can fit their nurture ac-
cording to their Nature.

11

That town w'ch thousands of enemys
w'th out hath not been able to take
hath been deliuered up by one tray
tor w'th in, and that man w'th all the
temptations, of Sathan, could not
hurt, hath, been foild by one lust
w'th in

12

Authority w'th out wisedome is like
is like a heavy axe, w'th out an edg
fitter to bruise, then polish

The reason why christians are so loth
to exchang this world for a better, is
because they haue more sence then faith
they se what they inioy, they do but
hope for that wch is to come

.L: 6 8 ς 14

If we had no winter the spring would
not be so pleasant, if we did not some
times tast of adversity, prosperity would
not be so welcome

15

A low man, can goe upright, under
that door, wher a taller is glad to
stoop; so a man of weak faith and
mean abilities, may undergo a
crosse more patiently then he that
excells him, both in gifts & graces

16

That house wch is not often swept
makes the cleanly inhabitant soone
loath it, and that heart wch is not
continually purifieing it self is no
fit temple for the spirit of god
to dwell in

17

Few men are so humble, as not to be
proud of their abilitys, and nothing
will make them more, then this,
what hast thou, but what thou hast
received? come giue an account
of thy stewardship.

18

He that will vntertake to climb vp a
steep mountain wth a great burden
on his back, will finde it a weary-
some if not an impossible task
so he that thinkes to mount to heaven
clog'd wth the cares and riches of this
Life, 'tis no wonder if he faint by
the way.

19

Corne till it haue past through the
Mill and been ground to powder, is not fit
for bread, god so deales wth his ser-
vants, he grindes them wth greif and
pain till they turn to dust and
then are they fine manchet for his
Mansion.

20   9

God hath suteable comforts and sup-
ports for his children according to
their severall conditions, if he will make
his face to shine upon them he then
makes them lye down in green pas-
tures and leades them beside the
still waters, if they stick in deepe
mire and clay, and all his waues
and billowes goe ouer their heads
he then leads them to the Rock wch
is higher then they

21   !

He that walks among briars and thornes
will be very carefull, where he sets his foot
And he that passes through the wil-
dernes of this world, had need ponder
all his steps.

22 22 23 4 5 6 7 8 9 "o
want of prudence as well as piety
hath brought men into great inconuen-
iencys, but he that is well stored wth
both, seldom is so insnared

b

23

The skilfull fisher hath his
severall baits, for severall fish. but
there is a hook under all, Satan
that great Angler hath his sun
dry baits for sundry tempers
of men, w^th ~~he discerns there~~
they all catch gredily at ~~their~~
but ~~none~~ few perceiues the hook
till it be to late.

24

There is no new thing under ye sun
there is nothing that can be sayd or
done, but either that or something
like it, hath been done and sayd
         both
before —

25

An aking head requires a soft
pillow, and a drooping heart
a strong support,

26

A sore finger may ~~please~~ disquiet
the whole body, but an vlcer with in
destroys it, so an enemy so with out may
disturb a commonwealth but differ=
tions with in ~~destroy~~ it.

27   27   27

It is a pleasant thing to behold the
light, but sore eyes are not able to
look upon it, the pure in heart shall
se god, but the defiled in conscience
shall rather choose to be buried vn=
der rocks and mountains then to
behold the presence of the lamb

28   28

wisedome with an inheritance is
good, but wisedome without an
inheritance, is better, then an in=
heritance without wisedome

29   29

Lightening doth vsually preceed
thunder, and stormes raine .

and cracke do not often fall
 till you threatning

30

yellow leaues signe want of sap
and gray haires want of moisture
so dry and saplesse performances
are simptoms of little spirituall
vigor

31

Iron till it be throughly heat is vn
capable to be wrought, so god sees,
good to cast some men into the furnace
of affliction and then beats them
on his anuile into what frame
he pleases

32

Ambitious men are like hops
that neuer rest climbing soe
long as they haue any thing to
stay vpon, but take away their
props and they are of all the
most deiected

Much Labour ...... the body, and
many thoughts .... the minde
man aimes at profit en the one &
content in the other but often
misses of both, and finds nothing
but vanity and vexation of spirit

34

Dimne eyes, are the concomitants of
of old age, and short sightednes
in those eyes that are of a Republique, fore-
tels, a declining state.

35

we read in Scripture of three sorts of
Arrows the arrows shot out of a bow of an enemy
the arrow of pestilence, and the arrow
of a slandsrous tongue, the two first
kill the body, the last the good name
the two former leave a man when he
is once dead, but the last mangles him in
his graue

36

Sore labourers haue hard hands
and old sinners haue brawnie
Consciences .

37

wickednes comes to its height by
degrees, He that dares say of a sin
a lesse sin, is it not a little one?
will ere long say of a greater
Tush god regards it not

38

Some children are hardly weansd
although the teat be rub-d wth
wormewood or mustard they will
either wipe it off or else suck.
down sweet and bitter togethsi
So is it wth some christians wn
god imbitters all the swees of
this life, that so they might
feed vpon more substantiall
food, yet they are so childishly
sottish that they are still hug
-ing and sucking these empty
brests, that god is forced to
hedg vp their way wth thornes
or: lay affliction on their loynes
that so they might shake hands

wth the world, before it bid
them farwell

39

A prudent mother, will not cloth
her little childe, in a long and
cumbersome garment, she there
fore sees what euents it is like
to produce, at the best, but falls
and bruises, or perhaps some what
worse, much more will the alwise
god proportion his dispensations
according to the stature and
strength of the person he bestowes
them on. large indowments of ho
nour, wealth, or a healthfull
body would quite ouerthrow some
weak christian therfore god cuts
their garments short, to keep them
in such a trim, that they might
rū the wayes of his commandements

40

The spring is a liuely emblem of
the resurrection, after a long
winter we e.

18 The leaveless tree and dry stock
at the approach of the sun, do re
sume their former vigor and grac
try in a more ample manner then
what they lost in the Autumn
So shall it be at that great day
after a long vacation, when the
Sun of righteousnes shall appear
these dry bones shall arise in far
more glory, then that wch they
lost at their Creation, and in this
transcends the spring, that their
leafe shall never fade nor their
Sap decline

                    41

A wise father will not lay a burden
on a child of seven yeares old, w^t
he knows is enough for one of twice
his strength, much lesse will our
heavenly father (who knows our
mould,) lay such afflictions upon
his weak children as would crush
them to the dust, but according

to the strength he will proportion
the load, as god hath his little
children so he hath his strong
men, such as are come to a full
stature in christ, and many times
he imposes weighty burdens on
their shoulders, and yet they go
upright under them, but it mat
ters not whether the load be more
or lesse if god afford his help

42

I have seen an end of all perfectiō
(sayd the royall prophet) but he ne-
ver sayd, I have seen an end of all
sinning; what he did say, may be ea
sily sayd by many, but what he did
not say, cannot be truly uttered by
any.

43

fire hath its force abated by water
not by wind, and anger must be al
layed, by cold words and not by
blustering threats

44

A sharp appetite and a through
concoction, is a signe of an

healthfull body, so a quick recept
=ion and a deliberate cogitation
argues a sound mind

45

we often see stones hang wth drops
not from any innate moisture, but
from a thick ayre about them
so may we somtimes see, marble
... floors seem full of
cohesion, but it is not from any
... growth, but from
... such Clouds that impends
them, wch prodiviss these sweat
-ing effects :

46

8 The words of the wise saith Solom:
are as nailes, and as goads, both
vsed for contrary ends, the one
holds fast, the other puts for-
ward, such should be the precep:
of the wise musters of assemblys
to their hearers, not only to bid
them hold the form of sound doc-
-trin, but also, so to run that
they might obtain

A shadow in the parching sun, &
a shelter in a blustering storme
are of all seasons the most wellcom
So a faithfull friend in time of
adversity, is of all other most
comfortable

§

There is nothing admits of more
admiration then to observe
dispensation of things amongst
the sons of men, betwixt whom
he hath put so vast a disproportion
that they scarcly seem made of the
same lumps, and sprung out of the
loynes of one Adam, some set in y
highest dignity, that mortality is
capable off, and some againe so base
that they are viler then y earth
same so wise and learned, that they
seeme like Angells among men, and
some againe, so ignorant and so rich
that they are more like beasts then
men, some pious saints, some in-
carnate Deuills, some exceeding
beauty full, and some extreamly deformed

some so strong and healthfull yt
their bones are full of marrow &
their breasts of milk, and some
againe so weak and feeble, that
while they liue, they are accounted
among the dead, and no other
reason can be giuen of all this
but so it pleased him, whose
will is the perfect rule of righ-
teousnesse,

49

The treasures of this world may
well be compared to huskes, for they
haue no kernell in them, and they
that feed vpon them, may soon
stuffe their throats, but cannot
fill their bellys, they may be
choaked by them, but cannot be
satisfied with them.

50

Somtimes the sun is only sha-
dowed by a cloud, that wee

cannot se his luster, although we
may walk by his light, but when
he is set, we are in darknes till he
arise againe, so god doth sometime
vaile his face but for a moment
that we cannot behold the light
of his Countenance, as at some other
time, yet he affords so much light
as may direct our way, that we
may go forwards to the citty of
habitation, but when he seemes to
set and be quite gone out of sight
then must we needs walk in dark
nesse and se no light, yet then
must we trust in the lord and
stay upon our god, and when y
morning (wch is the appointed
time) is come the Sun of righte
-ousnes will arise wth healing in
his wings .

5 1

The eyes and the eares are the
in lets or doores of the soule, through
w[ch] Innumerable obiects enter, yet
is not that spacious roome filled
wth neither doth it euer say it is
enough, but like the daughters of
the horsleach, crys giue giue, &
w[ch] is most strang, the more it receius
the more empty it finds it selfe, and
sees an impossibility, euer to be
filled, but by him, in whom all
fullnes dwells

52

Had not the wisest of men, taught
vs this lesson, that all is vanity
and vexation of spirit, yet our
owne experience wadd soon haue
speld it out, for what do we obtaine of
all these things, but it is wth Labour
and vexation, when we inioy it them
is wth vanity and vexation, and if
we loose them they are lesse then vanity &
more then vexation, so that we
haue good cause. often to repeat

That sentence, vanity of vanityes
vanity of vanityes, all is vanity

§ 3

He that is to saile into a farre
country, although the ship, cab-
bin and provision, be all conve-
nient and comfortable for him
yet he hath no desire to make y
his place of residence, but longes
to put in shore at that port wher
his bussines lyes, a christian is
sailing through this world unto
his heavenly country, and heere
he hath many conveniences and
comforts of desire but he must beware
of desiring to make this the place
of his abode, lest he meet with such
tossings that may cause him to
long for shore, before he sees land
we must therfore be heer as strangers
and pilgrims, that we may plainly
declare that we seek a citty above
and wait all the dayes of our ap-
pointed time till our change shall
come,

54

He that neuer felt what it was to
be sick or wounded, doth not
much care for the company of the
phisitian or chirurgian, but if
he perceiue a malady that thre-
-atens him wth death, he will glad-
-ly entertaine him, whom he sligh-
-ted before, so he that neuer felt
the sicknes of sin, nor the wounds
of a guilty Conscience, cares not
how far he keeps from him that
hath skill to cure it, but when he
findes his diseases to disquiet
him, and that   he must
needs perish if   he haue
no remedy, will vnfeignedly bid
him welcome, that brings a plaister
for his sore, or a cordiall for his faint
ing;

55

You read of ten lepers that were
Cleansed, but of one that re-

turned thanks, we are more rea
dy to receiue mercys then we
are to acknowledg them, men
can use great importunity when
they are in distresses and
shew great ingratitude after
their successes, but he that or-
dereth his conuersation aright
will glorifie him that heard
him in the day of his trouble

56

The remembrance of former de
liuerances, is a great support in
present destresses, he that de li-
uered me sath dauid from the
paw of the Lion and the paw
of the Beare will deliuer mee
from this vncircumsised philistin
and that hath deliuered mee
saith paul, will deliuer me, god
is the same yesterday, to day
and for euer, we are the same

that ~~are~~ stand in need of him, to
day as well as yesterday, and so
shall for euer,

57

great receipts, call for great re-
turnes, the more that any man is
intrusted wth all, the larger his
accounts stands vpon gods score
it therfore behoues euery man so
to improue his talents, that when
his great master shall ~~appeare~~, (call him to reckning he
may receiue his owne wth advan-
tage

58

sin and shame euer goe together
He that would be freed from the
last, must be sure to shun the cum
pany of the first

59

God doth many times, both reward
and punish ~~to~~ for one and the same
action, as we see in Jehu, he is re
warded wth a kingdome to the
fourth generation for takeing

veangence on the house of Ahab
and yet a little while (saith god,
and I will avenge the blood of
Jezebel upon the house of Jehu, he
was rewarded for the matter, and
yet punished for the manner, wch
should warn him, that doth any
speciall service for god, to fixe his
eye on the command and not on his
own ends. lest he meet wth Jehus reward
reward, wch will end in punishment

60

He that would be content, wth a
mean condition, must not cast his
eye upon one that is in a far better
estate then himself, but let him
look upon him that is lower then he is
and if he se, that such a one beares
pouerty comfortably it will help to
quiet him, but if that will not do
let him look on his owne unworthynes
and that will make him say wth Ja-
cob, I am lesse then the least of
thy mercys ..

Corne is produced w:th much la-
bour, as the husbandman well
knowes, and some land askes
much more paines, then some other
doth to be brought into tilth, so
all must be ploughed and harrowed
some children like sowre lands are
of so rough and morell a disposition
that the plough of correction must
make long furrows on their back
and the harrow of discipline goe
often ouer them before they bee
fit soile, to sow the seed of mora
lity, much lesse of grace in them
But when by prudent nurture they
are brought into a fit capacity, let
the seed of good instruction and ex
hortation be sown in them, in the
spring of their youth, and a plenti
full crop may be expected in the
harvest of their yeares.

As man is called the little world
so his heart may be cal'd the little com
monwealth, his more fixed and reso
lued thoughts, are like to inhabitants
his slight and flitting thoughts are
like passengers, that trauell to and fro
continually, here is also the great
Court of iustice erected, wch is alwey
kept by Conscience, who is both accuser
witnes and iudg, whom no bribes can
peruert, nor flattery cause to fauour
but as he finds the euidence, so he
absolues or condemnes, yea so Abso-
lute is this Court of Iudicature that
there is no appeale from it, no not to the
Court of heauen it self for if our consci
ence condemn vs, he also who is grea
ter then our Conscience will do it much
more, but he that would haue boldnes
to go to the throne of grace to be
accepted there, must be sure to carry
a Certificate from the Court of con
science that he stands right there —

63

He that would keep a pure heart
and lead a blamlesse Life, must
set himself alway in the awefull
presence of god, the considera
-tion of his allseeing eye will
be a bridle to restrain from
evill, and a spur, to quicken
on to good dutys, we certainly
dream of some remotnes betwixt
god and us, or else we should not
so often faile in our whole
Course of life as we doe, but he
that wth David, sets the lord al
-way in his sight will not sinne
against him.

64

We see in orchards, some trees soe
fruitfull, that the waight of
their Burden is the breaking of
their Limbes, some again, are but
meanly Loaden, and some haue
nothing to shew but leaues only,
and some among them are dry stocks
so is it in the Church wch is gods
orchard, there are some

eminent Christians, that are soe
frequent in good dutys, that many
times, the weighty therof impares
both their bodys and estates, and ther
are some (and they sincere ones too)
who haue not attained to that fruit
fullnes, altho they aime at perfection
And again there are that haue
nothing to commend them, but only
a gay proffession, and these are but
leauie christians, wth are in as much
danger of being cut down, as the dry
stock, for both cumber the ground

65

we se in the firmament there is but one
Sun, among a multitude of starres
and those starres also, to differ much
one from the other in regard of bignes
and brightnes yet all receiue their light
from that one Sun, so is it in the church
both militant and triumphant, there
is but one christ, who is the Sun of
righteousnes, in the midest of an innu
merable company of Saints, and those
Saints haue their degrees, euen in that

life, some are Stars of the first magni
-tude, and some of a lesse degree, &
others (and they indeed the most in
number) but small and obscure, yet
all receive their Luster (be it more
or lesse) from that glorious Sun that
inlightens all in all, and if some
of them shine so bright while they
moue on earth, how transcendently
splendid shall they be, when they
are fixt in their heauenly spheres;

66

Men that haue walked very extraua-
gantly, and at last bethink themselues
of turning to god, the first thing to th
they eye, is how to reform their wayes
rather, then to beg forgiuenes for their
sinnes, nature lookes more at a Compen
sation then at a pardon, but he that will
not Come for mercy wth out mony &
wth out price but bring his filthy ragges
to barter for it, shall meet with
miserable disapointment, going
away empty bearing the reproch.

67

All the works and doings of god
are wonderfull, but none more awfull
then his great worke of election and
Reprobation, when we consider how
many good parents haue had bad chil
-dren, and againe how many bad pa-
rents haue had pious children, it
should make us adore the Soueraintÿ
of god, who will not be tÿed to time
nor place, nor yet to persons, but takes
and chuses when and where and
whom he pleases, it should also teach
the children of godly parents to walk
with feare and trembling lest they
through vnbelef fall short of a pro-
mise, it may also be a support to such
as haue or had wicked parents that if they
abide not in vnbelef, god is able to
graffe them in, the vpshot of all
should makes us with the Apostle to
admire the iustice and mercy of god
and say
how vnsearchable are his wayes
and his footsteps past finding out

The gifts that god bestows on the
sons of men, are not only abused
but most Commonly imployed for a
Clean Contrary end, then that wth
they were giuen for, as health wealth
and honour, wth might be so many
steps to draw men to god in consider
-ation of his bounty towards them, but
haue driuen them the further from
him, that they are ready to say, we are
Lords we will come no more at thee
If outward blessings be not as wings
to help us mount upwards, they will
Certainly proue Clogs and waights
that will pull yoww downward

All the comforts of this life, may
be compared to the gourd of
Jonah, that notwthstanding
we take great delight, for a
seafon in them, and find their

shadow very comfortable, yet there
is some worm or other, of discontent
of feare or envie that Lyes at the root
wch in great part withers the
pleasure wch else we should take
in them, and wcch it is that we
perceive a decay in their greenes
for were earthly Comforts permanent perfect
who would Look for heavenly .5

∇0

All men are truly sayd to be tenants
at will, and it may as truly be sayd
that all men have a lease of their
lives, some longer some shorter, as it
pleases our great Landlord to let;
All have their bounds set, over wch
they cannot passe, and till the expi-
ration of that time, no dangers no sick
-nes no paines nor troubles, shall
put a period to our dayes, the Cer
tainty that that time will come, to-
gether, wth the uncertainty, how
where, and when, should make us to
number our dayes as to apply
our hearts to wisedome, that

36 When wee are put out of these
houses of clay, we may be sure of
an everlasting habitation that
fades not away.

71

All weak and diseased bodys, haue
hourly mementos of their mortality
But the soundest of men, haue likwise
their nightly monitor, by the Embleam
of death, wᶜʰ is their sleep (for so is
death often called) and not only their
death, but their graue, is liuely re
presented before their eyes, by be-
holding their bed, the morning may
mind them of the resurrection,
and the sun approaching, of the
appearing of the Sun of righte-
ousnes, at whose Comeing they shall
all rise out of their beds, the long
night shall fly away, and the day
of eternity shall neuer
End, seeing these things must be
what manner of persons ought
we to be, in all good conuersation

72

As the brands of a fire, if one seve
rede will of themselues goe out
altho you use no other meanes to ex-
tinguish it, the distance of place to ge
ther with length of time (if there be
no ...) will coole the affecti-
ons of intimate friends, though there
should be no displeasure betweene
them

73

A good name, is as a precious oynt
ment, and it is a great favour to
haue a good repute among good
men, yet it is not that, which commen
us to god, for by his ballance we
must be weighed, and by his Judg-
ment we must be tryed and as he pas
ses the sentence, so shall we stand.

74

Well doth the Apostle call riches
deceitfull riches, and they may tru
-ly be compared to deceitfull friends
who speak faire and promise much

But perform nothing, and so leaue
these in the Lurch that most rely
-ed on them, so is it with the welth
honours and pleasures of this world
wch maiserably deludge men and
make them put great confidence
in them, but when death threatens
and distresse lays hold upon them
they proue like the reeds of Egipt
that pierce instead of supporting
like empty wells in the time
of drought that those that go to
finde water in them, return with
their empty pitchers ashamed,

75

It is admirable to consider the
power of faith, by wch all things
are (almost) possible to be done, it
can remoue mountaines, if need were
it hath stayd the course of the sun
raised the dead, cast out divels,
reversed the order of nature, quen
-ched the violence of the fire, made

the water become firme footing, for
peter to walk on, nay more then all
these, it hath over come the omnipotent
himselfe, as when Moses intercedes
for the people, god saith to him let
me alone; that I may destroy them
as if Moses had been able by the hand
of faith, to hold the ever lasting
armey of the mighty god of Jacob
yea Jacob himselfe when he wrest
led with god face to face in perill
let me go, saith that Angell I will
not let thee go replys Jacob till
thou blesse me, faith is not only thus
potent but it is so necessary, that
without faith there is no salvation
therfore wth all our seekings and
gettings, let us above all seek to
obtain this pearle of price

76

Some ... interpret by their ...
and ... as they Israelites
... by the Canaanites, had de-
stroyed them, but put them under
tribute, for that they could no (as
they thought) w:th lesse hazard
and more profit, but what was
ye Issue, they became a snare unto
them, prickes in their eyes and
thornes in their sides, and at last
overcame them, and kept them un-
der slavery, so it is most certain
that those who are disobedient
to the Command of god, and en-
deavour not to the utter... to dri-
ve out all their accursed in-
mates, but make a league with
them, they shall at least fall in
to perpetuall bondage under them
untill their great deliverer Christ
Jesus come to their rescue.

71

God hath by his providence so
ordered, that no one Country hath
all Commoditys wthin it self,
but what it wants, another shall
supply, that so there may be a mu-
tuall Commerce through ye world
As it is wth Countrys so it is with
men, there was neuer yet any one
man that had all excellences, let
his parts naturall and acquired
spirituall and morall be neuer so
Large, yet he stands in need of some-
thing wch another man hath (perhaps
meaner then himself, wch shewes
perfection is not below, as also that
god will haue vs beholden one
to another.

my hand. & dear mother intended to
haue filled up this Book wth the
like Observations but was preuented
by death.

42

A true Copy of a Book left by my
dear & dear mother to her children
& found among some papers after
her death.   113

            To my dear children.

This Book by Any yet unread,
I leave for you when I am dead,
That being gone, here you may find
What was yr living mothers mind.
Make use of what I leave in Love
And God shall bless you from above.
                                    A. B.

My dear children./
I knowing by experie. yt ye exhortat. of
parents take most effect wn ye speakers
leave to speak, and these espec. sink &
deepest wch are spoke latest, & being
ignorant whether on my death bed I shall
have opportunity to speak to any of you &
much lesse to all, thought it ye best whilst
I was able to compose some short matter,
(for wt else to call you I know not) and
bequeath to you, that when I am no
more with you, yet I may bee daly in yr
remembrance, (Altho' yt is take least & my
aim in not I now doe) but yt you may
gain some spiri: Advantage by my
experie. I have not studyed in this you
read to shew my skill, but to declare ye
Truth, not to sett forth my self, but ye Glory
of God. If I had minded ye former it had
bin perhaps better pleasing to you, but
being ye last is the best, let it bee best
pleasing to you.
The method I will observe shall bee this —

114 I will begin with Gods dealing wth mee
froe my childhood to this Day.

In my young years about 6. or 7. as I
take it I began to make consc. of my
wayes, & what I know was sinfull as
lying, disobedc. to parents. etc. I avoyded
it. If at any time I was overtaken wth
ye like evills, it was a great trouble, & I
could not rest till by prayer I had
confest it unto God. I was also troubled
at ye neglect of private Dutyes tho: too
often tardy yt way. I also found much
comfort in reading ye Scriptures, espec:
those places I thought most concerned
my Condition, and as I grew to have
more understanding, so ye more solace I
took in them.

In a long fitt of sicknes wch I had on
my bed I often communed wth my
heart, and made my Supplicatn. to the
most High who sett mee free from that
afflictn.

But as I grew up to bee about 14. or yr
I found my heart more carnall, & sitting
loose from God, vanity & ye follyes of
youth take hold of me.

About 16. the Lord layd his hand sore
upon mee & smott mee wth ye small pox
when I was in my afflictn. I besought the
Lord, and confessed my pride and
vanity and he was entreated of mee, and
againe restored mee. But I rendered not
to him according to ye benefitt rec.

After a short time I changed my
condition & was marryed, and came into
this Country, where I found a new
world and new manners at wch my heart
rose, But after I was convinced
it was ye way of God, I submitted to it
& joined to ye chh. at Boston.

After some time I fell into a lingering
sicknes like a consumption together wth
a lamenesse wch correction I saw the

the Lord sent so littell and my me c doe mee
good: and it was not altogeather ineffectuall.
It pleased God to keep mee a long time &
without a child wch was a great greif to
me, and cost mee many prayers & teares before
I obtaind one, and after him gave mee many
more, of whom I now take ye care, yt as I
have broyght you into ye world, and wth great
paines, weaknes, cares & feares broyght you
to this, I now travail in birth again of you
till Christ bee formed in you.

Among all my experiences of gods gratious
dealings wth me I have constantly observed
this yt he hath never suffered me long to sit
loose fro him, but by one afflictin or other
hath made me look home, and search wt
was amisse. So usually ther it hath beene
wth me that I have no sooner felt my
heart out of order, but I have expected
correctin furit, wch most comonly hath
been upon my own person, in sicknesse &
weaknes, paines, etc. or on my soul in
doubts & feares of Gods displeasure, and my
sincerity towards him. somt. he hath smott
a child wth sicknes, somt. chastised by
losses in estate: and these I'multi crosses:
in great mercy I have been the times of my
greatest getting and advantage, yea I have
found them ye times wn ye Lord hath
manifested ye most love to me. Then have
I gone to searching, and have said wth David
Lord search me and try me see what wayes of
wickednes are in me, and lead me in ye way
everlasting: and seldome or never but I have
found either some sin I lay under wch God
would have reformed or some duty neglected
wch he would have performed. and by his
help I have layd vowes and bonds upon my
soul to perform his righteous comaunds.

If at any time wee are chastened of God
take it as thankfuley and joyfully as in greatest
mercyes, for if yee bee his yee shall reap-

reap the greatest benefit of it: ~~and I haue~~
it hath bvin no small supplie to me in times
of darknes when ye Almighty hath hid his face
from me that yet I haue had abundance of
sweetnes and refreshment after affliction
and more circumspection in my walking after I
haue been afflicted. I haue been with God
like an untoward child, that no longer then
his rod was upon my back, or at least in
sight, but I haue bin apt to forget him
and my self too. Before I was afflicted. I r
went astray, but now I keep thy statuty.

I haue had great xpve of Gods hearing
my prayers and returning comfortable answers
to me, either in grantinge ye thing I
prayed for, or else in satisfying my mind
without it, and I haue been confident it y
hath been from him, because I haue found
my hart throughe his goodnes enlarged in
thankfullnes to him.

I haue often been perplexed yt I haue not
found that constant joy in my pilgrimage
and refreshing which I supposed most of the
servants of God haue, although he hath not
left me altogether without the witnes of his
holy spirit who hath oft given me his word yt
sett to my soul that it shall goe well with
me. I haue somt. tasted of yt hidden
Mannay yt ye world knowes not, & haue
sett up my Ebenezer, and haue resolved
whatso my self yt yet such a promis, yt yet
tast of sweetnes ye gats of Hell shall
never prevail; yet haue I many times
findinge & droopinge and not enjoyed that
felicity that sent I haue done but when
I haue bin in uerknes and seen no light, yet
haue I desired to stay my self upon ye Lord,
and when I haue been in sicknes & pain,
I haue thought if ye Lord would but lift up
ye light of his countine upon me altho'
hee ground me to powder it would bee but
light to me, yea oft haue I thought wore
in hell it self and could there find ye loue
of God toward me it would bee a Heaven

and could I haue bene in Heauen without
ye Loue of God it would haue bene a Hell to
me for in Truth it is the absence and presence
of God ye makes Heauen or Hell.

Many times hath Satan troubled me concer-
ning ye verity of ye scriptures, many times
by setting me how I could know whether there
was a God, I neuer saw any miracles to
confirme me, and those weh I read of howded
know but they were feigned. That there
is a God my reason would soon tell me by the
wondrous worckes that I see, the wise framerey
of Heauen & ye earth, the order of all things &
night and day, sumer & winter, Spring and
Autumne, the dayly prouiding for this great houshold
upon ye earth, ye preseruing & directing
of As to its proper End, other considerations of
these things would arle amazement certainly
resolue me that there is an Eternall Being.
But how should I know he is such a God as I
worship in Trinity, & such a Sav[io]r as I rely
upon &c. this hath thousands of times bene
suggested to me, yet God hath helpd me ouer.
I haue argued thus wth my self, That there
is a God I see, If euer this God hath revealed
himself it must bee in his word, and this must
bee it or none. Haue I not found y operation
by it that no humane Invention can worck
can work upon ye soul, hath not Judgments
befallen Diuers who haue scornd & contemd
it hath it not bene preserued thro: All Ages
maugre all ye heathen Tyrants & all ye
Enemyes weh haue opposed it? Is there any
story but what weh showth the beginnings
of times & how ye world came to bee as
wee see, nor wee not know ye prophecyes
in it fulfilled weh could not haue bene so
long foretold by any but god himself?
when I haue got ouer this Block yt haue I
another putt in my way, & that admitting
bee ye true God whom wee worship, and it
bee his word, yet why may not ye Popish
Religion bee ye right, they haue ye same god
the same christ ye same word, They

48 they only enterprett it one way or another.

This hath some. stuck with me, and more it would, but ye arrin foolery, that are in their religi: together with their lying miracles, and cruell persecutions of the Saints, will admitt more of as they become yn yet not so to bee dealt withall.

The consideration of these things and many ye like would soone turn me to my own religi: again.

But some new Troubles I haue had since ye world hes been filled with Blasphemy, and Sectaries, and some who haue't been acct. Sincere xtians haue been carryd away wth them, that some. I haue said, Is there ffaith vpon ye Earth) & I haue not known what to think; But then I haue remembred the words of Christ that so it must bee, and that if it were possible ye very elect should bee deceiued. Behold faith or Savt. I haue told you before. that hath stayd my heart, and I can now say, Return o my Soul to thy Rest, vpon this Rock xt Jesus will I build my faith, & if I perish, I perish; But I know all ye Powers of Hell shall never prevail against it. I know whome I haue trusted, and whome I haue beleived, and yt he is able to keep yt I haue committed to his charge.

Now to ye King, Immortall, Eternall & invisible, the only wise God, bee Honor, & Glory for ever and ever,

                              Amen.

This was written in much Sicknesse and weaknes, and is very weakly & imperfectly done, but if you can pick any Benefitt out of it, It is the mark that J aimed at

Here follow severall occasionall
meditations. &c.

1.

By night when others soundly slept
And hath at once both ease and Rest
my waking eyes were open kept
And so to lye I found it best.

2.

I sought him whom my Soul did Love
with tears I sought him earnestly
He bow'd his Ear down from Above
In vain I did not seek or cry.

3.

My hungry Soul he fill'd with Good,
He in his Bottle putt my tears,
my smarting wounds washt in his blood,
And banisht thence my Doubts & feares.

4.

What to my Savi.e shall I give?
who freely hath done this for me,
I'le serve him here whilst I shall liue
And Loue him to Eternity.

For deliver. from a feaver.

When sorrowes had begyrt me round,
And paines within & out
when in my flesh no part was found
Then didst thou rid me out.
My burning flesh in sweat did boyle
my aking head did break,
From side to side for ease I toyle,
So faint I could not speak.
Beclouded was my Soul with fear
of thy Displeasure sore,
Nor could I read my Evidence
wch oft I read before.
Hide not thy face from me I cry'd
From Burnings keep my Soul.
Thou know'st my heart, and hast me try'd
I on thy Mercyes Roul.

50 O heal my Soul thou know'st I said,
    The flesh consume to nought
    what tho: in dust it shall be laid
    To Glory t' shall bee brought.
    Thou heardst, thy rod thou didst remove
    And spar'd my Body frail,
    Thou shew'st to me thy tender Love
    my heart no more might quail.
    O praises to my mighty God
    praise to my Lord I say,
    Who hath redeem'd my Soul from pitt
    praises to him for Aye.

        From another Sore fitt.

    In my distresse I sought ye Lord
    when nought on Earth could comfort give
    And when my Soul these things abhord
    Thou Lord thou saidst unto me Live.

    Thou knowest the sorrowes yt I felt
    my plaints & groanes were heard of thee
    And how in sweat I seem'd to melt
    Thou helps't and thou regard'st me.

    My wasted flesh thou didst restore
    my feeble loines didst gird with strength
    yea when I was most low and poor
    I said I shall praise thee at length.

    What shall I render to my God
    for all his Bounty shew'd to me
    Even for his mercyes in his rod,
    where pitty most of all I see.

    my heart I wholly give to thee
    O make it fruitfull faithful Lord
    my life shall Dedicated bee
    To praise in thought, in deed, in word.

    Thou know'st

Thou know'st no life I did require
Longer then still thy Name to praise,
Nor ought on Earth worthy Desire
In drawing out these wretched Dayes.
Thy Name & praise to celebrate
O Lord for aye is my request
O graunt I doe it in this state
And then with them which is the Best.

          Deliver'd from a fitt of ffAINTing.

Worthy art thou o L'd of praise,
But ah! 'tis not in me
My sinking heart I pray thee raise
So shall I give it thee.

My life as Spider web's cutt off
thus fainting have I said
And living man no more shall see
But vndr in silence layd.

My feeble Spirit thou didst revive
My Doubting thou didst chide
And tho as dead mad'st me alive
I here a while might ' bide.

Why should I live but to thy praise
My life is hid with thee
O Lord no longer bee my Dayes
Then I may fruitfull bee.

          Meditations when my Soul hath been
          refreshed with the Consolations weh
          the world knowes nott.
Lord why should I doubt any more wn
thou hast given me such assured pledges
of thy Loue. First thou art my Creator,
I thy creature, thou my master J thy
servant, But hence arises not my comfort
thou art my Father J thy Child, Yee shall my
Sons and Daughters saith ye Lord Almighty ——

52 Christ is my Brother, I ascend unto my Father,
and your Father, unto my God and your God —
But least this should not bee enough, thy maker
is thy husband. Nay more, I am a member of
his Body, hee my head. Such priviledges had
not ye word of of grath made them knowne
who or where is the man that durst in his
heart have presumed to have thought it?
So wonderfull are these thoughts that my
spirit failes in mee at ye consideration y'of,
and I am confounded to think that God who
hath done so much for mee, should have so
little from mee. But this is my comfort, when
I come into Heaven, I shall vnderstand &
p'fectly what he hath done for mee, and then
shall I bee able to praise him as I ought. &
Lord knowing this hope let mee purify my
self as thou art pure, and let mee bee no
more afraid of death, but when I desire to bee
dissolved and bee with thee which is best of
All.

July. 8th. 1656.

I had a sore fit of fainting wch lasted 2
or 3 dayes, but not in yt extremity wch at
first it took mee, and so much the longer it
was to mee because my dear husband was
from home (who is my cheifst comforter
on Earth) but my God who never failed
mee was not absent but helped mee, and
gratiously manifested his love to mee, wch I
dare not passe by without Remembrance, it it may
bee a support to mee when I shall have
occasion to read this hereafter, and to others
that shall read it when I shall possesse that
I now hope for, yt so they may bee encouraged
to trust in him who is the only portion of
his Servants.

I Lord let mee never forget thy Goodnss,
nor question thy faithfulnss to mee, for thou
art my God, & thou hast said and shall not
I beleive it —

Thou hast given me a pledge of yt Inherite
Thou hast promised to bestow upon me . O never
let Satan prevail against me but strengthen
my faith in Thee, 'till I shall attain yt end
of my hopes, Even yt Selvatõ. of my Soul.
    Come Lord Iesus, come quickly.

What god is like to him I serve
Or what Savt. like to mine?
O never let me from thee Swerve
For truly I am thine.

My thankfull mouth shall speak thy maiᵉ .
My tongue shall talk of thee
On high my heart o doe thou raise
For what thou'st done for me.

Goe worldlings to your vanities
And heathen to your Gods
Let them help in Adversities
And sanctifye their rods,
my God he is not like to yᵉ
your selves shall judges bee,
I find him Love, I know his powᵈ.
A Succourer of mee.

Hee is not man yᵗ he should lyᵉ.
Nor Son of man to unsay
His word he plighted hath on high
And I shall live for aye.
And for his sake yt faithfull is
That dy'd but now doth live,
The first and last yt lives for aye,
mee lasting life shall give.

My soul rejoice thou in thy god
Boast of him all yᵉ Day,
Walke in his Law, and kisse his Rod
Cleave close to him alway.

54 What tho: thy outward man decay,
Thy inward shall waxe strong,
Thy body vile it shall bee chang'd,
And glorious made ere-long.

With Angels-wings thy soul shall mount
To Bliffe unseen by Eye,
And drink at unexhausted fount
Of Joy unto Eternity.

Thy teares shall all bee dryed up
Thy sorrowes all shall fly,
Thy sinns shall ne'r bee summon'd up
Nor come in memory.

Then shall I know what thou hast done
For mee unworthy mee,
And praise thee shall ev'n as I ought
For wonders that I see.

Base world I trample on thy face,
Thy glory I despise,
No gain I find in ought below
For God hath made me wise.
Come Jefus quickly, Bleffed Lord
Thy face when shall I fee
O let me covet each hour a Day
Till I diffolved bee.

August. 28. 1656.

After much weaknes & fickness when my
spirit were worn out, and many times
my faith weak, likewise the Lord was
pleased to uphold my drooping heart, and to
manifest his Love to me. and this is that
which stayes my soul that this condition y^t
I am in, is ye best for me, for god doth
not afflict willingly, nor take delight in
greiving ye children of men, so hath no r
benefit by my adversity, nor is he ye better
for my profperity, but he doth it for my r
Advantage, and y^t I may bee a Gainer by it.

55

And if he knoweth that weaknes, of a frail body; ye
fitt to make me a veffell fitt for his vfe why
should I not bare it ye nor only willingly
but joyfully; of the Lord knows I dare not
defire that health yt fout. I haue had, least my
heart should bee drawn from him; and fett
vpon the world.
How I can wait, looking every day when my
faue shall call for me. Lord graunt yt while
I live I may doe yt service I am able in
this frail body, and bee in continual expectation
of my change, and let me never forgett thy
great Love to my soul fo lately expressed,
when I could lye down wth bequeath my foul
to thee and Death feem'd no terrible thing.
O let me ever fee thee that art invisible
and I shall not bee unwilling to come tho:
by fo rough a Messenger.
                    May – 11.
                    ✠ ✞. 1657.

I had a fore ficknes and weaknes took hold of
me wch hath by fits lasted all this spring
till this 11. May. yet hath my God given me
many a respite, & some ability to pförme ye
Dutyes I owe to him, and the works of
my family.
Many a refreshment haue I found in this
my weary Pilgrimage, and in this valley of
Baca many pools of water, ĝhat wch now I
chrisly labour for is a contented thankfull hrt
vnder my affliction & weaknes feing it is ye
will of God it should bee thus. who am I yt
I should repine at his pleafure efpeciaing
it is for my fpiritt advantage. for I hope
my foul shall flourish while my body decayes
and ye weaknes of this outward man shall
bee a meanes to strengthen my inner-
man
yet a little while and hee that shall
come will come and will not tarry.
                    May. 13. 57.

56

May. 13. 1657.

As Spring the winter doth succeed
And leaves the naked Trees doe dresse
The earth all black is cloth'd in green
At sun-shine each their joy expresse.

my Sins returnd with healing wings
my Soul and Body doth rejoice,
my heart exults & praises sings
To him that heard my wailing voice.

My winters past my stormes are gone
And former clowdes seem now all fled
But if they must Eclipse again
I'le run where I was succoured.

I have a shelter from ye storm
A shadow from ye fainting heat
I have accesse unto his Throne,
Who is a God so wondrous great.

O hast thou made my pilgrimage
thus pleasant fair and good,
Blest me in youth and Elder Age
My Baca made a springing flood.

I studious am what I shall doe
To show my Duty with delight
All I can give is but thine own
And at ye most a simple mite.

Sept. 30. 1657.

It pleased god to visit me with my old
Distemper of weaknes and fainting, but
not in y^t sore manner somt. he hath.
I desire not only willingly but thankfully
to submit to him for I trust it is out of
his abundant Love to my straying Soul wch
in prosperity is too much in love wth y^e
world. I have found by experience I can
no more live without correction then
without food. Lord with y^y correction

give Instruction and amendment, and then thy Broakes shall bad welcome, I haue not 57
been refined in ye fournace of affliction as
some haue been, but haue rather been
preserved with Sugar then brine, yet will
he preserve me to his heavenly kingd:.

Thus (dear children) haue yee seen ye many sick—
—nesses and weaknesses that I haue passed thro': to
ye End yt if you meet with the like you
may haue recourse to ye Same God who hath
heard & delivered me, and will doe ye like
for you if you trust in him; And when he
shall deliuer you out of distresse forget not
to giue him thankes, but to walk more closely
with him then before, this is the desire of
yr Loving mother. A. B.

In ye Same book were vpon
Speciall occasions the poems. &.
wch follow added.

_____

Vpon my Son Samuel his goeing for
England Novem. 6. 1657.

Thou mighty God of Sea and Land
I here resigne into thy hand,
The Son of prayers, of vowes, of tears,
The child I bare'd for many years.
Thou heard'st me then and gau'st him me
Heare me again, I giue him Thee.
He's mine but more O Lord thine own
for Sure thy Grace on him is Shown.
No friend I haue like thee to trust
for mortall helpes are brittle Dust.
Preserve o Lord from Stormes & wrack
Protect him there & bring him back:
And if thou shalt Spare me a Space
that I again may see his face
Then shall I celebrate thy praise
And Blesse the for't Even all my Dayes.

58　If otherwise I goe to rest
Thy will bee done for that is best
Perswade my heart I shall him see
For ever happyfy'd with Thee.

May. 11. 1661.

It hath pleased God to giue me a long
time of respite for these 9 years that I
haue had no great fitt of sicknes, but this
year from ye middle of January till may
I haue beene by fitts very ill & weak. The
first of this month I had a feauer sea te
vpon mee with indeed was the longest and
sorest yt euer I had lasting 4 dayes, and ye
weather being very hott made it ye more
tedious, but it pleased ye Lord to support
my heart in his goodnes, and to heare my
prayers and to deliuer me out of aduersity
But alas I cannot render vnto ye Lord
according to all his louing-kindnes, nor
take ye cup of Saluation wth Thanksgiuing
as I ought to doe. Lord thou yt knowest
all things know'st that I desire to testifye
my thankfullnes not only in word, but in
deed, that my conuersation may speake
that thy vowes are apon me.

My thankfull heart wth glorying tongue
Shall celebrate thy name
who hath restor'd, redeem'd, recur'd
ffrom sicknes, death, & pain.

I cry'd thou seem'st to make some stay
I sought more earnestly
And in due time thou succour'st me
And sent me help from high.
Lord whilst my fleeting time shall last
Thy goodnes let me tell,

And now experve J have gain'd
my future doubts repell.

An hūble, faithfull life O Lord
for ever let mee walk
Let my obed⁰ testefye
my praise lyes not in Talk:

Accept o Lord my simple mite
for more J cannot give
what thou bestow'st J shell restore
for of thine Almes J live.

For the restoration of my dear Husband
from a Burning Ague. June [too] 1661.

When feares and sorrows me beset
often did'st thou rid mee out
when heart did faint & Spirits quail
Thou comforts me about:
Thou rais'st him up J feard to loose
Regaū'st me him again
Distempers thou didst chase away
wth wrought didst him sustain
my thankfull heart wth pen record
the goodnes of thy God,
Let thy obed⁰ testefye
He taught thee by his rod.
And wth his staffe did thee support
that thou by both may'st learn
And 'twixt ye good and evill way
At last thou might'st discern
Praises to him who hath not left
my soul as destitute
Nor turnd his Ear away from mee
But graunted hath my Suit.

Upon my daughter Hannah Wiggin
her recovery from a dangerous feaver.

Blest bee thy name who did'st restore
  To health my Daughter dear
When death did seem ev'n to approach
  And life was ended near't

Graunt shee remember it & bee't ever
  And Celebrate thy praise
And let her Conversation say
  Shee loues thee all thy Dayes.

On my sons Return out of
England. July. 17. 1661.

All praise to him who hath now turn'
  my feares to Joyes, my sighes to song
my teares to Smiles, my Sad to glad
  Hee's come for whom I waited long.

Thou did'st preserve him as he went
  In raging stormes did'st safely keep
did'st that ship, bring to quiet port,
  The other sank low in the Deep.

From Dangers great thou did'st him free
  of Pyrates who were neer at hand
And order'st so the adverse wind
  That he before them got to Land.

In country strange thou did'st provide
  And friends rais'd him in every place
And Courtesies of Sundry sorts
  From such as 'fore nere saw his face.

In sicknes when he lay full sore
  His help & his Physitian wert
When royall ones yt time did dye,
  Thou heal'dst his flesh & his heart

From troubles and Incumbers thou
without (all fraud) didst sett him free
That wthout scandall he might come
To th' Land of his Nativity.

On Eagles wings him hither brought
Thro: want and dangers manifold
And then hath granted my Request
That I thy Mercyes might behold.

O help me pay my vowes o Lord
That ever I may thankfull bee
And may sett him in mind of what
Tho' st doat for him, & so for me.

In both of hearts erect a frame
of Duty & of Thankfullnes,
That all thy favours great receiv'd
Our vpright walking may expresse.

O Lord grant that I may never
forgett thy Lovingkindnes in this o
Particular, and how gratiously thou
hast answered my Desires.

Vpon my dear & loving husband his
going into England. Jan. 16. 1661.

O thou most high who rulest All
And hear'st the prayers of thine
O hearken Lord vnto my suit
And my Petition signe.

Into thy Everlasting Armes
of mercy I commend
thy servant Lord. Keep & preserve
my husband my dear friend.

At thy command o Lord he went
Nor nought could help him back
Then let thy promis joy his heart
o help and bee not slack.

Vphold my heart in thee o God
thou art my strenght and stay,
thou seest how weak & frail I am,
Hide not thy face away.

I in obed to thy will
o thou knowest did submitt
It was my duty so to doe
o Lord accept of it.

Yet thankfull my for merceys past
Impute thou not to me
o Lord thou know st my weak desires
was to sing praise to thee.

Lord bee thou Pilott to ye ship
And send them prosperous gailes
In stormes and sicknes Lord preserve
thy goodnes never failes.

Vnto thy work he hath in hand
Lord grant thou good successe
And favour in thir eyes to whom
He shall make his addresse.

Remember Lord thy folk whom thou
To wildernesse hast brought
Let not thine own Jnheritance
Bee sold away for Nought.

But tokens of thy favour give,
with Joy send back my Dear
That J and all thy Servants may
Rejoice with heavenly chear —

———— Lord let.

Lord let my Eyes see once Again
Him whom thou gavest mee
That wee together may sing praise
ffor ever unto thee.

And the Remainder of o'r Dayes
Shall consecrated bee
With an Engaged heart to sing
All praises unto Thee.

In my Solitary houres in my dear husband
his Absence

O Lord thou hear'st my dayly moan
And see'st my dropping teares.
My troubles all are thee before
My Longings and my feares.

Thou hitherto hast been my God
Thy help my Soul hath found
Tho: losse and sicknes mee assailes
Thro: thee I've kept my ground.

And thy Abode tho'st made w'h mee
w'th thee my Soul can talk
In secret places, Thee I find
where I doe kneel or walk.

Tho: husband dear bee from mee gone
whom I doe love so well
I have a more beloued one
whose comfort far excell.

O stay my heart on thee my God
vphold my fainting Soul
And when I know not what to doe
I'll on thy mercyes roll.

64 My weaknds thou do'st know full well,
Of Body and of mind
I in this world no comfort have,
But what from Thee I find.
Tho: children thou hast given me
And freinds I have alsoe
Yet if I see Thee not thro: them
They are no Joy, but woe.
O shine upon me blessed Lord
Ev'n for my Savers sake
In thee alone is more then All,
And there content I'll take
O hear me Lord in this Request
As thou before ha'st done
Bring back my husband I beseech
As thou didst once my Sonne.
So shall I celebrate thy praise
Ev'n while my Dayes shall last
And talk to my Belov'd one
Of all thy Goodnes past.
So both of us thy kindnes Lord
with praises shall recount
And serve thee better then before
Whose Blessings thus surmount.
But give me Lord a better heart
then better shall I bee
To pay the vowes weh I doe owe
tih ever unto Thee.
vnless thou help wt can I doe
But still my frailty show?
If thou assist me Lord I shall
Return thee what I owe.

In thankfull acknowledgmt for yt
Lrs I rec'd . from my husband out of
England .

O Thou that hear'st yt prayers of thine
And'mongst ym hast regarded Mine,

Hast heard my cry's, & seen my teares 65
Hast knowñ my doubts and all my feares,
Thou hast releiv'd my fainting heart
Nor payd mee after my desert
Thou hast so store him safely brought
For whom I thee so oft besought
Thou wast the Pilott to the ship
And rais'd him up when he was sick
And hope thou'st given of good successe,
In this his Buisnes and Addresse.
And if thou wilt return him back
Whose presence I so much doe lack,
For all these mercyes I thee praise
And so desire Ev'n all my Dayes.

In thankfull remembre for my dear husbands
safe Arrivall. Sept. 3. 1662.

What shall I render to thy Name
    Or how thy praises speak
My thankes how shall I testefye?
    O Lord thou know'st I'm weak.
I ow so much so little can
    Return unto thy Name
Confusion seases on my soul
    And I am fill'd with shame.
O thou that hear'st prayers Lord
    To thee shall come all flesh,
Thou hast me heard & answered
    My plaints have had accesse.
What did I ask for but thou gav'st
    What could I more desire
But thankfullnes even all my dayes
    I humbly this Require.
Thy mercyes Lord each morn so great
    In number nombe[r]les,
Impossible for to recount
    Or any ways expresse.

                        — helpe thy

66 O help thy Saints A sought thy fface
J' Returnd unto thire praise
And walk before thee as 'they ought,
In strict & upright wayes.
This was the last thing written in that
Book by my dear & hond. Mother.

Here followes some verses upon ye Burning
of or house, July. 10th. 1666. Copyed out of
a loose Paper.

In silent night when rest J took
For sorrow neer J did not look,
J wakened was with thundring nois
And Piteous shreiks of dreadfull voice.
That fearfull sound of fire and fire,
Let no man know is my Desire.
J starting up ye light did Spye,
And to my God my heart did cry
To strengthen me in my Distresse
And not to leave me succourlesse.
Then coming out beheld a spacc
The flame consume my dwelling place.
And when J could no longer look,
J blest his Name yt gave & took,
That layd my goods now in ye dust
Yea so it was, and so 'twas just.
It was his own it was not mine
Far bee it yt J should repine,
He might of all justly bereft,
But yet sufficient for us left.
When by the Ruins oft J past
My sorrowing eyes aside did cast
And here and there ye places Spye
Where oft J sate and long did lye.
Here stood that trunk, and there y' chest,
There lay that store J counted best,
My pleasant things in ashes lye
And them behold no more shall J

Under thy roof no guest shall sit,
Nor at thy table eat a bit.
No pleasant tale shall 'ere be told
Nor things recounted done of old.
No candle 'ere shall shine in thee
Nor bridegroom's voice ere heard shall bee.
In silence ever shalt thou lye,
Adieu, Adieu, All's vanity,
Then streight I 'gin my heart to chide,
And did thy wealth on earth abide
Didst fix thy hope on mouldring dust
The arm of flesh didst make thy trust
Raise up thy thoughts above the skye
That dunghill mists away may flie.
Thou hast an house on high erect,
Fram'd by that mighty Architect,
With glory richly furnished,
Stands permanent tho: this bee fled.
It's purchased, and paid for too
By him who hath enough to doe.
A prise so vast as is unknown,
Yet by his gift is made thine own,
Ther's wealth enough, I need no more,
Farewell my pelf, farewell my store.
The world no longer let me Love,
My hope, and Treasure lyes Above.

.Ad Sim. Bradstreet filium
charissimum meum.

.In posteris Parentes vitam per
petuam faciunt, & in liberorum
imitatione, mores diuturnos.
Naturaliter tamen posterita
ti inest, *dispositio* in magis, defectus majorum
quam virtutes imitari. Sed a
te, meliora, mi Fili, expecto.
Tu enim, petiisti, ut Scriptione
tibi legendum, aliquid, cum
ab oculis detraherer, committe
rem. His igitur sequentibus
meditatiunculis, nihil venit in
mentem, tibi idoneus, mihi nihil
facilius. Qualia sunt addico
tibi. Parva ab amicis accep.
tabilia sunt dona, multo magis,
a filiis piis. Cogitationes aliorum
quibus nullas nisi verè maternas
darem, studiosè vitavi; quas, magni
estimandas, credo, mei causâ, futu
ras, licet seipsis, parvas fuerint.

Largiatur tibi in hac vitâ grati
am suam Jehovah, & posthâc gloria
coronam donec, ut in Die judicii
............, gaudioque summo, appii
am — Sic Deum continuò sup
plicè rogat

      Tua amantissima.
Parens
      Ann Bradstreet

Mar: 20: 1664.

Hæc Epistola Romano Sermone
versus est à Simone Bradstreet
hujus Excellentissimæ Fæminæ
Pronepote cum sequentibus
Meditatiunculis ———

Meditationes divinæ & Ethicæ

1. Est nihil oculis visibile, homi
num nulla actiones, nullum acqui
situm bonum, nullum præsens vel
futurum malum, a quibus omni
bus Animi Salutem & utilitatem
promovere non possimus. —
Et ille homo, non minus Sapi
ens, quàm prius est, qui tales
fructus ab eis carpit.
                queant.

2. Plurimi, bene loqui, at pauci
        bene agere. Majores in spe
culatione, quam summus in actione.
Ipse autem reverà Christianus
est qui in utrisque proficit. —

3. Iuventus est capiendi, ampliandi
ætas media, & utendi senectus, opti
ma Opportunitas. Iuventus remissa,
ignorantem facit mediam ætatem,
& ferè, senectutem, utroque vacuam red
dunt. Et cujus est tantum vani
tate & mendaciis cibus, cubitum
mœstus est eundum —

Meditationes Divinæ & Ethicæ

4. Ut navis quæ nimium vela petit sub-
timia, nullamq; habens vel levem suburr-
ram, citò evertitur, sic homo multa
scientia ac doctrina, sed gratia & pruden-
tia parva, præditus ab imis ruina profundita-
tibus non procul abest. ——

2.

As weary pilgrim, now at rest
Hugs with delight his silent nest
His wasted limbes, now lye full soft
That myrie steps, have trodden oft
Blesses himself, to think upon
his dangers past, and travailes done
The burning sun no more shall heat
Nor stormy raines, on him shall beat
The briars and thornes no more shall scratch
nor hungry wolves at him shall catch
He erring pathes no more shall tread
Nor wild fruits eate, insteed of bread
for waters cold he doth not long
for thirst no more shall parch his tongue
No rugged stones his feet shall gaule
nor stumps nor rocks cause him to fall
All cares and feares, he bids farewell
and meanes in safity now to dwell
A pilgrim I, on earth, perplext
with sinns with cares and sorrows vext
By age and paines brought to decay
and my Clay house mouldring away
how long so be at rest
soare on high among the blest

This body shall in silence sleep
Mine eyes no more shall ever weep
No fainting fits shall me assaile
nor grinding paines my body fraile
with cares and fears ne'er cumbred be
Nor losses know, nor sorrowes see
what tho my flesh shall there consume
it is the bed Christ did perfume
And when a few yeures shall be gone
this mortall shall be cloth'd upon
A Corrupt Carcasse downe it lyes
a glorious body it shall rise
In weaknes and dishonour sowne
in power tis raised by Christ alone
then soule and body shall unite
and of their maker have the sight
such lasting ioyes shall there behold
as eare ne'er heard nor tongue e'er told
Lord make me ready for that day
then Come dear bridgrome Come away
                    away

Aug. 31 g 1